# London's Contemporary Architecture +

## a map-based guide

### Ken Allinson

#### Fourth edition

D0243110

Architectural Press is an imprint of Elsevier
Linacre House, Jordan Hill, Oxford OX2 8DP, UK
30 Corporate Drive, Suite 400, Burlington MA 01803, USA

First published 1994 (Ken Allinson and Victoria Thornton)
Second edition 2000 (Ken Allinson and Victoria Thornton)
Third edition 2003 (Ken Allinson)
Fourth edition (Ken Allinson) 2006
Reprinted 2007

Copyright © 2006, Ken Allinson. Published by Elsevier Ltd. All rights
reserved.

No part of this publication may be reproduced, stored in a retrieval system
or transmitted in any form or by any means electronic, mechanical, photocopying, recording or otherwise without the prior written permission of the
publisher

Permission may be sought directly from Elsevier's Science & Technology
Rights Department in Oxford, UK: phone (+44) (0) 1865 843830; fax (+44)
(0) 1865 853333; email: permissions@elsevier.com. Alternatively you can
submit your request online by visiting the Elsevier web site at http://else-
vier.com/locate/permissions, and selecting Obtaining permission to use
Elsevier material

Notice
No responsibility is assumed by the publisher for any injury and/or damage
to persons or property as a matter of products liability, negligence or otherwise, or from any use or operation of any methods, products, instructions
or ideas contained in the material herein. Because of rapid advances in the
medical sciences, in particular, independent verification of diagnoses and
drug dosages should be made

**British Library Cataloguing in Publication Data**
**A catalogue record for this book is available from the British Library**

For information on all Architectural Press publications visit our
web site at www.books.elsevier.com

ISBN-13: 978-0-75-066818-7
ISBN-10: 0-75-066874-1

Printed and bound in Italy.

Book design, all photos and drawings by Ken Allinson except as noted.
Graduate Centre photo on cover by Myles Cummings.
**Acknowledgements:**
Jean Fisker, for her considerateness as well as her professionalism.
Victoria Thornton, for her assistance and support at every step.
Everyone at Open House.
All those individuals, architectural practices and other organisations who
have loaned material for publication.

ELSEVIER

## Who is the guide for?

This guide suggests what is good, contemporary and accessible, but it also lists other examples of notable architecture when it are nearby, regardless of historic period.

It is a guide for those of you who enjoy experiencing architecture, whether you are a Londoner or a visitor with a limited amount of time to see what the city has to offer.

## How to use the guide

Buildings have been listed geographically, into the areas and neighbourhoods you might want to visit. They are divided between contemporary buildings of primary interest and other buildings that are 'nearby' – a description including both other modern and historical buildings (at the bottom of the pages).

Buildings are located on maps at the beginning of each section. It is recommended that you use acopy of the 'London A-Z' to assist in finding exact locations, using the address provided.

# The City

'Bank is a place where something like eight roads crush together at a single focal point like jobbers onto a good deal. This is the geographical and symbolic heart of British capitalism, at the centre of a City Conservation Area (that now covers over one third of the City) and a wonderful group of buildings by architects of significance. At one time it was rather important to have an address within ten minutes walk of here (in effect, within the old city walls). Whilst the most dominant and prestigious building is now the Bank of England, the design product of John Soane and one of Britain's better known inter-war architects, Herbert Baker, it is the Royal Exchange that best establishes the principle of historical continuity and was for a long time one of the most important buildings in the City. In addition, there is Dance's Mansion House, Stirling's No.1 Poultry, the Lutyens' Midland Bank, Hawksmoor's St. Mary Woolnoth, and Wren's St. Stephen Walbrook.

**1** The church of **St. Stephen Walbrook**, 1672 - 80, is among the better Wren churches in the City (on the south east side of Bank) — a centrally organised church damaged in wartime bombing and now fully restored with a modern

altar by Henry Moore (1972), sitting at the heart of an interior with distinctly 'Scandinavian blonde' overtones set against the dark browns of Wren's late C17 aesthetic (which still includes the pulpit). Worth a visit. The steeple is particularly fine, as are most of those on Wren's City churches.

**2** The **Mansion House**, with its squashed portico facing onto the Bank junction, is the official residence of the Lord Mayor of the City of London (nowadays little more than an symbolic figurehead who markets the City). It was designed by George Dance the Elder in 1739 - 52,

originally having two tall additions above the pediment line – lopped off (as if in some Freudian gesture) by his son, George Dance the Younger. The pediment sculptures depict the City defeating Envy and Bringing Plenty (one wonders what Foucault would do with that).

**3** The **Bank of England** is the most significant building at Bank. It is monolithic and fills the entire urban block, but should be read as two buildings: Sir John Soane's original work dating from 1788-1808, and Sir Herbert Baker's work which rises above the perimeter walls, from 1922 - 39. The former is a superbly articulated fortress, an original 'ground-scraper', filling the block, with few external openings in its expertly articulated perimeter wall. Behind it was a masterful complex inspired by the buildings of Ancient Rome, drawing daylight from above into rooms where clerks made up their books by lamp-light. By Baker's time, the architect could throw a power switch and achieve the same effect and his architecture removes Soane's work and rises up proudly in its place from behind the old walls. Quite properly, Baker has been vilified for obliterating Soane's masterpiece, but even his work has features to enjoy. (Especially if the Bank is open for Open House London — an occasion when you might be able to make comparisons with the similar grand interiors of Edwin Cooper's former Port of London Authority building at Tower Hill. Cooper has a former NatWest bank building on the opposite corner, done about the same time as the Lutyens building; he was the architect of the first custom-

design Lloyds building in the 1920's.) However, Soane's (mostly blank) walls are, in themselves, an architectural delight and worth a perambulation all the way around (and they include, on the northern side, a statue of the man himself).

*It was once considered of great importance to work within a ten minute walk of the Bank of England. This had less to do with convenience than some arcane relation to the old Roman walls and the traditional status of the City of London as a semi-autonomous state within a city. This juncture continues to exercise a curious influence and attract important architecture and architects — which ever way one turns there is an important building.*

**4** *Like Lloyd's of London, the **Royal Exchange** was, until recently, another exercise in cultural continuity masking architectural differences. The first Royal Exchange was founded as a place of international commerce and built 1566. It burned down in the Great Fire of 1666 and was then rebuilt, only to be burned down again in the 1830's. Each architectural exercise provided the same fundamental configuration of accommodation around a central court where people could meet. The original building had an arcaded court and the present building of 1841 - 44, by Sir William Tite has a central court that was covered over when the building was refurbished by Fitzroy Robinson in 1990. It was then converted again (2002) into a smart, European style court of expensive shops — in a sense returning the space back to its original intentions as a trading place (even if this is at a rather less strategic and more frivolous level).*

**5** *Edwin Lutyens was one of Britain's most acclaimed architects up to his death in 1944. This bank HQ he designed for **Midland Bank** (1924 - 39) and is a good example of the old man cheerfully fronting (literally and metaphorically) a design executed (millennium style) by others. Somehow, an irascible character comes through: look at the detailing and the Lutyens-designed little boy with goose. Try entering the bank hall from the side and leaving through the opposite side, attempting to deny the latterday tat that promotes financial services and the like — the old hall and all its pretensions is still there, not yet a cafe or bar. Also see Lutyens' **Brittanic House** building (1921 - 5) in Finsbury Square.*

**6** *St. Mary Woolnoth* (1716 - 27), at Bank, is especially noteworthy among the works of a man (Nicholas Hawksmoor) who served for a long time under Wren and finally came into his own relatively late in life. Despite its difficult site, the architectural elements are almost abstractly simple, underscoring the symbolic geometries that once had so much significance and embodying the C18 sense of the Sublime as something at once wonderful, awesome and terrible. It seems appropriate that this building should sit near to Stirling's **No.1 Poultry**. It is one of six churches by this architect: also see **St. George Bloomsbury** (just south of the British Museum); **St. George-in-the-East**, Wapping; **St. Alphege**, Greenwich; **St. Anne**, Limehouse; and, especially, **Christ Church**, Spitalfields. Also take time to compare this church with the Stirling Wilford building opposite — a distinct note of commonality crosses the centuries.

No. 1 Poultry, EC2.
James Stirling Michael Wilford & Associates,
1998. Tube: Bank.

# 7  No. 1 Poultry
## le coq on Poultry

Stirling & Wilford's design for No.1 Poultry began in 1985. By its completion in 1998 it was stylistically anachronistic: a strident post-modern building that might have been more appropriately completed ten years earlier. But that doesn't make it a bad design, or uninteresting.

    The building's developer, Lord Palumbo, is also a major figure in arts funding. His father began considering redevelopment of this difficult triangular site and its 1890, neo-Gothic buildings designed by John Belcher with a scheme drawn up by the late Mies van der Rohe in the mid-1960's (Mies died in 1969). The initiative proposed demolishing the existing set of rather small and well-formed buildings, aggregating the sites and replacing them with a large piazza and shoe-box tower — a not uncommon City development pattern, which drew the criticism from Prince Charles that the proposed building was a 'glass stump'. Controversy followed. Alternatives were put forward (notably by conservative interests and (the now Sir Terry Farrell), and Palumbo jnr. turned to Stirling and Wilford for another proposal – a stunning design that eventually won planning permission (this took place just after Stirling and Wilford's Staatsgalerie had opened in Stuttgart). And then Stirling died having a minor hernia operation.

    No. 1 Poultry is deliberately designed as a symmetrical, axial scheme whose flamboyant mannerisms are argued to contextually relate to its neighbours (Lutyens, Soane, Hawksmoor, Tite, Wren). Shops are on the ground floor and a mall at basement level links through to Bank station, the Tube and the DLR. The top level houses a Terence Conran terrace restaurant (Coq d'Argent) with terrace landscaping by Arabella Lennox-Boyd. In between are five floors of speculative office space. All this is organised around a central, open court (formally massed as a rotunda) which also allows the public to pass through the heart of the building and down to a lower level concourse connected to the Underground.

8   *The **Monument** on King William Street, EC3 commemorates the Great Fire of London, 1666, and is designed by Christopher Wren and Robert Hooke (1671 - 6). We no longer create such monumental civic obelisks inspired by the example of the Ancients in order to commemorate important contemporary events (perhaps Newcastle's 'Angel of the North' is an exception?) and one half expects to find a commercial sponsor's plaque at the base. The column used to greet visitors from the south until London Bridge was realigned and is worth a visit in order to experience*

*its peculiarity and scale at ground level, and to enjoy the view of the City from the top. Also try St Paul's, Tower 42, the 'Gherkin', Tower and Bridge, as well as the terrace restaurant at No.1 Poultry.*

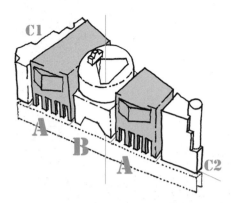

*The No.1 Poultry design bears within it the memory of both what was on the site previously and the original ideas of 1986, which sliced the site into four disparate parts, including the retention of the John Belcher corner building. This evolved into an A-B-A rhythm flanked by a western service end and a new eastern prow bearing elements of Belcher's design (including the clock and a salvaged terracotta frieze of 1875 by Joseph Kremer on the Poultry side). However, one difficulty with such architectural games is that they are front-end biased (toward the sensitivities of planners) and the experience depends entirely upon memory — and who can remember a building once it has been demolished? This means that — whatever the ostensible intent — Stirling's corner feature has to sustain itself on its own merits. The central element (\B' above) is a light-well and public right of way — don't let the security guards tell you it isn't when you get your camera out!*

The prominent corner turret looking toward Bank (which some critics with more erudition than common sense argue it to be a roguish quotation of a celebratory Roman rostral column!) is a satisfyingly strong piece of architectural gamesmanship formally reminiscent of what was there before. But if we can never remember what *was* there before, the gesture loses its meaning. In any case, such theatricality is a reminder of how, in other hands, a marriage between the developer's vanity and '80's Post-Modernism could produce rather peculiar designs. The building also appears to lack those elements of surprise and invention that made Stirling's earlier work so intriguing, as well as the deftness and humour one associates with this distinctly idiosyncratic architect – that witty irreverence lifting his work above the mainstream. Bemusement at the design's outmoded idiosyncracity had the media reporting that the building was designed in a spirit of derivative homage by a Stirling associate rather than the man himself. (But what is unusual in that? It was, in any case, posthumously completed by Michael Wilford & Associates, now also a closed practice. Such is the secret history of buildings, a clouded oral narrative which buildings themselves do little to elucidate.

The building joins the company of Lutyens' Midland Bank, Soane's Bank of England screen wall, Dance's Mansion House, Wren's St. Stephen Walbrook and Hawksmoor's rusticated facade of St. Mary Woolnoth as a notable architectural exercise at this most significant corner of the City. However, No.1 suffered the difficulty of completion after the recession of 1990 to 1994, an interlude engendering a massive redefinition of architectural fashions whose most notable feature was the termination of 15 years of architectural Post-Modernism and its overnight replacement by a revived, less baroque and theatrical Modernism (actually, more truly post-modern!), more likely to be inspired by work in Barcelona than Chicago. (Although, ironically, Mies is back in fashion! See the Foster building on Gresham Street). However, times change and in a few years this strong design might become respected for what it is, rather than disparaged for being merely outmoded.

**9** *This (the Former **Barclays Bank** HQ, GMW, 1994) has to be one of the least distinguished buildings in the City — a Post Modern design completed in 1994 when everyone (including developers) had gone somewhere else. But it's interesting and is by GMW, who have so many buildings in the City. The peculiarities of this headquarters building includes references to Stirling (the neo-Egyptian cornice, from his Stuttgart Gallery), to Otto Wagner (the late C19 Viennese gold decorations on the cornice), and to Rogers*

*(the Lloyd's atrium top). But see it in context, not just with the other buildings in the adjacent alleys, but in terms of GMW's City output that includes the former Banque Belge, the Commercial Union and the ground level lobby of Tower 42.*

**10** *The former **Banque Belge**, GMW, 1975 is on the corner of Bishopsgate and Leadenhall EC. It is a very elegant attempt to make the bottom / middle / top equation work in the Georgian manner: almost entirely with well considered geometrical proportions. But perhaps it should be much taller – in which case it might have put the Commercial Union to shame. The entrance canopy on Leadenhall is a later addition of about 1999. Compare it with that building, with the rather bizarre, neo-Gothic Minster Court, the Barclays Bank HQ on the corner of Lombard and Gracechurch (1994), and the base of Tower 42 — all of them by GMW. That collection makes a fascinating history of changing architectural fashions as well as a record of a changing City.*

# 11 The Lloyd's '86 Building: an exercise in continuity

Lloyd's of London, Lime Street, EC3
Richard Rogers Partnership, 1978–86
Tube: Bank

The now ageing, 47,000 sq.m. Lloyd's 1986 Building is established as a Modernist icon and has become an accepted part of the City fabric, even if it is now overtaken in the glamour stakes by newer neighbours such as Foster's St. Mary Axe building (the 'Erotic Gherkin'), Rogers' own Lloyds Register around the corner, and suffering a degree of internal abuse. As a design, the building makes little sense located outside the context of the client's status and history: one of the most prestigious, respectable, and long-established institutions within the secretive world of the Square Mile, an insurance market where so-called 'Names' gamble their wealth against the possible misfortune of others through the medium of insurance underwriters and brokers. It was after one of the worst periods of such misfortune and the beginning of a new mass market for insurance that Lloyds found itself needing and able to move itself from premises in the Royal Exchange to a new, custom-designed building in

*Photo: Nick Cooney*

*Lloyd's seen from inside the upper part of 30 St. Mary Axe (the 'Gherkin'.)*

Leadenhall Street. That was in 1923 and the completed '1928 Building' was designed by Sir Edwin Cooper (1873 - 1942). The fundamental organisation of this building (a large and high trading floor, with a formal entrance used by few and a secondary entrance used by most people, with cores at the corners) was followed through in each of the subsequent buildings Lloyd's constructed, including the Rogers' design.

The 'grand manner' Portland stone entrance portico in Cornhill is now all that remains of the 1928 Building. From its entrance vestibule a passage led to a palatial, square, double-height hall, 1500 sq.m. in size, lit by a central roof light and huge, suspended light fittings, and dressed in Subiaco marble. At its centre was the 'caller's rostrum' and the famous Lutine Bell: rung, by tradition, whenever a ship was sunk. A secondary underwriter's entrance in Lime Street served as a kind of rear door to the Room (as the market hall was called).

Within eight years of moving into the 1928 Building Lloyd's was expanding into an adjacent building and, after WWII, business had grown to such an extent that a gallery was considered for the Room. However, this proposal was superseded by a scheme to completely rebuild the adjacent building according to the designs of Terence Heysham (1897 - 1967): what was to become the '58 Building'.

Like its predecessor, the 1958 Building was fundamentally a tall, marbled, top-lit space complete with an array of hanging light fittings; upper floors were for support staff. Lloyd's had been able to expand horizontally, stretching the Room into the largest air-conditioned volume in Europe. They were also able to provide a gallery (for the relatively newer, non-marine insurance markets, such as cars and aviation), to bring along the rostrum for the Lutine Bell, and also the timber linings and plasterwork of a 1763 country estate dining room designed by Robert Adam – which became the linings of the 'Adam Committee Room' in a new Committee Suite. The underwriting space was now about 4100 sq.m.

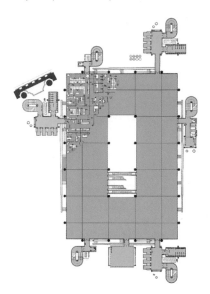

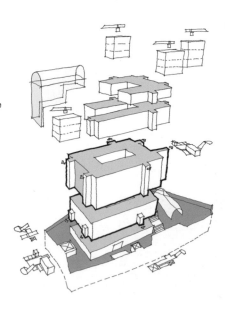

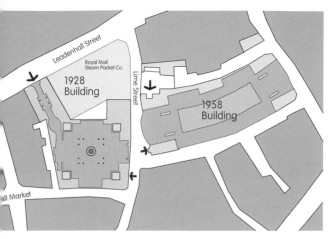

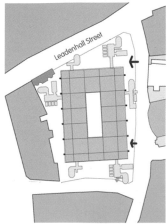

By the early 1970's the need for additional accommodation had returned and the Lloyd's Committee initiated a search for architects who might design a building to last, not 25 years again, but 125 years! The outcome was a Richard Rogers Partnership design for the site of Cooper's building, a scheme which allowed Lloyds to retain the 1958 Building for support staff (later converted by DEGW, who added two large and separate basement food courts — for the underwriters and the Lloyd's staff. By late 2002 this building was scheduled for demolition).

Like its predecessors, the 1986 Building – as it became known – is all about the Room. Recreating it on the 1928 Building's site meant that expansion had to be vertical rather than horizontal. The single gallery Heysham designed now became five galleries of insurance market. The roof lights of the 1928 and 1958 Buildings now became a cathedral-like atrium. The marble was reinvented as high specification concrete and the circular, hanging light fittings as sophisticated, specialist-designed, fittings ubiquitously provided for all interior spaces: Room, galleries, offices and even the Chairman's suite on the upper floor. In the latter, the Adam Room was recreated in all its wondrous and incongruous glory as a classical building accommodated within the Rogers' edifice – an odd Post-Modern note in an otherwise radically Hi-tech design.

The most controversial aspect of the architecture is undoubtedly the decision to locate all services on the exterior. This daring rationale ostensibly derived from the need to keep the market floors entirely clear of intrusions and has been hailed as both romantic (akin to Gothic cathedrals) and truly modern (one of the most advanced technological edifices in the western world). However, debate concerned with the merits and demerits of oil rig aesthetics has carried another sub-text. The cultural values of Lloyd's, as a rapacious, capitalist City institution with deeply conservative instincts (after moving into the 1986 Building they retained the basement of the 1958 Building as a practice shooting range), proved, in the long run, to be profoundly at odds with those of its left-wing, egalitarian architects fresh from completion of a *grand projet* in Paris. The project's history saw an apparent exemplar of

designer–client relations become an adversarial battle between modernist architects and their more reactionary, public school clients – particularly when it got down to who sat (more advantageously) where and on what within the stacked trading galleries. Discontent became rife, focusing on all kinds of design issues.

Problems included a bright blue carpet which was replaced by a biscuit-coloured pattern worthy of a tawdry provincial office; a special design (by Eva Jiricna) for the 'boxes' at which the underwriters sat – diluted to accord with demands they should be just like the old, teak and uncomfortable boxes of the 1958 Building; window 'sails' designed by Jiricna for the Captain's Dining Room (the Underwriter's formal dining space) – unceremoniously removed whilst her granite floor was covered by more tawdry carpet.

In the background were political and financial difficulties threatening the future of the market and paralleling the last years of building completion. These continued and, by 1994, the building had been sold to a German developer – an act soon to be followed by a massive financial claim against the Rogers' Partnership for problems with the external pipework and the sale of the '58 building (now demolished and being replaced by, you guessed it, another Foster team design). A common denominator between designer and client, one concerning a love of risk, daring and an ambition to make public statements had not overcome cultural disparities and the misfortunes of fate. Will the building last or slowly deteriorate, possibly to be replaced by something more economic?

*Compare with other nearby Rogers' designs:* **K2** *(at St. Katherine's Dock),* **100 Wood Street***, and* **Lloyd's Register of Shipping***. Also compare with the first significant office building after Lloyd's —* **Channer Four** *and the building in Soho, at* **Broadwick Street***.*

# The City

**12** *Leadenhall Market (Horace Jones, 1881), on the east side of Lloyds, stands as the masterful reinvention of a poultry market which has been here since the C14. Jones (1819 - 97) quietly exhibits a fine architectural gamesmanship which establishes the potential of the heartland of the City's urban blocks. For example, the ostensible formal geometry of the scheme is anything but that in reality and Jones cleverly insinuates his big idea into the surrounding fabric with a series of local and contingent moves. Examine the manner in which he (joyfully?) extends southward from the central crossing, reaching out architectural tentacles, pushing the facade concept as far as it will go — even where there is no building behind because of 'rights of light' issues — in an effort to reach out to the surrounding streets that define the urban block. There is an urbanity here that perhaps awaits the socio-economic conditions that will bring the market back to life outside of a narrowly defined lunch-time trade to City workers. Remove the parking and get a farmers' market in here? As an example of good backlands utilisation, Leadenhall and similar places (such as Bow Lane) implicitly offer a severe criticism of City redevelopment patterns that pool sites in favour of ever larger buildings and denude formerly rich backland places of their vibrancy. You can walk from here westward through a series of alleys to Bank, passing bland walls of white ceramic brickwork (to reflect daylight) and circular plaques that remind one there was once a pub or coffee house on this site. However, on the way you will also touch upon areas such as that behind St. Peter's church, where this same vibrancy and a mix of building scales is still (just) maintained, indicating what is still possible. These examples are severe criticism of the Planners' '50's and '60's enthusiasm for decks and bridges (as at the Barbican), and for monsters such as Broadgate, Spitalfields and Canary Wharf, all of which deny organic change (both as intention and future possibility).*

*Right: Jones' exercise in stretching the façade to places where it becomes pure theatre.*

**13** *The **Commercial Union** building (GMW 1969), is a classic example of the post-war, North American tower-and-piazza equation that makes a comparison with a later generation's values across the road at Lloyds as well as with the likes of (less well designed) 1960's City towers that lined London Wall. It's an elegant building that was sympathetically but entirely reclad after the IRA bomb that went off at the nearby Baltic Exchange in early April 1993 (the bomb that prompted a rebuilding resulting in Foster's 'erotic gherkin').*

*The major criticism is the usual one for such an architectural equation: the piazza is not entirely unpleasant, but remains a rather inhospitable place.*

**14** *Like its contemporary neighbour (the lower, former **P&O Building** to the immediate west, now sporting a cheerful 1998 piazza entrance canopy lit by fibre-optics) the CU once had one of those 1st floor decks ('pedways') beloved of the LCC's '50's and '60's planners, waiting to link into a spreading City network that, in 1965 was planned to be 35m in extent. Go around the corner to Leadenhall St. and you will see this dream literally come to an abrupt halt up against a 1929 Midland Bank by Lutyens, manifesting the presumption that the bridge would naturally leap from the former P&O building across the gap and that Lutyens' 'grand manner' bank would, in time, fall down before its utterly inevitable progress. The largest example of this dream is, of course, the Barbican. Other parts of the pedway system still remain (e.g. just south of Broadgate).*

*Above: View to the entrance.*

## 30 St. Mary Axe: enigmatic exotica

In 2003 the City finally got a building to outpace the Lloyd's '86 building designed by a Richard Rogers team: Foster's 'erotic gherkin' — opposite Lloyds and adjacent to GMW's elegant Commercial Union building (120m), and counterpointing Col. Seifert's still elegant Tower 42 a few blocks away (183m; formerly the NatWest Tower, the building that has dominated the City skyline since 1981).

Whilst the overwhelming reality of the 180m high, 40 storey building (76,400 sq.m.) is its dramatic sculptural form and its dominance of the skyline, a key feature of the building's internal organisation is its spiralling light-wells that wind around the building and cut across the simple, circular plan providing a perimeter of office 'fingers' around a central core — visible from afar as a wrapping, tonal banding to the building's triangular glazing pattern. The Buckminster-inspired form enjoys all kinds of instrumental rationalisation: it is described as 'environmentally progressive', the light-wells allowing light to penetrate and they can ventilate the offices thus reducing air conditioning loads (all assisted by an aerodynamic form that sets up appropriate pressure differentials); the stiff diagrid skin relieves the conventional bracing function of the central core; the glass skin is ventilated; the glazing allows full perimeter views, the tapering geometry reduces reflections and wind disturbance at ground level — which also benefits from an otherwise enlarged public space on a comparatively tight site (as at the Ark).

Like the best of Foster's work (the design is actually attributed to Ken Shuttleworth, Foster's partner at the time of the design), the architecture has a self-evident clarity about it. Unfortunately, the diagrid is heavily encased with fire protection and the internal lining is on an orthogonal grid (perhaps, in part, explaining the dark glass). The plan is always shown at the fattest point and the atria are actually very small at the bottom and top. In fact, they disappear altogether in the upper floors. Also, someone somewhere in the design process awoke to the fact that tall, winding atria make good fire chimneys and the Gherkin's atria only stretch between 2 - 5 floors before being cut off — not quite the original dream. Such pure forms also suffer a difficulty Fuller acknowledged with geodesic domes: how do you get in? He suggested one dives under the perimeter. Here, the Foster team have made a cut-out in the skin, forming a lobby (which bears unexpected references to Alvar Aalto's work). To top it all, early 2005 saw a few of the windows exploding or falling out! This produced interesting measures at the piazza level, but it is usually deserted anyway (except, that is, for architectural tourists).

Nevertheless, despite some gripes, this is a remarkable piece of design. However, there is something you should know: there was once an early '90's IRA bomb that devasted this area. The blast took place in front of the Baltic Exchange — a building fondly preserved by

*Above: the adjacent church of St Helen's Bishopsgate, a nun's church dating from 1200, recently renovated by Quinlan Terry.*

*Below: the ground floor plan of 30 St Mary Axe.*

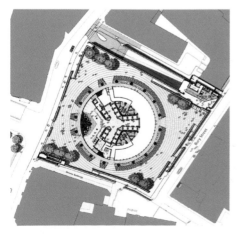

**15** the conservation lobby. But it was so badly damaged that there was no choice but to demolish it, placing its splendid central market room into wooden crates. The intention was that any new building on the site would have to include this room. Clearly, the proposal was a developer's nightmare. But the City planners were clever: they negotiated the constraint by agreeing with the site owners for an example of architectural design that was so excellent no one could object to it not including the old parts of the Baltic Exchange. Hence Foster and the Gherkin.

However, none of this explains the strange attraction / aversion the Gherkin evinces. Its rocket-shaped form has a brooding, enigmatic quality and when the building opened for the Open House London event in 2004 there was a five hour wait in a queue that was over 1km long. Most people simply wanted to get to the top, to an amazing double height glass room with incredible views. But it is externally that the building — sitting back within its security zone of open piazza area — serves the metropolis as some equivalent to the Roman ceremonial columns, to obelisks and other such devices that range from neolithic standing stones to that thing in Kubrick's *2001* movie. Such aspects arguably bear more attractiveness than a design which, at the level of tactile habitability, has been considered to be as barren as any other work from the Foster office. Visit it and make up your own mind.

*At the time of writing arrangements can be made to visit the building, but only in small groups. But is is not cheap. Note: you can similarly pay to access Lloyds.*

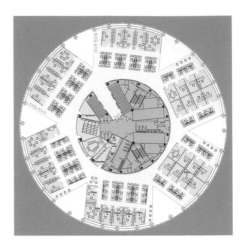

**16** *Just north of Lloyds, through an alley off St. Mary Axe, in Bury Street, EC3, sits a remarkable building: the **National Employer's House** designed by the Dutch architect H.P. Berlage in 1914, after a US visit (engendering a Sullivan inspiration). This is a building designed for tight City streets and has to be seen obliquely, when the green glazed facade mullions (spaced at 1.3 m centres and sat upon a brick base) read as a solid wall of tiling. Then move along and watch the windows reveal themselves. The mullions decrease in size, ostensibly manifesting the decreased loads being carried. (The 'Gherkin' piazza rather destroys this effect*

*by suggesting a full-frontal approach rather than an oblique one.) The small lobby is about all that exists of the original interiors. Go around the corner where the building pops out again and see the wonderful corner sculpture by Joseph Mendes de Costa.*

*Left: the building in construction.*

*Below: the ground level arcade that extends around the base of the building - a place that should be welcoming and pleasant, but doesn't quite pass 'the cappuccino test' of attractiveness and comfortability.*

## Plantation Place

**17**

Fenchurch Street, EC3
Arup Associates, 2004
Tube: Bank/Monument/Tower Hill

This is a bit of a beast, reminiscent of Denis Lasdun's effort just north of the Barbican (Milton Gate) i.e. its all glass — plus decorative stone fins (the planners insist on stone). But it is not unattractive, has a splendid upper level garden terrace, enjoys superb views and is extremely well detailed. In brief, the building replaces Plantation House — a scene of trading in exotic goods for generations — and the challenge to its designers was to articulate a massive bulk as a series of discrete parts. They strive to do this vertically in a familiar divide between the lower and upper parts — the latter all glass; the former decorated with stone fins. They also divide the urban block between north and south parts, with an alley in between (where we find an art installation called 'Time & Tide', by Simon Patterson and featuring pictures of the Moon's surface). But it is the southern facades that are by far the most intriguing and successful (those belonging to Plantation Place South; 14,215 sq.m. net)

in their striving to express a more tectonic kind of façade. It then becomes all the more regrettable that, immediately one leaves the street, the façades reduce to something comparatively cheap 'n' cheerful. This might accord with a long City tradition of how to treat the alleys and backlands

but it doesn't help such places become more important and it is a distinct betrayal of modernist ideals that had aspired toward a different set of values — compare this, for example, with the work of Hopkins at Bracken House. Also compare with the work of this same practice at Broadgate, where the strategy of stone on the lower façades and a breakout to aluminium and glass on the upper parts (now commonplace) was first explored (as a variation on the podium and tower theme).

*It is well worth exploring the many alleys around here — a backlands that reveals a surprising degree of neglected potential within the City. The above is on a route from Bank to Leadenhall Market. It includes leftover reminders of a once rich cultural history that has now disappeared and been replaced by a blue plaque and a security camera. That such a potential is not exploited is, in part, because the City has no interest in tourists or residents - the very people who might enrich its monoculture. The reasons are simple: tourists get in the way, as do residential leases which prevent rapid change.*

# The City

**18**   *Minster Court (Mincing Lane, EC3; GMW 1991; tube: Tower Hill): the three buildings of this 59,000 sq.m. complex (the 'London Underwriting Centre')* form a 'groundscraper': low and flat, filling the urban block and respecting street lines. Targeted at the insurance market (Lloyd's is around the corner), it's also an idiosyncratic re-creation of those C19th battles between the Classical and Gothic traditions – this time complete with neo-Gothic entry court pillars straight off the CAD screen ('wireframe' representations that will surely date the building precisely to any future archaeologist) and three horses of the Apocalypse straight from the early 1980's London exhibition of the horses from St. Mark's Square in Venice. The forecourt with its large glazed roof and in between spaces are described as 'public'. They're not, and are gated off at weekends. Beyond them are bars and restaurants. One's principal complaint has to be that the theatre doesn't go far enough. The piers and arches, for example, are disturbingly non-structural and one longs for a Michael Hopkins version of the same game (it would be real!). However, behind the façade games, the three blocks of offices conform to what has been the accepted convention for office design for some time: access floors, suspended ceilings, 1.5m interior planning grids, etc. The façade itself conforms to another fashionable convention of the 1980's: granite cladding, a symbol of robustness and durability, superseded in the 1990's by a softer fashion for limestone.*

*     This building is worth comparing with other GMW City architecture over the years: the elegant* **Commercial Union** *building opposite Lloyd's, the former* **Banque Belge** *building (the low block on the corner), the former* **Barclays Bank HQ** *on Gracechurch Street (a most peculiar, bombastic mix of Otto Wagner, Terry Farrell and Jim Stirling), and the new lobby to the* **NatWest Tower**. *These buildings provide a unique record of changing architectural fashions within one practice.*

**19**   *The Institute of Chartered Accountants is a building to be read in three stages. The first was a much-praised building designed by John Belcher (1883–89), in Great Swan Alley, EC2, north of Bank. Forty years later and in another era his ageing partner, Joass, added an eastern extension – exactly like Belcher's earlier work. Another 35 years later William Whitfield (master planner of Paternoster Square) came along to make major additions. Rather incongruously, he again extended the Belcher and Joass facade in the original manner, turned a corner and added a lively baroque door feature which appears to say: "There you are Mr. Belcher: I can also do it as well as you, in your language." And then, in the same breath, he switches to the current 'served & servant' Modernism of the late 1960's: expressed functional elements differentiated from the office floors, Brutalist concrete, large areas of glass, etc. Few buildings exhibit such a skilful architectural gamesmanship (but see Horace Jones at Leadenhall). It's a rare and artful, old fashioned skill (similar but not the same as the self-conscious display of mannered gamesmanship exercised by Venturi at the Sainsbury Wing) that can be a source of joy to practice and experience. Absence of such an ingredient to practice arguably empties it of irony and extracts joy from its seriousness.*

## Lloyd's Register

71, Fenchurch Street, EC3
Richard Rogers Partnership, 2000
Tube: Bank

At a plot ratio of 8:1 overall and 11:1 (build area to site area) for the new build parts, the Lloyd's Register of Shipping building is a dense piece of development, squeezed into the site of existing premises like jam injected into the heart of a donut. The building is large and the design is clever: a professional achievement that simultaneously satisfies the requirements of City planners, the client and the passer-by in the street. Lloyd's wanted lots of space. The planners wanted old buildings and façades retained. And, as passers-by, we all want something to engage and enjoy. This design certainly does that. Old and new are married together in a complex manner that — as with all good design — appears effortless and, as a solution, self-evident. Which, of course, it isn't. As at Wood Street (same Director in charge) the conservative street experience belies a much more robust and bloody-minded reality deeper within the site. But the architects have achieved this magnitude of building and high density with a sensitivity to scale. This is especially evident in the entry court — a former churchyard: tight, cramped, over-powered by soaring glass lifts that silently glide up the side of the building . . . and yet it is comfortable and pleasant — in fact, a refreshing experience.

The Register goes back to 1689, sharing common roots with Lloyd's insurers (for whom, Rogers did the '86 building). However, the Register established its own identity in the late C18 and by 1901 it had its own building, designed by T. E Collcutt (described as 'arts & crafts baroque'). Lloyd's later expanded into nearby buildings and, in the 1920's acquired and demolished the church of St. Katherine Coleman, building more accommodation. And they kept on growing. In 1993 Lloyd's intended to move its 1300 staff out of the City, but this failed to come to fruition and it was decided to remain in the City, rebuilding on the existing site with a brief for a 24,000 sq.m. (net area) building, a minimum net/gross ratio of 70% (actually quite generous, but reflecting the site difficulties), a high plot ratio (which, as built, is 8:1 overall and 11:1 for the new parts), and the potential for a significant amount of sub-letting (which has turned out to be about 50%). To which the Rogers' team added an energy-efficient element.

*Lloyd's Register may have been completed fourteen years after its much more expensive relation, the Lloyd's '86 building, but it shares many of the basic features and details, as 88 Wood Street and K2, two other buildings by the practice in the City area. Also see the Broadwick Street building and Channel Four.*

The Collcutt building is the one that sits on the corner of Fenchurch Street and Lloyd's Avenue, and which has been so cleverly integrated into the new facilities designed by a team led by Graham Stirk (as for 88 Wood Street) so that the better parts of the old building have been retained. Apart from integrating new and old in this manner, the design strategy is similar to that of the Lloyd's '86 building and 88 Wood Street: an 80:20 equation as managers say, in which most of the accommodation is simple and rational, whilst the remaining part is complex. For example, the principal part of the accommodation is a series of 'wedges', two of which rise to 14 stories; the remainder is in the refurbished old buildings (which included adding another storey to the Grade II Listed Collcutt building). On Fenchurch Street, between the East India Arms on one corner and the Collcutt building on the other, sits a building that the architects and their client intended

**20** to demolish and replace with a glass pavilion. But the planners refused. And they were right, because it is the contrasts that make this overall configuration work so well. The 'wedges' are nominally 9m wide (but tapered) with atria in between. However these intermediate atria are not consistent divisions and the planning results in some very deep floor plates at the lower levels. The key point to be made is that these structures attempt to be as rational and consistent as possible, whilst finding discrete points at which they knit together with existing buildings and similar site constraints.

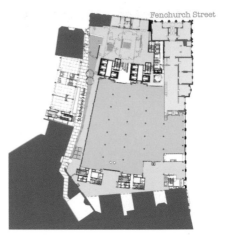

Fenchurch Street

The structure is mostly precast concrete with some elements poured on site to form a composite structure. Wherever possible, this is exposed so that it can play a role in providing thermal inertia. This allows night-time cooling and so reduces the peak heat gain / cooling issue during office hours (when computers and lights are heating the place up). These spaces are serviced by a deep plenum computer floor — into which fresh air is pumped — and by a ceiling level light beam / chilled beam fitting that obviates the need for the dreaded suspended ceiling. It also means the architects could provide a coved section to the ceiling soffit (to reflect light). As with 88 Wood Street the new parts have floor to ceiling glazing, providing excellent views and lots of daylight obviated when necessary by external, motorised louvres. Each cladding element is 3m. x 3.250m; there is an inner sheet of laminated glass plus an outer one of solar protective glass; the assembly is shaded by motorised, perforated aluminium louvres. These louvres are tracked, so they can be slid sideways to clean the window glass. The external lift cores are supported on steel frames and clad in glass — and it is these features that enliven and articulate the building.

**21** It is on a triangular site at the east end of Fenchurch Street, EC3, confronting car drivers arriving into the City from the east, that Terry Farrell offers us a solution to the corner problem to be read as a set of interpenetrating bodies, a kind of metaphorical architectural 'hinge' (1987). The building is an avowedly Post-Modern composition, together with a strong, implied classical arrangement of base, giant order, cornice and attic storey. The cramped entrance lobby around the side, on Leadenhall Street, struggles to offer us an impressive experience but, overall, the building is so much better than other, contemporaneous offerings from the Po-Mo lobby. (Whatever did happen to all that Po-Mo and Hi-tech stuff people got so excited about in the '80's and was so effortlessly absorbed by the beast of the metropolis.) Compare it with Stirling & Wilford's later design at Bank.

**22** The **Port of London Authority** at **10 Trinity Square,** EC3 was designed by Sir Edwin Cooper (1912, architect of the first Lloyd's building). His baroque wedding cake, designed as the managerial home of the PLA, stands high and proud, looking over the former, busy but troubled dock areas, as if its imperialist bombast might bear upon the workers even as its massing proudly welcomed ships into the Pool of London beneath the Tower of London. Neptune looks down upon the scene from his niche on high and the street level offers 'grand manner' gestures that are attractively urbane in scale. A touch of that imperialist bombast still exists on an upper level in this building; a suite of ornate executive dining and meeting rooms which remind one of how some people lived in the City until comparatively recently.

Photo: Nigel Young / Foster & Partners

Photo: Nigel Young / Foster & Partners

*The atrium's wall of glass stops about 3-4m above the paving, producing a sheltered but still outdoor area.*

## Tower Place

Foster's publicity for this rather elegant 42,000 sq.m. office building claims it as a reinvention of the famous, early '70's Wills Faber design replacing taller and 'insensitive' 1960's designs, and the medieval grain of small buildings and streets. Two triangular plan buildings are linked by a superb large atrium: "the stone and glass facades . . . allow maximum daylight penetration, while blade-like aluminium louvres provide solar shading and add a shifting textural layer to the facades." Actually, it is the 'atrium' semi-enclosed outdoor space which makes the project special. This incorporates 20m high façades and 3.56-metre-long borosilicate tubes which transmit wind loads from the façades to the steel columns supporting the roof structure. The needles have a load-bearing inner tube and a protective outer tube, with PVB sheeting between the two and with steel end components. A tensioned steel cable was inserted in each tube to resist wind suction.

*Underneath the atrium deck is a large coach park. And on the deck are sometimes difficult security guards who insist upon telling everyone they can't take photos (which is an improvement on when the building opened, when they didn't allow any tourist to even stand still). In fact, there are well-marked public rights of way (look for the studs) and they can't stop you doing whatever you want within those areas (which are, in effect, the public highway. I have had it in writing from the City Planning department). This difficulty is met all over the capital, especially in the City: at Canary Wharf, at Broadgate, at Merrill Lynch, Minster Court, etc. The problem is that what appears to be entirely public is actually private, with public access. Sometimes (as at Merrill Lynch and Minster Court) you will find gates closing off areas during the weekend. It all reminds one of the law at the end of the C19th. which forced owners to remove the gates in typical London squares which prevented the riff-raff from entering. Now we are getting gated communities all over again, courtesy of the late 20th.c. privatisation movement.*

## Tower Hill Environs

Horrible name, but a rather nice development which uplifts the game of tourism and is one of the best examples in London of how to handle a public place (which receives some 5m visitors per annum). Previous issues of this guide showed a Terry Farrell Po-Mo barn-like building housing, appropriately, a McDonald's. It has been swept away by this 'second bite at the cherry' that is more Barcelona-correct than Inigo-Jones-barn, but how refreshing that is. There is not a lot to say about the simple elegance of this scheme which provides a restrained backdrop to the Tower, providing toilets, ticket booths, an education centre, external performance spaces (sometimes in the former moat), etc., and also complements the Foster building immediately behind (Tower Place), which provides underground parking for visitors and coaches. *A not entirely dissimilar exercise by this same practice was at Denys Lasdun's National Theatre foyer areas.*

Photos: Morley von Strenberg

## 25 K2 (London Bridge House)

Tower bridge Approach, St. Katherine's Dock E1
Richard Rogers Partnership, 2005
Tube: Tower Hill / London Bridge

Being the last of the great dock projects, St. Katherine's was also the smallest and most expensive, but enjoyed a location adjacent to the Tower, on the eastern edge of the City of London. This meant that, after the dock closed in 1969, St. Katherine's was among the first areas to be redeveloped. However, more than a few fine warehouses disappeared and a somewhat ordinary office building was erected called the World Trade Centre. K2 is rather more splendid: a 16,000sq.m. replacement sitting on a prominent corner site. In essence, K2 is very simple — this is what the Rogers' team are good at: a rectangle split in two by a central, glass roofed atrium (crossed by bridges), thus enabling the building to be used by one or many tenants. This atrium terminates at a central lift core — making circulation eminently obvious (a fundamental aim of most Rogers' buildings), and the exterior is articulated at each corner by escape stairs and service lifts (cf Lloyd's '86, Lloyd's Register, and 88 Wood Street, as well as Channel 4). It is only when one sees these masters of the game at work that one realises how inept and overworked are most commercial office buildings. The output may bear strong family similarities (especially in the detailing), but each design expresses a sound analysis resulting in a simple diagram: fine examples of Vitruvius' 'intent' and 'expression of the intent'. The building's major 'architectural feature' is the manner in which the central atrium space is projected forward in order to announce its presence and the entrance to the building — a feature that bears a general similarity to the strategy employed at the Rogers-designed Channel 4 building of some years ago. This is a not unimpressive look-no-hands exercise which just stops short of appearing overstructured but which, as at C4, lends the building strong branding as well as playing orthodox architectural games. Some of those games are around the problematic entrance area, where the architects were challenged to exercise a proverbial inventive wit in order to cope with the different access levels.

(The structure — like almost all speculative office buildings in the City — is conventional steel frame, concrete filled columns, steel permanent shuttering to concrete floors, etc.)

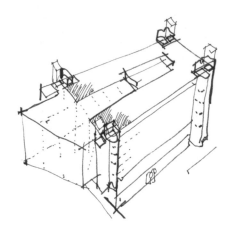

26 The **Tower of London** and **St. Katherine's Dock** are tourist attractions that are not unworthy of an architectural enthusiast's attentions. The Tower, for example, is interesting when construed as a village — which, in effect it is, with many people living there (their homes visible when walking the ramparts). On the embankment side, against the Thames, one enjoys fine views to City Hall and More London, as well as of Horace Jones' Tower Bridge. And you can walk from here through to St. Katherine's (and well beyond, into Wapping, if you feel energetic). The hotel here is arguably less horrific inside than outside, but the finest building left in the docks is the former warehouse with clock tower now converted into apartments (the Ivory House, George Aitchison, 1860). The brick wall surrounding much of the dock remains one of the last examples of such security measures that once contained all the docks. Most of the housing in the dock is by Renton Howard Wood Levin Partnership. This includes the 1977 buff brick, low-rise / high-density public housing as well as the mid-1990's wall of private residences around the dock's northern side. Other housing to the south-east is by the London County Council (LCC), of the 1930's, giving the housing historian a good example of housing over the last 70 - 80 years (including some old warehouse conversions along the river).

## Women's Library

Old Castle Street, E1
Wright & Wright Architects, 2001
Tube: Aldgate East

Housing a significant international collection, the Women's Library (a part of the Metropolitan University) uses a layout that responds to the client's requirements for highly accessible and secure private space coupled with the need for stringent environmental control in some areas. The building consists of an exhibition hall, seminar room, educational facilities, reading room, archives, cafe, offices, friends' room and garden. The most public spaces are on lower floors, with increasing security as one moves up through the building. Servicing requirements, coupled with the need for primary spaces such as the exhibition hall, led to the plan form. This consists of a series of large rooms, one on each floor, framed by two structural cores, which contain the circulation and services. This is set back from the washhouse wall, with ancillary accommodation between old and new. The combined resolution of the structure, environmental control and functions of the building led to a complex section of heavyweight construction.

The spaces intertwine in section so the uniqueness of each of the building's main functions is reflected architecturally. The spatial manoeuvres within the building are highly complex to reflect this uniqueness. For example the exhibition hall consists of overlapping spatial relationships and axis, while the reading room, a calm, white room is the only symmetrical space in the building. Design ideas are carried through from the strategic design to the smallest details, such as ironmongery and window details. Nine artists worked with the architects, eight of them making staircase panels representing a well-known woman.

*At the time of writing, a Law Library (also by Wright & Wright) faced in red brick had just been completed near the Women's Library. (Both are a part of the London Metropolitan University.)*

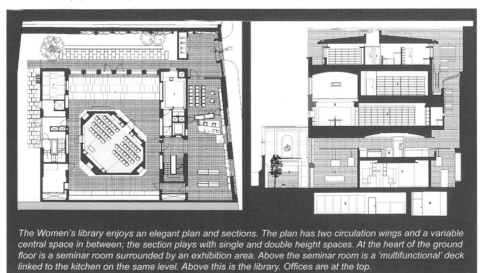

*The Women's library enjoys an elegant plan and sections. The plan has two circulation wings and a variable central space in between; the section plays with single and double height spaces. At the heart of the ground floor is a seminar room surrounded by an exhibition area. Above the seminar room is a 'multifunctional' deck linked to the kitchen on the same level. Above this is the library. Offices are at the top.*

# 28 Spitalfields: edge city

The current redevelopment of the former Spitalfield market area is about the City expanding into the East End and, in the process, demolishing parts of a former fruit and vegetable market founded in 1683 whose current buildings are from around 1928. (The landlord of the property is the Corporation of London — the City — and the Planning Authority is Tower Hamlets.) When originally proposed, the market buildings were neglected and unwanted. But un-suited entrepreneurial interests alien to financial trading started to provide food-stalls and the like in the old buildings; then there was a temporary opera facility ... (the market recently claimed to enjoy more visitors than the Tate Modern). What developers seemed incapable of providing was happening all on its own. But instead of embracing this, they bluntly promoted their instrumental mind-set and there began a controversy with the community which still continues in a zone mediating between Broadgate and the utterly different (but changing) nature of the area around Brick Lane (some of which includes gentrified late C17th. terraces such as Fournier Street, together with Nicholas Hawksmoor's recently renovated Christ Church).

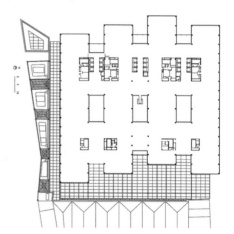

The EPR-designed office building on Bishopsgate (immediately opposite Broadgate and the entrance to Liverpool Street station) is nearly 26,000 sq.m., was the first of the post-recession redevelopment (1999) and is in marked contrast to the architectural Post-Modernism of Broadgate, revealing the change in developers' tastes in the intervening period. The shape reflects planning constraints that allowed height on Bishopsgate and required low mass on the Spitalfield side. And, in 2000, Foggo Associates completed an 18,550 sq.m. office building called **280 Bishopsgate**, north of the EPR building. (Foggo was a design partner at Arup Associates and in charge of their contribution to Broadgate.) But the heart of the redevelopment is a large Foster scheme of some 70,000sq.m. of offices and 4,700 sq.m. of retail space called **1 and 10 Bishops Square, E1.** This has, for a long time, been at the centre of a heated debate about change in the area which bears parallels with the battle seen at Covent Garden in the early '70's, and later at Coin Street.

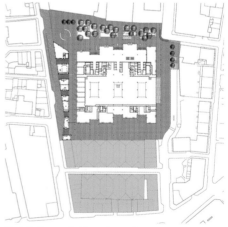

Lyons Sleaman and Hoare are responsible for refurbishing the remaining market spaces.

*Above right:* plans of the Foster building at Spitalfields. *The scheme cleverly seeks to mediate between Broadgate and the market, between instrumentally-minded capitalist financiers and the Bangladeshi community of Brick Lane, effectively extending the City eastward (a continuation of an expansionist theme noticeable since the mid-1980's). Inevitably, this changes values, customs, and the culture of the area, particularly within the old market itself. The base of the Foster design fulfils a disguise function to some of the more harsh contrasts of this equation: retail and market below, wrapping two sides of the building (complete with a public art management programme); huge office spaces above* (for City lawyers). *The scheme is strategically clever, but (as happens too often with a Foster building) it is let down by its detailed execution as opposed to its strategic intent. The place isn't exactly a comfort zone. But see it. Walk, for example, from Broadgate, through Spitalfields to Fournier Street and Brick Lane, and beyond to David Adjaye's Idea Store and to Alsop's building at the Royal London Hospital.*

# Bloomberg's:
## Reuters on steroids

Citygate House, 39–45 Finsbury Square, EC2
Foster and Partners / Julian Powell-Tuck, 2001
Tube: Moorgate

This is really a building to see on the inside, but you can get into the building's public art gallery and gain views through to the inner workings (otherwise try the Open House London weekend event). On the outside it is two buildings: a 'grand manner' building from the 1920's adjacent to a new 17,000 sq.m. commercial office building from Foster's studio (bizarrely posing as SOM circa 1960 via Ungers), unified by Julian Powell-Tuck's superb interior work (which includes coloured floor coding which can be seen from the street).

The drama of these interiors stems from Bloomberg's expressive culture: as if the former market leader (Reuters) woke up one morning to find it was an ad agency on something pharmaceutical. Bloomberg is actually a sophisticated number crunching factory and information service for financial institutions, but it's all high-energy stuff where staff are well paid, well served and given environments complete with swanky training facilities, a rolling art programme, large exotic aquaria on each floor (one of the largest collections in Europe, needing two full-time marine biologists to look after it), a lobby that doubles as a free cafeteria and more monitor screens than people.

In fact Bloomberg TV is everywhere — including the toilets and inset into cafeteria benches. Take it away and the affective energy level would drop dramatically. And much of the production takes place in Bloomberg's basement studios whose informality and economy is guaranteed to send shock waves through some media visitors. The cleverness resides in the fact that the TV epitomises everything that Bloomberg is and thereby becomes a celebratory device that permeates the entire ambience of the place. It is not every culture or architectural project that allows the

designer to reach through to the heart of a culture and manifest it in such a fun and dramatic manner. Oddly enough, it is not intrusive — it's wall-paper.

What strikes one about Tuck's work is that he has managed to realise something 'authentic': a one-to-one match between culture and design. It might not be the BBC (who, on the visits I have made with them, are stunned by the economy of the production facilities), Reuters or any ad agency one can think of, and it might not be a culture or design to your liking (this is the raw end of capitalism), but the authenticity of the design sings through and commands one's respect. And the more one thinks about that point, the more one becomes curious about what 'good' design really is. Without good styling, the realised design won't command respect; but the presence of good styling alone will not achieve this — something more is needed. Perhaps that something is a note of self-celebration. But what is this when it is not Sartre's 'bad faith'? This is easily recognisable, if only intuitively: that 'dung' note which suggests something is not right, that one is experiencing a pretence . . . On the other hand, such an impoverishment may be the authentic nature of some cultures. But to expressively grasp the essence of a culture and to be able to manifest this as an intrinsic part of a commodious design — that's arguably quite clever.

**30** **85 London Wall,** EC2 is designed by the Casson Conder Partnership, 1990. It is a pleasant, rather small building (5,085 sq.m. gross) and sits at the opposite end of the spectrum to the size and 'footprint' of buildings such as Minster Court, those at Broadgate, or Foster's 'gherkin'. It is for the smaller organisation and professional user and was executed in an unfashionably anachronistic manner, employing pre-cast stone and concrete panels in order to achieve a rather collegiate look for this conservation area, as if it really belonged in Oxford or Cambridge. The stone is Portland and Juane limestone. The building is worth comparing with William Whitfield's work at Richmond House or Powell & Moya's QEII Conference Centre.

# 31 Broadgate: a battle of giants

Broadgate/Eldon Street EC2
Arup Assoc. & SOM, British Rail Architects.
1984–92
Tube: Liverpool Street

The Broadgate story embraces issues of large scale urban change, architectural politics (a battle between modernist traditions and post-modernist sentiments), and a common ground probably unacknowledged by either of the main protagonists. The narrative begins with No.1 Finsbury Avenue, on Wilson Street, one of the first developments to be targeted at a specific market (financial trading), designed by Arup Associates and their first adventure designing speculative office buildings. Finished in 1984, No. 1 was the 'foundation stone' of a scheme put together by two of London's then most prominent developers (Lipton and Bradman) and British Rail. In brief, the master plan demolished a small station and amalgamated its services into an adjacent one (Liverpool Street), in the process unlocking the potential to develop a large tract of land on the edge of the City of London.

The master plan was put together by Arup Associates under Peter Foggo, but only the first half of the building programme was designed by them. The developer laid down stringent requirements and told his professionals how they were to design the buildings. Foggo reached a point where design constraints and the pace of development imposed upon him prompted a resignation and he left to set up his own practice (tragically dying of a brain tumour not long afterwards, in 1993). Meanwhile, in stepped SOM (Skidmore Owings and Merrill), an American firm simultaneously working on the Canary Wharf development in Docklands. Whilst Foggo was a part of that tradition concerned with honesty of construction, design integrity and those kinds of design values reaching back through the Arts and Crafts movement to Morris, Ruskin and Pugin in the last century, SOM's loyalties were to the historically-oriented eclecticism of an architectural Post-Modernism born in the USA in the 1970's.

The designs of these two firms demonstrate a disparity of values guaranteed to cause one another severe discomfort. The common denominator was the developer, Stuart Lipton, who imposed his own standards upon the design and construction teams, insisting the buildings were clad in granite and that the interiors – whatever the external styling – conformed to a well-researched set of ideas concerning the modern office building of the mid-1980's. However, whilst Arup used the granite as a self-evident form of decoration, with open joints indicating that the stone is in no way load-bearing and getting rid of it as soon as possible (reverting to a picturesque skyline of aluminium cladding), SOM attempt to make the granite appear load-bearing, as it might have been used 100

**Broadgate Plan**

Broadwalk House

1. Exchange Square
2. Finsbury Avenue Square
3. Broadgate Circle

Primrose Street

Appold Street

Finsbury Avenue

Liverpool Street Station

Bishopsgate

Octagon Arcade

*Top: view to Exchange House – surprisingly, this is a design that withstands changing fashions possibly better than other buildings at Broadgate.*
*Above: view up Bishopsgate toward Liverpool Street Station. The Foster development (see p.36) is opposite, within Spitalfields.*
*Adjacent top: view down the Bishopsgate colonnade.*
*Centre right: the mix of old and new in Liverpool Street Station (by the now defunct British Rail Architects department).*
*Bottom right: the Botera sculpture.*

years ago.

Arup's masterplan is rooted in the tradition of the West End squares of the later C18. There are three of them. The first – where we find No. 1 Finsbury Ave. – was originally characteristically British in character, moody and informally planted, with moss growing between the dank cobblestones (which the management periodically attempted to eradicate with doses of chemical). But it was all recently changed when an underground facility (gallery? restaurant?) was constructed. Now the square is rather bland. The buildings around this square are all by Arup, although the entirely brown ones on two sides are technically a part of the earlier development and do not have the ubiquitous granite overlay (they are part of the No1. Finsbury Avenue development, also by Arup).

The last square constructed is formal and axial, deriving inspiration from the *beaux arts* traditions in which American practice has its roots (and to which Post-Modernism returned, turning its back on the Bauhaus influences of the immediate post-war period). The detailing is 'big' and redolent of the Chicago from where it emanated, although there are distinct hints of H.H. Richardson's work in the rusticated sandstone of the landscaping. Broadgate Exchange – the building flanking the northern boundary – has to straddle the rail tracks and is made up of deep floor-plates carried by four huge parabolic arches, two of which plough through the centre building, whilst the other two articulate the exterior.

Between these two squares sits a third, the Arena, designed by Arup but with an American influence (Rockefeller Center). Like Exchange Square, it offers lunch-time events to entertain the Broadgate workers. In winter it becomes an outdoor ice-skating rink, complete with brightly attired kids and thumping music. However, underlying this C20 reference are other, historical inspirations. This is — or rather was — a columnated Roman ruin, the kind of ivy-covered, banked amphitheatre architects such as Palladio, Piranesi, Gibbs and many others would visit in order to draw inspiration from the Ancients and to rekindle what we always interpret as lost knowledge and remote origins. This is the ruins of monasteries destroyed in the Reformation, now overgrown and profoundly romantic. From this perspective, Arup and SOM meet together, even if they do come from entirely different directions. But the owners have seen the Arena as an opportunity to provide the additional retail space so obviously missing from the original scheme, and so Fogo's romantic dream has been somewhat buried beneath an over-building serving boozy traders. Such additions were needed, but one regrets the loss of a more profound cultural content. In between these poles sits the design of the redeveloped Liverpool Street Station, by the former British Rail Architects Group. It is at once old and new, old rebuilt to be new and new dressed up to appear old. The entrance on Bishopsgate is a self-conscious attempt to recreate Guimard's Metro entrances in Paris, now with cast-steel joints and glass covering. The old roof of the station has been extended in the manner of the original construction. Old-looking brick towers are new concrete ones clad in stick-on brick. Part of the old hotel (now a McDonald's) looks too new to be true; in fact, it was taken apart and rebuilt brick by brick. The forecourt is styled with four large light fittings straight out of the then-influential public works in Barcelona. It's a well executed, if heady mix of values.

*The art at Broadgate includes work from Richard Serra, Fernando Botero, George Segal, Barry Flanagan, Jim Dine, Xavier Cobero, Stephen Cox, Bruce McLean and Jaques Lipchitz — all of which dares the late Phillip Johnson's condemnation of 'turds in the plaza' (an unlikely criticism from such a man!). The Canary Wharf curators argue the Broadgate policy is old hat i.e. not into art as Post-Modern entertainment churn (ephemeral rather than permanent).*

*Broadgate can be compared with Spitalfields, Canary Wharf, Merrill Lynch, Minster Court, Paddington Basin, Kings Cross, Regent's Place and More London, together with a host of smaller developments re-writing the urban landscape of London.*

## 32 Helicon

1 South Place, EC2
Sheppard Robson, 1996
Tube: Moorgate

This confident 22,000 sq.m. speculative office building is of interest because it was one of the first significant buildings built after the early 1990's recession and because it helped to define re-established Modernist fashions. It also manifests current enthusiasms for glass as well as a concern with energy conservation and the control of solar gain as a functional basis for architectural articulation. For example, some façades are triple glazed, incorporating a 900 mm gap with aluminium louvres and acting as a thermal flue that can be opened at the top in summer and closed in winter. The plan has four service cores on the perimeter, whilst floor spaces are arranged around a central atrium beginning at level three, above a retail element at the lower levels. It was fresh at the time as a post Post-Modern and post-recession exercise indicative of values that have persisted to this day.

## 33 Winchester House

Deutsche Bank, London Wall, EC2
Swanke Hayden Connell Architects, 1999
Tube: Liverpool Street

The sleek London home of the largest bank in the universe (Deutsche Bank) is a well-respected speculative office building designed by the American firm Swanke Hayden Connell and fitted out by Pringle Brandon, offering the tenants accommodation that includes three open floor plates of 4600 sq.m., each with 650 people (described as 'a dealing factory'). On London Wall it streams along the street as a huge, gentle wave with delicately detailed aluminium windows that curve around the corner and punctuate the wall of Lussac limestone cladding. On entry into the grand lobby and between deals the building users can gaze upon expensive art work (including work by Anish Kapoor, Rachel Whiteread and James Rosenquist, etc.) that, no doubt, reassures them they are far from being Philistines, even in the workplace. The building is not weathering well, but remains a good example of the type (have a look around the rear).

The rear (Great Winchester Street) façade makes more of an effort to articulate itself. Internally, Deutsche Bank has a very impressive art collection, starting with the Rosenquist housed in the lobby: 'The Swimmer in the Econo-mist'.

**34** The spaces between the old warehouses (from the mid C18th) and the new, rather ordinary modernist office buildings (by Richard Seifert, 1978 - 85) at **Cutlers Garden**, E1, just to the east of Liverpool Street Station, are the key to the pleasures of this complex on the edge of the City. In an understated way, the development manages to achieve more than similar schemes. Here is the virtue of comparative reticence and the care with which quiet and calm urban spaces (with landscaping by Russell Page) have been reinvented from former industrial warehousing. Unfortunately, they're semi-private and the security guards sometimes let you know it. Have a look, but beware of questions about your camera.

**35** **Gibson Hall** (1864 - 5), by John Gibson, on the corner of Bishopsgate and Threadneedle, is a fine example of Victorian, neo-classical banking architecture designed as the HQ of a bank that replaced a neo-Palladian mansion formerly on the site. Externally, the hall is a fine, single-storey screen of large arched windows and giant order columns topped by allegorical statuary (worth comparing with the Bank of England). Inside, there is a large banking hall whose counters were not removed until 1982, after which time the place became an assembly hall and rentable venue. The adjacent Threadneedle Street has many 'grand manner' bank buildings from 1850 - 1920, now becoming death masks as their insides are hollowed out and rebuilt.

## 30 Finsbury Square

Eric Parry has completed an office on the east side of Finsbury Square that includes an unusual attempt at a west-facing office stone-clad facade — a screening that is worth examining (and trying to figure out). That's it: a speculative office building fronting the east side of the square — but not many such buildings sport such a well designed facade. Bizarrely, the balconies are not accessible to staff in case someone jumps off ! ; such is the contemporary Health & Safety mentality. Finsbury Square itself is a sadly neglected place that should be a principal City amenity. *Compare this with Plantation Place South and with a similar Parry exercise at Paternoster.*

27 - 30 Finsbury Square, EC3
Eric Parry, 2002
Tube: Moorgate

## Moorhouse

This is more like what we expect from the Foster office: slick, simple, incorporating a bold sculptural gesture (in this case, the curve in plan and in section on the south and east sides).

    The 19 storey, 30,500 sq.m. building (with 16 upper level office floors) coincidentally twins itself with No.1 London Wall, but is free of the constraint to lock itself into the 1950's 'pedway' system. But it otherwise defines itself as a latter-day version of the neo-Miesian / Corb manner 'showboxes' that once lined Route Eleven (now London Wall). Like those earlier buildings it is, for external observers, an exercise in town-planning elegance, together with a currently fashionable off-set grid pattern to the side facades (also see 100 Wood Street). Floors are approximately 1250-1900 sq.m. and the rent being asked (typical for early 2006 in the City) was @£50 per sq.m.

    At the base of the building is a new Crossrail station (Crossrail No1 Line, a part of the east-west line being constructed and about to become one of London's major construction projects). In typical architectural prose Lord Foster said about the building: "In contributing to the development of Crossrail line 1 — an essential addition to London's public transport network — Moorhouse illustrates that a single building can have wide-ranging urban implications. How people travel to and from work makes a greater contribution to sustainable architecture than any individual energy-saving features".

*Moorgate was once one of the principal City gateways, demolished (together with other gates etc) in 1761. It was burnt down in the 1666 Great Fire (togetehr with Ludgate, Newgate and Temple Bar), rebuilt and then demolished in the 1760's.*

*You could cover most of the City on a 'Foster' tour: Moorhouse, Spitalfields, No.1 London Wall, 100 Wood Street, 10 Gresham Street, 33 Holborn Circus, Tower Place, 30 St Mary Axe (the Gherkin), and the new building opposite the Lloyd's '86 building.*

Moorhouse, 117 Moorgate EC2
Foster & Partners, 2005
Tube: Moorgate

## 38 Milton Gate

1 Moor Lane, EC2
Sir Denys Lasdun, Peter Softley & Partners,
1991 Tube: Barbican

Like the National Theatre, Milton Gate betrays Denys Lasdun's fascination with diagonals and castles, as well as a peculiar lack of interest in entrances. Milton Gate is a block-filling, 20,000 sq.m. office building, cut by a diagonal route leading into an inner atrium, the exterior being entirely clad in green, double-walled glazing. It might be an intriguing technical and aesthetic exercise with both literal and metaphorical 'green' ambitions, but the design fails to appreciate the message it sends out: corporate defensiveness easily engenders a consequent sense of alienation. In this sense the building is, like his IBM office building adjacent to the National Theatre, less than a huge success. However it is by an architect who could produce some stunning work and — we admit — many people love it. (It also appears to be a precursor to the upper parts of Arup Associates' monster, Plantation Place.)

**39** Colonel' Seifert's **Tower 42** (completed between 1970-81), at 25 Old Broad Street, EC2, has been — until recently — one of the City's least missable buildings and once the headquarters of the NatWest Bank (called the NatWest Tower). The building towers 183 m high and cantilevers its floors from a massive concrete core – so massive that its builders argued it to be as much steel reinforcing as concrete (and had the greatest difficulty placing what concrete there is). Consequently, the plan offers a thin periphery of offices (similar to the Smithson's Economist Building). However, the intelligent London pigeon will notice that the plan is

that of the NatWest Bank's logo (although no one is any longer quite sure which came first).

After the IRA bombing of 1993 which prompted much rebuilding and refurbishment in this area, the ground floor area (free of columns because all loads come to ground via the core) was given a large glazed lobby, designed by GMW and the entire building was rebranded, reclad and internally refurbished rather than demolished (too difficult and expensive). The transatlantic rebranding is no doubt aimed toward the presence of many US organisations in the City since deregulation in the mid-1980's. Internally, Fletcher Priest did the upper level restaurant and cafes (see FP's Sedley Place off Oxford Street, and compare this restaurant with the upper level of Foster's 'gherkin'.).

**40** **Bunhill Fields** is one of those relatively lost parts of London — and probably should remain so if you are not a fan of old graveyards. But if solitude midst the metropolis has an appeal to you, give it a try. It is located between City Road and Bunhill Row and has been a public open space since 1867 and its packed gravestones are said to give an idea of what central London graveyards used to be like. On the other hand you may like to simply enjoy the place as a respite from a surrounding buzz, especially on a summer's afternoon. (There is a similar place in north Holborn, off Judd Street, called **George's Gardens**. Also try '**Postman's Park**', in the City, off Aldersgate.)

**41** A curiousity: **Fox**, the umbrella shop facade (1937; 118 London Wall, east of the Foster Moorhouse building), is by someone called Pollard. Its Vitrolite (a special kind of black glass, popularised in the inter-war years), stainless steel and neon façade remain an idiosyncratic delight.

Church gate, St Olave, Seething Lane

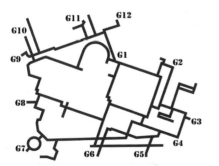

Knowingly or not, the Barbican reasserts a defensive, castle-like motif as a strategic aspect of its planning concept. Its perimeter is littered with 'gates' and its interior with walkways.

1. Alban Gate (Terry Farrell)
2. 88 Wood St. (Rogers)
3. 100 Wood St. (Foster)
4. Police Station (McMorran) + St Albans Tower (Wren)
5. 25 Gresham St. (Grimshaw)
6. Guildhall (Giles G. Scott)
7. 10 Gresham St. (Foster)
8. St Ann & St Agnes (Wren)
9. St Lawrence Jewery (Wren)
10. St Giles
11. Barbican (Chamberlin Powell & Bon)
12. NO.1 London Wall (Foster)

## Wood Street Group: haunted modernism

It is commonplace to note that what was once radical becomes, with hindsight, considerably less so and more deeply embedded in history than we had initially thought. For example, the '86 Lloyd's building, when looked at closely, becomes an exercise in continuity; history and context assert themselves. It's a theme Peter Ackroyd takes up in what at first appears a rather fanciful manner in his excellent *Biography of London*: the notion that the city has a living character that surreptitiously asserts itself and affects what is done within its domain. Take the Wood Street area for example. Currently, it is a fascinating grouping of buildings, many of them very recent and including designs from Foster, Rogers, Farrell, and Grimshaw. These buildings can all be seen to be accommodating themselves to historical memory, traditions and the detritus history has left as a proliferation of churches, their towers, former graveyards, pieces of Roman and medieval defensive wall, and streets that have their historical roots in Roman and later Medieval times. For example, the Wood Street area of London was once a Roman fort; its principal north-south axis is now Wood Street and at its northern end was a gateway that became known as Cripplegate (adjacent to St. Giles Church, which still stands, now within the Barbican).

The physical manifestation of this rich history was badly damaged (and in many instances obliterated) in the Blitz of World War II. Christopher Wren's church of St. Alban's, for example, survived only as a tower — the one that now stands in the centre of a widened street — and one has to imagine a scene that for many years took on a curiously romantic character as nature populated the ruins (of what had formerly been a garment area of large Victorian warehouses) with grasses and pretty wild flowers. David Kynaston describes the Barbican area as, for many years, 'virtually a wild heath, littered with the remnants of a commercial civilisation'. But the LCC planners saw it all as a massive opportunity to march optimistically into the future, taking the relaxed building controls of the mid-1950's as an opportunity to offer the City a realigned London Wall ('Route Eleven', the making of which unearthed hundreds of human skulls) and the Barbican.

And yet, in the 60 years since the Blitz and its devastation, the area has increasingly settled back into a manifest history. The Barbican — as an unconscious reinvention of the Roman fort — carefully knits its way around old Roman walls like an elephant avoiding eggshells; the Guildhall reconstructed its ruinously damaged halls and demarcated the line of a recently discovered Roman amphitheatre in the paving of its piazza; McMorran's police station reinvented the prisons of the street; Alban Gate attempted to recreate Cripplegate; and modern temples to Mammon from Foster, Grimshaw and Rogers nestle up against preserved former churchyards.

# The City

**42** *The **Barbican**, Silk Street, EC1 by Chamberlin Powell & Bon, is a classic 1950's dream of regeneration, replacing an area that was heavily bombed during WWII. A key planning concept at the time concerned enthusiasms for elevated pedestrian walkways and decks. When debated in 1959, one City Deputy suggested that, 'opposition to elevated walkways was based on prejudice' and that 'once people were up on the walkways there was no need for them to come down at all — until they wanted to go home'. The notion developed into plans for a thirty mile City network, only abandoned after the early 1970's property boom collapsed and alarmed conservationist sentiments were reversing the lack of perceived value in anything Victorian or the City's medieval street pattern, significant parts of it obliterated by highway widening schemes that accompanied the pedway scheme. The concept was meant to slowly insinuate its way across the City as buildings were replaced and remnants can still be found in unlikely locations, e.g. opposite the north side of Lloyd's, waiting for Lutyens' Midland Bank building to be demolished. It was a planning concept that entirely missed the opportunity to develop the network of City back streets and alleys (as at Leadenhall Market or Bow Lane), allowing pedestrians a choice: either to tackle the traffic and fumes, or wind one's way through back streets alive with the kinds of activities developers deny and frequently replace by blue plaques noting the former location of a coffee house or some such.*

*The Barbican development itself (1957 - 79) is one large, 'gated' deck serving private apartments, an arts centre and schools, at the heart of which is a central landscaped area complete with lake, ornamental medieval church (St. Giles) and what the Pevsner guide now describes as a 'thrillingly vertiginous crossing' slung at high level between gigantic concrete columns (visitors no doubt following the painted yellow lines on the paving so they don't get lost whilst seeking the arts centre). The composition comprises tower blocks and terraces, all of it monolithic and 'brutalist', providing an experience that mixes exhilaration with hesitation. No one says so, but its success owes, one suspects, as much to a sustained middle-class content as any design feature.*

*The Barbican's Waterside Cafe was refurbished in 2002 by Allford Hall Monoghan Morris. The same architects are also responsible for a current masterplan for the arts centre (and they have continued to do interior work since then, removing some awful additions to the original work and generally restoring the centre to habitability and lending it a more civil tone).*

## Alban Gate:
## strange twins at the portal

The developer for Alban Gate argued that replacing a 1960's shoe-box office tower (Lee House) was not feasible unless the new building could be much larger. Farrell's idea was to acrobatically use air-rights over London Wall and provide two linked towers totalling 35,000 sq.m. of office space for multiple lettings, all within the planner's height constraints. The Post-Modern outcome is no longer in fashion and Farrell's compositional concerns have commanded respect but not affection. However, the towers themselves — the parts up there — are only one half of what was going on and what Farrell was attempting to achieve.

Always an urbanist, Farrell brought his own agenda to the project and attempted to design the building as a new gateway up onto the Barbican deck — a reinvention of the medieval Cripplegate that had been located slightly north, adjacent to St. Giles Church in the heart of the Barbican development. His intention was that the planners should be persuaded to landscape and pedestrianise Wood Street and he could then provide a sweep of stairs up to the deck level and partially heal the divorce between the Barbican and the rest of the City. It never happened and the resulting difficulties at the lower levels are an uncomfortable compromise. Where is the front door? At ground level or up on the deck level? (It is at ground level, but around the corner, in Monkwell Street.) It simply doesn't work, but Farrell might have pulled it off and he should be praised for having had the vision and commitment to attempt a redress of the legacy that 1960's planners had left to the City.

The building belongs to the same era as others by Farrell especially Embankment Place (1991) and MI6 Building (1992) and what the architect sees as the building's principal merit — its then fashionable, neo-Michael Graves compositional play with step-backs, granite and glass – is what many others dislike about the scheme. But in this concern he is hardly different to the best Modernists, men such as Lubetkin, who were profoundly concerned that Modernist ideology neglected compositional issues. The problem is that his designs are read as bombastic and over-worked — a kind of shoulder-padded 'Gucci architecture' strutting its stuff and ironically, given his genuine concern with populist themes, unloved.

As a champion of Post-Modernist architectural values during the 1980's Farrell was among the best. But this building (1991) is the gravestone of a set of stylistic values that vanished overnight with the recession then swallowing the construction industry. When it emerged a few years later (around 1995) the Post-Modern themes that had dominated architectural debate from about 1975 (very much a North American import) had been dismissed and forgotten, apparently never to be spoken of again (even by developers). Everyone had become Modernist: a new kind of post-Post-Modernism, minus the appetite for 'ironically' mining history for themes and features.

*The obvious comparisons are with the building's neighbour, **88 Wood Street** — a building Farrell criticises as 'non-contextural' — and with the **25 Gresham Street** building by Farrell's former partner, Nicholas Grimshaw.*

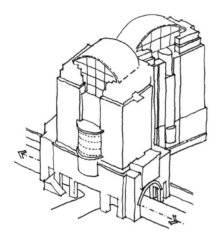

**44** *Golden Lane, EC1, immediately north of the Barbican and preceding it in design, is a classic post-war example belonging to an era when few self-respecting architects would dream of working for a 'commercial' (i.e. private) practice and most wore a left-wing, humanist bias on their sleeve. It is designed by Chamberlin, Powell & Bon (1952–62) as something distinctly urbane, without garden suburb association. The principal block has a remarkable roof-line which lifts the less expressive architecture of the lower parts. Ignored or derided for years, the development — like many similar '50's and '60's schemes — is now prime home-hunting territory for young architects.*

## 45  88 Wood Street

88 Wood Street, EC2
Richard Rogers Partnership, 2000
Tube: Moorgate, St. Paul's, Barbican

The partners who brought Lloyd's to realisation are the mature men of the practice and some of them have even retired, with Rogers himself as a Lord of the Realm more involved with political and strategic issues than the details of buildings, leaving a younger generation to take over the firm's values (in this instance, Graham Stirk). At 88 Wood Street, the outcome is a building that many people consider to be one of the better office buildings in London.

The design was begun in the heady 'bubble' years of the late 1980's with Japanese client (Diawa) and planning permission was granted in 1992 for 18,000 sq.m. of lettable office space. But the building only got as far as foundations (locked into an existing telephone exchange that was, for a time, listed) before the early '90's recession hit. When the client returned it was with a brief for a building of 24,000 sq.m. lettable space within the same building geometry. Four extra floors were cleverly insinuated by means of reducing the floor thickness and partly by moving air conditioning plant to the basement. Construction began again in 1995 with Diawa taking nine of the floors and now requiring a large service pavilion to be provided on the south side of the building — a 'blind' building that subsequently had to be glazed and converted when Diawa decided not to move in after all. When completed at the end of 1999, the building comprised three terrace blocks rising in steps from 8 to 18 storeys, arranged to fit a difficult site geometry and serviced by six perimeter access cores. These also have toilets, provide primary services distribution, fire escapes, etc., and in this sense are very similar to the Lloyds building. The strategy is the same: offer a regular and rational, usable geometry of space within the peculiar shape of the site, and to design the service cores in the left-over spaces around the perimeter. (*Also see Channel 4, Lloyd's Registry and K2.*)

**46** *The **Guildhall**, EC2, is the home of the Corporation of London, with a layered architectural history dating back to 1411. Older parts damaged during WWII, carefully restored and extensively added to with additions by Sir Giles Gilbert Scott, Son & Partner (1880–1960). The comparatively provincial looking 1955–58 north block bears comparison with his Bankside power station (now the new Tate Modern); the detailing is similar. The long block on the west side, undertaken after Scott's death, is a mere eight years later (1966–69), and designed by the same practice now, apparently, led by an opportunistic younger generation in the office with different ideas to the old man. The result is classic, high quality 1960's: lots of prefabricated concrete that steps out at the upper levels, nodding toward medieval traditions. This wing helps to form the piazza in front of George Dance's C18 Gothic / Indian façade. The **Guildhall Art Gallery** (2000) that sits on the eastern side of the piazza in front of the old*

*Guildhall frontage is a high-quality but rather bizarre Post-Modern building designed by Richard Gilbert Scott (the grandson of Giles Gilbert Scott, who worked on the restoration of the Guildhall), thus continuing a peculiar line of patronage. The original was destroyed in WWII and the new one is as much reception facility as art gallery and has a link on its northern end into the old parts of the Guildhall. The City runs a marketing suite on the gallery's south-east corner which includes a wonderful model of the City area, used for marketing purposes and therefore only accessible by arrangement (try Architectural Dialogue or Open House London). During the construction of the gallery, Roman foundations were uncovered that demonstrated this was where they had an amphitheatre. This has become the prompt for an occasional fancy dress celebration of this City heritage within the piazza.*

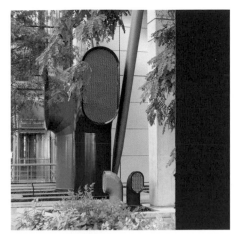

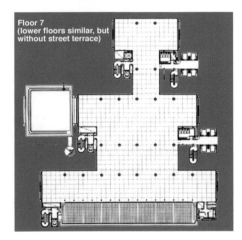

Floor 7
(lower floors similar, but
without street terrace)

Despite Farrell's contention that the building is 'non-contextual', it is distinctly so on the Wood Street frontage, where the height is kept down to something like the general height of frontages along the street. The building then cleverly and systematically rises up in two-storey increments to 18 storeys on the western frontage — a height that more or less matches the bulk of Farrell's adjacent building. This was allowable so near to St. Paul's Cathedral because the building effectively sits within the visual 'shadow' of Farrell's building. (Other noteworthy neighbours — such as Foster's 100 Wood Street and the Sheppard Robson building opposite that — did not have this advantage.)

A major characteristic of the design is its extensive glazed perimeter. This is partially shaded by the cores on the south side and by the restricted frontage on the west but heat gain is, in any case, obviated by triple-glazing and an air extract system that draw the air heating up between the panes of glass before it enters the building. The pure, white glass then allows spectacular views all around — off-setting the depth of the floor-plate at some points. (The irony, of course, is that these two factors — daylight and aspect — can be at odds with one another in a modern office building loaded with computer screens.)

The lobby area is another of the building's dramatic features, stretching from the east through to the west façade, looking out on to London Wall along the building's northern flank. Its long internal wall is of polished plaster.

The 33,000 sq.m. gross building is on a conventional 1.5m grid, its structure alternating 15 x 6m bays with 10 x 6m bays of in-situ, post-tensioned concrete. External bracing — articulated on the north and south ends — stabilises the building. The service cores (normally what stabilises a building) are themselves stabilised by the building frame.

Old-fashioned Modernist values (truthfulness, readability and the like) are coincidentally illustrated by things such as the coloured steel structure and air vents: red for foul air, blue for fresh — although you would be forgiven for thinking of them in terms of mama, papa and the babies.

**47** *The Wood Street area appears to be dotted with old churches and left over parts such as towers and graveyards (e.g. **St. Albans**, a Wren church and tower of 1602 - 7, which survived the Fire but not WWII; only the neo-Gothic tower remains in Wood Street). Among these, the buildings that are most important are two Wren churches: **St. Lawrence Jewry** (right; 1671 - 80; damaged in WWII and restored by Cecil Brown, 1954 - 7) and **St. Agnes & St. Anne** (far right; 1677 - 87; to the east of St Lawrence). Like most of the 23 remaining Wren churches in the City (he built St. Paul's and 51 churches over a period of 46 years; the Victorians destroyed 19 and WWII took out another 9), what you experience is a lot of restoration work (and sometimes contention re authorship — St. Anne's is*

*sometimes attributed to Hooke), but nevertheless often impressive and definitely a part of the character of the Wood Street area. Some people make a comparative study of the churches and their experience of Wren's gamesmanship in applying his aspirational values and dealing with particular circumstances certainly enlivens the subject and brings it alive. (Try a visit to the Guildhall bookshop to see what is available on the subject.)*

## 48  100 Wood Street

100 Wood Street, EC2
Foster and Partners, 2000
Tube: St. Paul's; Bank; Barbican, Moorgate

Foster and Partners' eleven storey, 20,405 sq.m. contribution to the grouping in Wood Street is a sandwich of offices in between two entirely different facades, addressing two different urban demands. Venturi would approve. The east facade (on Wood Street) is an exercise in good manners, encouraged by the City Planners who insisted upon Portland stone, a height restriction and cutbacks at the upper level — the latter being interpreted by the Foster team as a major opportunity to get away from the offset of glass and stone on the facade and indulge in what they love best: a curved and triangulated construction that vaults over to the west side of the building. But if you were to quickly dart through the retained medieval alley to see what was happening on the St. Mary Staining side, you get a surprise: the vaulting has disappeared and an entirely different game is going on that seeks to respect another planning demand: this time to allow daylight onto the former churchyard. The facade becomes a dramatic curved and raked exercise ostensibly propped by large cast columns akin to the 'giant order' of an arcade. (One can't but help remember an early Jim Stirling scheme that involved a leaning façade.) But look behind the glass and you see inner columns that reveal the outer ones as at least a conceit and possibly downright fakes. Here, too, the building has to cope with some significant neighbours: the rear ends of Rogers' 88 Wood Street, a Sheppard Robson building in Noble Street, and Nicholas Grimshaw's 25 Gresham Street — not to mention fragments of Roman and medieval wall that are just opposite. They all jostle together around the focal point of the green grass and tree of the churchyard.

One increasingly likes this building, but possibly for the wrong reasons. There is a self-evident narrative to it that says something about the politics of creation about which most other buildings remain mute. And with its '50's fashion on the Wood Street side, its *moderne* diagrid barrel-vault, and its sub-Jim Stirling west side, the building is a rich mix — which is possibly why the Foster office keeps quiet about it.

**49**  *Directly opposite 88 Wood Street sits the* **Police Station** *designed by McMorran and Whitby. This is pure architectural Mannerism, but of a refined and cool pre-Venturi genre. As constructed, the station was intended to serve that central one third of the city so badly Blitzed in 1941. As a part of the 1960's rebuilding that included the adjacent Route Eleven and Barbican, it belonged to a promised future. As a design, the station belonged to the 1930's rather than the 1960's. And as an institution strongly imbued with pride, ceremony and the hierarchical mores of a City Police force with a long history, it was the swansong of an era:*

*fifteen years later it had been reinvented as a specialist support facility to the other stations in the Square Mile and its police talk nostalgically about the old days. The design was idiosyncratic even in 1966. At a time when capitalist interests in the City were breaking new ground by embracing post-war Modernism, McMorran was offering the Police a courtyarded Italian Renaissance palazzo (simultaneously conforming to the accepted development convention of a tower and podium). The latter was the courted villa, including stables for 16-18 hand police horses, and prominent vents disguised as chimneys; the tower was a tall block whose upper half was given over to residential accommodation for unmarried officers (separate sexes, of course). On the outside it's Portland stone, while the inner court is faced*

*in London stock bricks. However, the detailing — African hardwood doors and sash windows, for example — is always well considered and as sturdy as the structure is deliberately Cold War bomb-proof. The lobby even includes stonework from Roman walls found during construction. (McMorran also designed the Old Bailey extension and a building on the west side of the Reform Club in Pall Mall. Sadly, he committed suicide just as the station was completed and the large hall on the station's piano nobile (the tall windows on Wood Street), was named after him — only to be renamed some years later.)*

## 25 Gresham Street

This — the first of Nicholas Grimshaw's efforts in the City — may be one of its better office buildings. The plan (1000 sqm.) is simple enough, but it splits the core in order to make arrival and internal movements a dramatic event by locating the lifts at the very front of the building. This (the south facade) is the key to the design. In typical Grimshaw fashion, it attempts some architectural acrobatics by cantilevering / suspending itself over the historic garden of St. John Zachary (a public area that was once part of a church burnt down in the Great Fire of 1666) and produces a novel and pleasantly informal entry area which is approached from the side rather than frontally. Compare its informality with Foster's 10 Gresham across the street. And note the design's integration of the garden. *(As an aside, Grimshaw was once Terry Farrell's partner, adding another competitive note to this grouping of buildings.)*

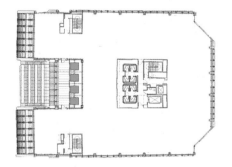

*25 Gresham's lobby area is truly novel within the genre of speculative office buildings and makes a bold attempt to make the entire office frontage an aspect of the urban issues at this part of the street. The cladding is the ubiquitous stone (in this case slate), now held in place by distinctly decorative stainless steel 'spiders' - a device that hovers between High-Tech and something truly more ornamental, perhaps making the cladding the least successful aspect of this otherwise fine building.*

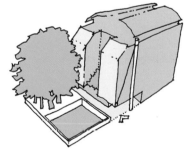

# The City

## 51 10 Gresham Street

10 Gresham Street, EC2
Foster and Partners, 2003
Tube: St. Paul's, Bank, Barbican, Moorgate

We were all awaiting a reaction to computer-generated curves and a nostalgia for the more brutal constructional verities of Mies van der Rohe to return to fashion. And here it is — from the Foster team, where Wood Street meets Gresham. There is even something Miesian about the scale of the fenestration, although the chamfered escape tower corners and attic stories (for planning reasons) hark back to a different theme in '60's design. It seems everyone is Po-Mo these days. But while scandal accompanied the revelation that Mies actually went around corners in a somewhat theatrical rather than functionalist manner, these architects are quite happy to go one step further and parody the whole game in aluminium cladding.

Despite all that, this 27,000 sq.m. office building (with a large central atrium) is actually quite good. It has comparatively narrow 18m. deep floor-plates clad in a 'ventilated façade' with wood Venetian blinds and a PR blurb that says lots about natural materials and turns the planners' constraints into positive architectural features. However, one can't but help comparing its pompous entrance (complete with Marilyn Monroe curves to the entry glazing) to the likes of Lloyd's Register, 25 Gresham, or even 88 Wood Street.

The building on the west is the Wax Chandler Hall, now separated off as a discrete 'grand manner' building with a public way between it and 10 Gresham (as if each symbolised the schizophrenic values of City workers: modernist neo-functionalism for 9-5, and 'grand manner' for in between-times socialising). However, on the south side there is an addition given over to a restaurant / cafe which sports a very New York water feature adding to the north American undertones.

## 52 No1 London Wall

No 1 London Wall, EC2
Foster and Partners, 2003
Tube: St. Paul's, Bank, Barbican, Moorgate

Squatting above and around new premises for the Worshipful Company of Plaisterers (entry on the Noble St. side; the remainder of the ground floor is service areas) are the flowing curves of this 19,308 sq.m. office building that makes quite a contrast with its neighbour, 88 Wood Street. It's small entry lobby is on London Wall, from where escalators take users up to the office floors (approximately 1900-1300 sq.m. net). Reception is on the 1st floor, where there is a central lift core serving the remainder of the building (and also a bridge link across to the Barbican, a part of the old 1950's 'pedway' system). It's interesting that facility managers aren't scared of curves these days (unlike when Erskine's Ark was built, not so many years ago).

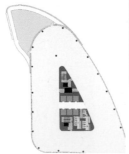

**53** **St. Paul's Cathedral** has to be London's principal work of architecture. It's large (155m long, 111m high), old (1675-1711), was designed by an English genius of note (Sir Christopher Wren), and has — particularly since its survival during WWII — come to serve as a symbol of all that is English. In town planning terms the building dominates central London and has engendered recurring controversy among supporters and detractors of its need

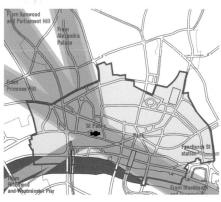

for metropolitan prominence. Viewing corridors from a variety of London vantage points impose constraints upon the development potential for tall buildings and issues of adjacency have been among London's more contentious architectural debates. This controversy became quite heated during Prince Charles' intense interest in the mid-1980's redevelopment proposals that came to a long-winded fruition as the Paternoster development (by a group of architects, under the general guidance of Sir William Whitfield).

Does the building merit such a status and attention? The design belongs to the tail end of an era when geometric symbolism embodied cosmological meaning, when Wren, the self-taught architect, was deeply conscious of the French concept of 'Natural' and Customary' beauties that Kant was to divide between the noumenal and the phenomenal, when London was becoming a boom-town and modernism (as we appreciate the term in a broad cultural sense) was manifesting itself even as many architects still pretended to a 'speculative', masonic knowledge. It's a building on the cusp, post Inigo Jones and pre the Adam Brothers and others (such as Chambers and Soane) who were the fathers of latter day professionalism.

As such it is a dry and mechanical design, something deeply intellectualised but hardly informed by the emotive content Wren's assistant, Nicholas Hawksmoor, was able to give his own church designs in the early C17th — buildings whose smaller scale is yet imbued with more feeling of an awesome 'sublime'. (Try reading Peter Ackroyd's 'thriller' about Hawksmoor.)

In truth, St. Paul's is a Gothic church in disguise (as Wren was painfully aware) and was hardly deemed to be architecturally radical, even by its author. And it now serves ritualistic bonding ceremonies between City and Monarchy and can't be treated lightly, but has to be subject to a careful interrogation and deconstruction of its meanings. A pleasant start at that is to not only visit the building but to climb through the innards of its dome to the viewing platform at the top — a journey of exposure within the structure of the thing.

***Viewing corridors*** to St. Paul's Cathedral impose tight constraints upon that key area wanting tall buildings: the City (see left). They push them towards natural areas of potential and possibility in the north-east part of the City (where the 'Gherkin' is located). Around the Cathedral itself are sacrosanct zones where everything must be relatively low (in effect, about 8 storeys).

Incidentally, it took as long to realise the British Library as St Paul's, and the architect of the latter became as disillusioned as that of the former. Projects such as the Royal Courts of Justice and Westminster Palace suffered similar fates. Similarly, areas such as Kings Cross have taken almost generations for schemes to come to fruition and the South Bank is only now enjoying a make-over that nevertheless stops short of the ambition of earlier schemes.

# 54 Paternoster: a fearful assemble

Paternoster Square, EC4
Various architects, 2001
Tube: St. Paul's

Otto Wagner once spoke of architecture as being a path that was troublesome and full of thorns. That sounds like a good description of the Paternoster Square development which was plagued ever since its post-war birth in an area devastated by the German Blitz of WWII. It had, historically, been an area of book publishers and over 6m. books were destroyed in the bombing. The replacement was another of those 'traffic-free precincts' designed over a car park, master-planned between 1955 - 62 by Lord William Holford, and executed by a number of architects (1964 - 7). Ideas for an '80's replacement scheme became bogged down by the interventions of Prince Charles and worthy schemes (e.g. by Rogers and Arup Associates) were rejected. Neo-Georgian, neo-Roman and neo-Florentian schemes were sampled, finally resulting in Sir William Whitfield being appointed to reconcile tastes and values (see his mention on the Institute of Chartered Accountants, work done in the mid-1960's).

*The central column, with MacCormac Jamieson Prichard behind.*

It is difficult to know exactly what Whitfield's contribution has been — apart, that is, from his own neo-fascist styled building (which is actually not so bad, but very oddly scaled, especially when facing St. Paul's), and the 23m. high central column with nothing much to celebrate except the end of a dogged project history. Perhaps it doesn't matter, but one has to see this development and compare it with Broadgate and Canary Wharf, as the other two obvious developments with which it must bear comparison. (Also, perhaps, Spitalfields and Merrill Lynch.) These are all unhappy beasts, demonstrating a speculative capitalist imperative which, in the case of Paternoster, met sentiment head on. The view down onto the rooftops from St. Paul's is dispiriting and, on the ground, the various colonnades all induce groans of disturbance (on the northern boundary they are

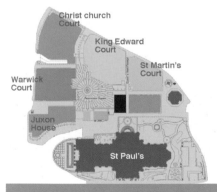

• *Christ Church Court : Rolfe Judd*
• *King Edward Court: Eric Parry (with Sheppard Robson).*
• *St. Martin's Court: Allies & Morrison*
• *Churchyard buildings by Whitfield with Siddell Gibson.*
• *Juxon House: Sir William Whitfield (with Sheppard Robson).*

*The Parry exercise in a fashionable, neo-Guiseppe Terragni look, but the massing somehow goes terribly wrong on this building, failing to provide the desired enclosure (not as good as thew building in Finsbury Sq.). And there is nothing complimentary to say about the colonnade in front.*

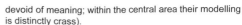

*View to St. Pauls and Temple Bar, with MJP on the right.*

*Whitfield and Heatherwick.*

devoid of meaning; within the central area their modelling is distinctly crass).

However, the development is arguably still more likely to integrate itself into the surrounding fabric than, say, Broadgate (and definitely the island of Canary). The basic urban design scheme is actually rather good: unremarkable, but carefully considered. And these are skilled architects at work (with a distinct Cambridge link): MacCormac Jamieson & Prichard, Allies & Morrison (far from their best work), Rolfe Judd, Eric Parry (with a building looking as if it were inspired by Terragni and thus offering us another dose of neo-fascism), and (along St. Paul's Churchyard) Whitfield with Siddell Gibson (the brick buildings — actually not all bad and possibly the most satisfying of them all). Sheppard Robson were in there helping Parry and Whitfield.

Finally — as the formal link between St. Paul's and the central court of Paternoster — we have a resurrected Temple Bar, freshly restored, like some scrubbed up old lady. This used to sit in the middle of Fleet Street, marking the boundary of the City and has a gory history (a place to spike the heads of traitors, for example). It was taken away in 1878 and held at a park in north London until this somewhat theatrical relocation (which somehow manages to undermine its authenticity). Thomas Heatherwick has a sculptural piece here (on the north side of the Whitfield building), disguising two cooling towers as an electricity substation.

Take a long look; it's not all bad and offers some lessons in the mis-channelling and over-working of well-intentioned creative abilities.

*Sculpture within the Whitfield arcade facing St. Paul's. Right: view to the Whitfield façade that couples St. Paul's west frontage.*

*Take your time, walk about and try to deconstruct the game. Apart from the viewing corridors, note the corners, the attempts to fracture monolithic façades and introduce variety and views (mini viewing corridors onto St Paul's). At this level, the archive is hard to argue with, and yet there is still a demoralised and exhausted undertone to the place, perhaps indicative of the project's fraught history and desperate attempts to be politically correct.*

Merrill Lynch & GlaxoSmith Global HQ, 2
King Edward St. EC1; Swanke Hayden Connell
Architects, 2001
Tube: St. Paul's

## 55 Merrill Lynch: City pride

The planning department of the City of London is particularly proud of two recent office buildings. Each — in entirely disparate ways — epitomises their aspirations for City architecture. The most obvious of this pair is Foster's Swiss Re building at 33 St. Mary Axe – what is colloquially known as the 'Erotic Gherkin'. Its merits are obvious, but it remains firmly within a typology of tower designs using a simple piazza:tower equation, much like the ageing Commercial Union building that sits opposite and represents what was, until the Foster building was completed, the best example of this type in the UK.

The other building the planners are proud of is very different: a building that necessarily keeps itself low in order to respect London's viewing corridors to St.... Paul's Cathedral clear. These corridors – giving views from most of London's high points, such as Parliament Hill on Hampstead Heath – force high buildings into a few locations and invariably require sites near St. Paul's to be carefully considered. The outcome is a complex set of development issues that can easily be imagined. These are epitomised by the reinvented Paternoster development on the Cathedral's northern side – an office complex that typifies a debate and controversy that has been prolonged for decades, draining the architects involved of their creative motivations.

Immediately to the north of Paternoster, however, is the pride of the planners: the London headquarters of the global American organisation, Merrill Lynch. They are housed in a custom-design complex of buildings striving to incorporate existing architecture and create a genuinely interesting set of disparate office spaces including the enormously deep trading floors characteristic of such organisations. The latter are reputed to be the largest in Europe, but Swanke Hayden Connell have managed to integrate them within an architectural whole that is not only full of architectural variety, but even intimacy.

The overall complex takes the form of a flexible *assemble* incorporating an old post office building, a set of old Victorian terraced buildings, and the site of a Wren church and its former graveyard (now one of the City's public gardens). It manages to incorporate servicing access, colonnades, an atrium, courtyards and a new public alley with great success and entirely without the depressingly monolithic qualities that dominates much of Canary Wharf, that other scene of North American influence in London. Although one entrance is dominant, the overall arrangement has been carefully considered so that it can be fragmented and dealt with as discrete parts. Merrill Lynch could leave and parts of the complex could even be severely altered, but without compromising the overall urban equation.

And while the planners can be pleased with the outcome, Merrill Lynch are also pleased with a set of office interiors that successfully provides open spaces full of the daylight and views that, again, one notes absent from most of the American models at Canary Wharf. There is even a fine roof garden hidden away (off the Board Room, of course).

But it is the in between spaces that are the delight of this complex, making another contrast — this time with Paternoster, across the road. The long alley that lies behind the Victorian buildings along Newgate Street is particularly welcome.

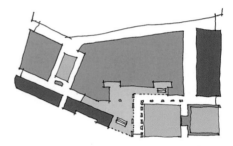

*The green parts in the diagram above are the old church and its former graveyard. The purple are the former Post office (on the east) and a terrace of integrated Victorian buildings. the remaining orange parts are the offices, with a large lobby at the centre of the complex. The alley between the southern range and the new blocks behind is a pleasant (if rather heavily secured) route that, in theory, should allow access all the way from east to west. In fact, one is forced to stop within the entrance lobby, where guards want to know what someone who constantly looks around and carries photographic equipment is doing there. Smile: you're on camera.*

**56** *This Arup Associates building at **80 Cannon St.** / Bush Lane dates from 1972 - 6 and employs an exo-skelton which leaves a column-free interior. This stainless steel structure is said to be water filled as fire protection (suggesting a bizarre boiling kettle if a fire ever takes place!). The base level was originally intended as a rail station — which was never realised and, unfortunately, someone later had the bright idea of infilling the lower parts with retailing. Well, it was a waste, wasn't it? And so a degree of imaginative effort is needed to locate its image back as it was.*

**57** *This five-storey 1973 - 7 office building (formerly Credit Lyonnais), designed by Whinney, Son & Austen Hall, sits opposite Bracken House (on the east side, **30 Cannon Street**) and is in marked contrast to it. The building sits on the site of a Wren church bombed in WWII and has been, until recently, distinctly unfashionable except among a minority. Some architects argue that the building's raked, prefabricated glass-reinforced cement façade is a lot more interesting than Bracken could ever be — a mimicking of earlier load-bearing façades of the type constructed by Seifert and its literally hollow theatricality is the stuff, one suspects, of Hopkins' nightmares.*

**58** *When the fish market moved out of **Billingsgate** (in Lower Thames Street, EC3), they left a building designed by Horace Jones in 1875 and considered to be ripe for redevelopment into deep trading spaces (this was the booming, deregulated City of the mid - 1980's). And then the prospective tenant – who was going to ferry staff from here to other offices across the river in London Bridge City – pulled out. What to do? The Richard Rogers team handling the conversion had artfully created mezzanines hanging from the existing structure, brought in diffused daylight via prismatic lenses, created habitable space within deep underground vaulting and, in the process, struggled against a melting permafrost which the stored, frozen fish of generations had formed in the mud beneath the Thames' waters. It was exasperating. Then came IRA bombs and the need for emergency City space, persuading needy tenants that these peculiar spaces had potential. Abortive project work is always painful for those involved and it was good that the building was finally used in a similar way to that intended. But that period ended and, at the end of 2002, Billingsgate's splendid spaces were being used for City parties; by 2005 not much had changed.*

*So what's wrong? The lower floors are literally cavernous but not quite Piranesian; but they'd make a great club. The ground floor with its mezzanines suspended from the original columns is spacious, but the City now has more choice. It would make a great . . . market . . . but it's on the wrong side of an urban race-track called Lower Thames Street. Hope lies in a revitalisation of the limited public walkway along the river frontage surely an opportunity to reinvigorate this fine building?*

*You can walk significant stretches of the riverside on the northern side these days. It's not quite as easy and pleasant as the south side and is relatively hidden away, but give it a try.*

# The City

## Bracken House

1 Friday Street, EC4
Michael Hopkins and Partners, 1991
Tube: Mansion House, St. Paul's

Bracken House is an example of architectural gamesmanship that assures you experts are at work. At the instrumental level there is inventiveness and expertise providing sound, functional office space but, as always, that is not what is interesting about the design, and certainly not where one finds the wit in a scheme that sent a notice to the profession: here was an architect — formerly a partner of Norman Foster — who was not going to be pigeon-holed into prevailing stylistic categories. Instead, Hopkins effectively made a declaration that he was cutting across the categories and wet and crusty materials as well as industrialised ones in the cause of good architecture and sound construction.

The original building, of which the north and south wings remain, was completed in 1959 as the home of the eastern-most of the 'Fleet Street' newspapers — the pink broadsheet that is the Financial Times — appropriately located within the City itself. In 1952 the FT's owner, Brendan Bracken, had asked his architect, Professor Albert Richardson, to provide a new building with a curved facade. Richardson obliged by quoting references to a Renaissance palace in Turin (the Palazzo Carignano) and giving Bracken a design comprising a central printing hall and two office wings (on the northern facade of which you can find a zodiac, featuring the head of Sir Winston Churchill, a rather bizarre and amusing homage to the great friendship forged between Bracken and Churchill during the war). In the mid-1980's the FT moved to a Docklands building designed by Nicholas Grimshaw (from where they have moved on), and the intention was to replace the old building with a new Hopkins design.

Again quoting the geometry of the Turin palazzo, Hopkins (with his fellow-director, John Pringle) proposed retaining the two wings but replacing the less interesting printing hall with a donut plan of offices radiating from a tight central atrium (which accommodated the lifts). Many of the key features of this new, central part relate back to the character of the two wings. For example, the attic storey carries through; the gunmetal cladding derives from the use of this alloy on the old windows; the geometry of the cladding bays derives from windows on the wings; and the stone piers on the ground floor are in the same pink 'Hollington' stone used by Richardson.

Underlying the 26,300 sq.m. design were two other contextual considerations. The first was that the new owners — Japanese bankers — had hoped to build much higher. However, the height restrictions imposed by proximity to St. Paul's Cathedral made the development rather expensive and demanded the designers squeeze the floor to floor heights. The second consideration concerned Prince Charles. His influence was everywhere – nowhere more so than around St. Paul's, an area ripe for redevelopment and subject to his close scrutiny.

Charles was of the not unreasonable opinion that contemporary facades tended to be thin and two-dimensional: their designers should return to the good days when thick, masonry cladding leaned against the steel frame of the building and carried its loads straight to the ground (rather than hanging the cladding off the steel frame, the modern practice). So Hopkins provided a load-bearing façade, but one that is stunningly contemporary. It's a gesture with wit, inventiveness and even humour, incidentally underscoring the fact that all good architecture is essentially contingent and rooted in time, place and circumstances, locking the mundane and the intellectual

*The Bracken House gunmetal façade (an alloy of zinc, bronze and lead) is a rare example of architectural gamesmanship, at once acrobatic and respectful of its contextual references and inspiration. The cantilevered, concrete floor slab naturally deflects and the cast metal façade takes the load of this deflection, levelling the floor. Loads from the upper levels pass down to the vertical tubes to the cast brackets at ground level. Being themselves cantilevered from a pivot, the vertical forces are counter-balanced by a steel tension tube on the opposite (rear) side. All the weight is borne by a stone pillar (no concrete is involved, except for the foundation). The entire arrangement neatly confronts the criticisms of Prince Charles in that contemporary façades are too thin and not articulated because they are not load-bearing.*

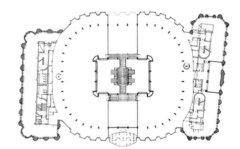

*Bracken is a composite of two buildings: the retained wings of the 1959 Financial Times building, looking — as did many City buildings of the period — as if they belonged to 1929, sandwiching the donut plan of a central part by Michael Hopkins. The latter replaces the former FT printing hall but cleverly picks up on a variety of features of the retained wings, reinventing them and making an elegant marriage of old and new. It's as if the two parts are engaged in some form of curious, frozen duet with one another.*

together as one voice: architectural design as an action of the moment.

The team set the external columns far back from the facade, so that the cantilevering concrete slab sags under its own load and has to be supported by the gunmetal cladding which takes out the deflection by propping the slabs and carrying the loads to ground. Well, to large cast, cantilevering brackets that 'catch' the loads with a quiet piece of acrobatics. Sat up stone piers (the real thing, of course, not stone facing to concrete) that match the Hollington stone of the '59 building, these brackets reach out to pick up the loads and are counter-balanced by stainless steel tie rods down the back of the piers.

At the heart of the interior sits a top-lit atrium with four lifts structured within large cast steel panels, bringing users out onto bridges studded with glass block — a device used at every level, including the roof, in order to keep the overall level down.

It's all rather clever and beautifully designed. And one has to add that not many architectures are informed and defined by such multi-level gamesmanship. Strangely, however, it already feels like a dated kind of Modernism whose tectonic concerns have been left behind in an era increasingly turning to decorative devices. (Compare it, for example, with Herzog & de Meuron's work.) Like Hopkins' work at Portcullis, one suspects it will take a while for people to be able to fully appreciate the merits of this building.

*A hallmark of the Hopkins studio has become steel plate lift enclosures. You can see something similar, for example in the 2005 St. Thomas' hospital building.*

**60** *This collection of buildings — from the south side of **Ludgate Hill** up Limeburner Lane to Fleet Place and Holborn Viaduct — are all designed by Skidmore Owings & Merrill and completed in the heady days of the late 1980's 'bubble economy'. Forming a grouping that totals some 50,000 sq.m. mounted on anti-vibration foundations and stretching some 1.5 km over realigned railway tracks going into Blackfriars station, they are designed as disparate buildings with varied in between spaces that are not without interest. However, the development betrays what the New York journalist, Neil Postman, described as a contemporary urge to amuse ourselves to death (the entertainment economy) – on this occasion in the form of SOM's notion of contemporary Modernism as a mix that includes the vaguely medieval black granite and stainless steel of 10 Fleet Place, sitting side by side with a mock beaux arts exercise of Santander House on the corner with Ludgate Hill. Behind the façades is a similar workplace equation, making outside appearances a skilfully executed chocolate box wrapping (which, to be fair, is hardly unusual these days).*

# 61 Salvation Army: hope at the bridge threshold

Queen Victoria Street. EC4
Sheppard Robson, 2005
Tube: Mansion House / St. Paul's

Parisians are likely to associate the Salvation Army with Le Corbusier and 1920's Modernism, so it is interesting to find the Army commissioning a new global headquarters on a rather prominent site in central London: within the City, near to St. Paul's Cathedral and at the entrance to Foster's Millennium Bridge. In fact the 'Sally', as it is colloquially called, has been on this site for well over one hundred years. But time and change have brought changes to the site and dilution to the needs of this Army of salvation which — now married to concepts of hot-desking and new ways of working — has meant a much reduced accommodative requirement. The large building they had occupied for so long was not only too big, but deemed to be inappropriate to an organisation that not only wants to be seen as evangelical and frugal, but also modern. Such were the key words given to their architects, Sheppard Robson.

Given a need to accommodate far fewer people on the site, Sheppard Robson engaged in a development strategy which located a new headquarter building on the site's most prominent corner and gave the other two-thirds over to a speculative commercial development which, in effect, has paid for the Sally's new premises.

The volume of the building is equally split between three upper levels of offices and three lower levels of public spaces and facilities. The latter includes a conference suite and restaurant; the former has the usual facilties and – on the building's principal floor – a suite given over to (and equally divided between) the General of the Army and his Chief of Staff. They, in turn, share offices with their wives (a significant aspect of their role) and are supported by a team of support staff (men, of course). At the heart of this executive suite is a fine chapel that projects out over the outer street that leads onto the Millennium Bridge. In many ways this simple room of glowing glass walls and a wooden ceiling is the gem of the building.

Below this suite are the public areas. These include a large basement conference and public cafe area above which the reception floor is propped on raked concrete legs (a device also used — rather less dramatically — on the Abbey building at Regent's Place, on Euston Road). The conference area actually sits beneath the bridge access walkway (see the section overleaf).

The other notable feature of the London Sally that draws people's attention is the façade treatment. This overlays the principal and west-facing façade with angled and 'fritted' glass panels that float well in front of the main, double-glazed, floor to ceiling windows. The architects originally had these along the northern side, too, but the developer objected to the blurring of views as well as a functionally unnecessary cost, so they were omitted.

Then, of course, there was the St. Paul's heights issue: air conditioning plant normally on the roof had to be accommodated within the main volume of the building.

Overall, this is an unusual client adapting to change and providing London with one of its more interesting examples of tradition married to contemporary realities.

Photos: Richard Waite

West               East

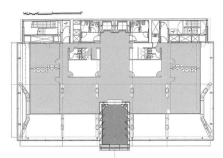

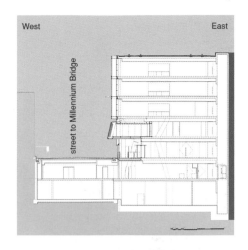

*The principal floor of the SA building is symmetrically occupied by the General and his Chief and Staff (and their respective wives). The organisation's chapel is centrally located, projecting over the street where throngs pass between St. Paul's and the Tate Modern.*

street to Millennium Bridge

*Drawings: Sheppard Robson, adapted by K.A.*

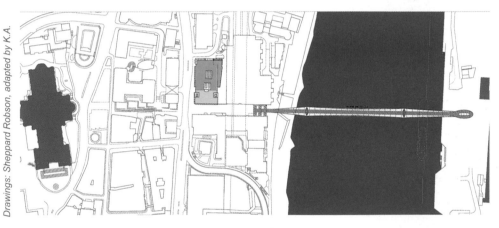

**62** The **Daily Express** building in Fleet Street is now no more than a highly impressive frontage with an equally impressive art deco entrance lobby. Behind it is a massive office building. But it was always thus: a smart face behind which stood the realities of newspaper production. The façade was designed by Sir Owen Williams, 1930 - 33, and was the first true curtain-walled building in London (black Victrolite glass spandrels in chromed metal framing). We are told that Williams originally wanted clear glass but was over-ruled by the building's owner, Lord Beaverbrook (or, been-a-crook, as this Canadian was characterised in his day). Its 'art deco' entry lobby was designed by Robert Atkinson and is quite special (perhaps the only 'deco' piece worth looking at in London). Decorated relief work on the walls is by Eric Aumonier.

Haberdasher's Hall, 18 West Smithfield, EC1
Michael Hopkins and Partners, 2002
Tube: Farringdon

*Haberdashers sits dep within the urban block
and provides accommodation around a cloistered
courtyard. The architecture is all about scale.
The oak panelled, double-cube livery hall with its
pitched roof is on the first floor.*

*A lime-
stone spiral
stairleads
from the
entrance up
to the piano
nobile where
most of the
public spaces
are located.
Oak is the
dominant
finish.*

## Haberdasher's

The Guilds remain a curiosity of City culture, many of them lost in history as well as rooted in it, and few of them desiring or managing to plausibly reinvent themselves — except for the Worshipful Company of Haberdashers, who have insinuated themselves into the urban fabric of Smithfield, deeply hidden away behind older buildings and within the heart of an urban block — giving its designers the interesting problem of how to cope with a very difficult site (entirely without street frontage) as well as any cultural and symbolic demands.

The contemporary Haberdasher's is as much rentable conference venue as club or ancient guild, demanding a balance between these disparate roles. Hopkins deals with such issues and the site by forming a central, 20m cloistered court dominated by the barn-like volume of the main hall that is on axis to arriving visitors — who then turn right and are taken up to the principal accommodation on a piano nobile via a spiral stair. Soft red brick, limestone and oak are predominant materials.

A fundamentally important keynote to the scheme is the handling of scale e.g. the diminutive arches of the cloister, topped by the taller windows of the first floor and, in the case of the hall, capped by a tall, pitched leaded roof with two dominant ventilating chimneys. It's where so many architectures go wrong and Hopkins' team have got it right. Having said that, there is no doubt that, as at Portcullis, Hopkins is here offering us his peculiar mix of old and contemporary values, courting the danger that the architecture ends up as metaphorically and emotionally dry as the construction is actually dry — which, perhaps, is exactly what clients such as Members of Parliament and Haberdashers want.

*Get in during Open House London if you can't make it at on any other occasion.*

**64** *St. Bartholomew's Church, West Smithfield, EC1, is usually offered to us because it is loaded with history: an Augustian priory, founded in 1123, partly destroyed in the Reformation, restored by various architects, notably Aston Webb, who added to the four bays of the aged choir (1886 - 98; see, for example, the transepts and west front). Forget all that and simply experience the building as a splendid mix of spaces, textures and other architectural qualities that have been layered, violently edited back, restored, and yet (somehow) have managed to retain architectural coherence and enormous character. What one experiences is, self-evidently, as much accident as design, but this hardly detracts from the satisfaction of the experience and — one must admit — its romantic undertones. The place feels like a cliched oasis midst the raw urbanity of equally large meat market bustling with huge multi-axle trucks loaded with bloody carcasses,*

*an equally large hospital, the frothy life of Farringdon media types who populate the local bars and restaurants, and a background of the Barbican. Leave all this; progress down the long path from the gate (under a house of 1595, restored by Webb), through the graveyard and the lobby, into the aisle and 13th c. nave where — if you are fortunate, all will be quiet and dappled sunlight will kiss the stonework. This is surely one of London's more pleasant architectural delights (like the John Soane Museum on a quiet day out of the tourist season). For example, on the right is a tomb of c.1405 wonderfully and irreverently slapped onto the C12th Norman construction as a paradoxical action that at once affirms and denies all concepts of order and harmony.*

*The Foster team's Holborn Circus design forms a 'big wrap' around this prominent corner, with stone fins as a notional ground floor 'rustication'.*

**65** The **Sainsbury Business Centre** *(38,400 sq.m.), at 33 Holborn Circus, EC1N, is a 2002 Norman Foster replacement for a '60's block once occupied by the Daily Mirror (designed by Sir Owen Williams). The usual competences are there, including a large atrium entrance backed by large office floors behind vast areas of glass. The ground floor has its glazing faced with limestone louvres, lending a base to the building and a different scale and character at pavement level. Being all glass, the building improves at night, when the façade (especially around the corner entrance area) slowly becomes transparent. But the real glitter — of a different kind — is across the road, in the jewelry shops of Hatton Garden, where all that romance about engagements and anniversaries, of a Jewish trading culture and the rest is embodied in an urban phenomenon that is a universe away from Foster's sanitised corporate beast and home for 2600 workers across the road.*

**66** The **JP Morgan building** *(John Carpenter Street, EC4; BDP, 1992; tube: Blackfriars) is a surreal Po-Mo building that reinvents the Renaissance palace as a deep-plan financial trading centre, over 66,000 sq.m. gross, with two trading floors of 4645 sq.m. each and 55% of its volume given over to services: a fortress buzzing with digitised financial trading involving sums one can hardly imagine. Fully one third of the floor space is underground, in order not to contravene height restrictions near to St. Paul's. Overall, the accommodation is split into two parts: a Main building and, across the road, an Island (support) building. The design grows out of the back of a rather grand Davis & Emmanuel school of 1880 which is used as a boardroom, as one might expect. It's big, transmogrifying the*

*palazzo model. Classical elements (such as the cornice) become carefully proportioned functional features and air conditioning grilles marry themselves into the idea of Baroque rustication. Knowingly or not, the architects have given us a theatrically phrased monument to their own patronage by the wealth and power of the occupying latter day princes. It's all rather Disney . . . and yet very real and not fantasy at all. Modish and 'structural' themes in architecture ('Customary' beauty and 'Natural' beauty, as the C17 termed it) are the appropriate informants of the scheme — perhaps not quite as someone like Sir Christopher Wren might intend it, but the principles are the same. But if you think such theatricality died between about 1990 - 4 (with the UK recession of about that date) then take a closer look at much of Foster's work, for example, from the last ten years. Buildings like 24 Gresham Street (sub-Mies) and that taken over by Bloomberg (sub-SOM, circa 1960's).*

**67** *Most of the original Smithfield meat market buildings (**Smithfield Market**, Charterhouse Street, EC1) were designed by Horace Jones (the Tower Bridge architect) and completed in 1831. What one now sees is HLM's 1994 renewal of the facilities in order to bring them into line with European Union standards. It didn't come cheap and HLM have taken the opportunity to offer an idiosyncratic mix of stainless steel modernism and a colourful renovation of Jones' sheds. Two new floors have been added within the existing frame, providing offices and facilities for the traders. A principal difficulty with the design is the peripheral glazed canopy which proclaims a reinvention of the facilities, but offers little else and clearly presents maintenance problems (it is always dirty), but bike couriers find it convenient.*

**68** *This already ageing folly in Farringdon (44 Britton Street, EC1 Janet Street-Porter / CZWG, 1988) sits on a corner site in an area better known for offices and studios. The design — which exemplifies the playful dimension of English Post-Modernism — emphasises the corner, plays vaguely contextural games with window arrangements, inscribes huge squares, offers an un-London blue glazed roof, and adds 'log' lintels that some critics have likened to a 'knowing' comment on the C18th Abbe Laugier's notes about architectural origins(!). The brickwork was Porter's idea of cast shadows and descriptions of the interiors by the owner are daffy, joyful and dominated by a jokey desire for the place to look 'wrecked'. It was an existential statement. But, for some reason architecture and frivolity invariably make poor bed-fellows. But it is clever and it is fun. Then the owner moved on. And so did architectural fashions.*

Right: The Reform
Club, on Pall Mall

# Whitehall & the West End

London's architectural geography has two principal poles or areas of focus about which everything else revolves. The first is the City of London. The second is Whitehall, where the church, the crown, court and government have always been located. The church was represented by Westminster Abbey, the crown by the palaces of Whitehall (and now Buckingham Palace and others), with government centred at Downing Street, off Whitehall itself.

Westminster is where Edward the Confessor founded a royal palace in the C11, adjacent to a Benedictine abbey of obscure origins, already a place where kings were crowned when the Normans conquered England. Later, the royal residence of the Palace of Westminster shifted to Whitehall Palace and the former residence became the place where the Lords and the Commons met. Most of Whitehall Palace was destroyed by fire in 1698, apart from Inigo Jones's Banqueting House. In 1834 the Palace of Westminster was also burned down, prompting a competition for new Houses of Parliament, 'in the Gothic or Elizabethan style'. This resulted in the present design, by Charles Barry and Augustus Pugin – in turn, damaged during WWII, restored by Sir Giles Gilbert Scott, and now supplemented by Portcullis House, designed by Sir Michael Hopkins.

As London expanded westward from the City and northward from Whitehall, the aristocratic estates of west London were speculatively developed into the set of Georgian streets and squares that characterise much of the so-called West End. The first of the latter included St. James' Square, Covent Garden, Lincoln's Inn and Bloomsbury Square, while the grander residential areas around Belgravia tend to be early or later C19. Many of the former residences have now been converted to offices, but significant areas remain in domestic or mixed use and some fine Georgian terraces exist in Bloomsbury (despite inter and post-war enthusiasms for 'comprehensive redevelopment' — visible, for example, around London University and at Brunswick Square). This area is more or less bounded by Piccadilly to the south and Marylebone Road to the north, and between Park Lane to the west and Kingsway to the east.

The private and speculative nature of the West End's urban developments is one of its important features. Even Regent's Street and Park were privately financed and it is only in the later Victorian period and the early years of the C20 that civic-minded 'improvements' cut new streets (such as Shaftesbury Avenue, the Aldwych and Kingsway) through the old fabric and created significant urban features such as the Embankments. One can't imagine such interventions being repeated.

Meanwhile, Whitehall consolidated as an area of government buildings adjacent to the royal palaces of the Mall and St. James', spreading west into the Victoria area (where you can also find the Richard Rogers' design for Channel Four). Perhaps the next (inevitable?) stage is this development will be the vacation of the palaces and their conversion into tourist venues (a process that appears to have already begun).

*Left: inside the central court to the Foreign Office.*
*Right: C17th and C18th buildings and 'Vitruvius Brittannicus': Inigo Jones — a key figure in the introduction of 'regularity' to London's urban fabric.*

# Whitehall and the West End

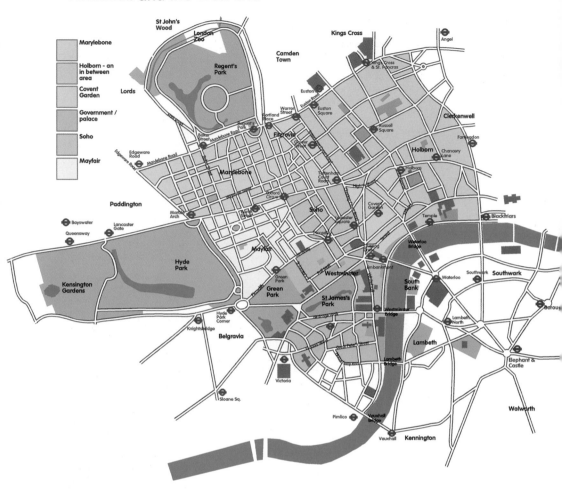

Legend:
- Marylebone
- Holborn - an in between area
- Covent Garden
- Government / palace
- Soho
- Mayfair

Map labels:
St John's Wood, London Zoo, Camden Town, Kings Cross, Angel, Regent's Park, Lords, Euston, Kings Cross & St. Pancras, Warren Street, Euston Road, Euston Square, Russell Square, Clerkenwell, Portland Place, Great Portland Street, Fitzrovia, Holborn, Farringdon, Baker Street, Marylebone Road, Regent's Park, Edgware Road, Edgware Road, Marylebone, Chancery Lane, Holborn, Tottenham Court Road, Paddington, Oxford Circus, Soho, Holborn, Temple, Blackfriars, Bayswater, Marble Arch, Leicester Square, Covent Garden, Lancaster Gate, Bond Street, Charing Cross, Queensway, Piccadilly Circus, Waterloo Bridge, Kensington Gardens, Hyde Park, Mayfair, Westminster, Embankment, Waterloo, Southwark, Southwark, Green Park, St James's Park, South Bank, Borough, Hyde Park Corner, Westminster Bridge, Lambeth North, Knightsbridge, Belgravia, Lambeth, Elephant & Castle, Victoria, Lambeth Bridge, Sloane Sq., Walworth, Pimlico, Vauxhall Bridge, Kennington, Vauxhall

*Horse Guards, Whitehall (St. James' Park side)*

# Whitehall & The West End

The West End has come to be defined as a central area ringed by older 'village' centres such as Knightsbridge, Notting Hill, Marylebone, St, Pancras, Angel, etc. — places of disparate architectural character and development opportunity. Even the central heartland is divided between the pretensions of St. James', the government quarter of Whitehall, an Oxford Street separated into distinct shopping halves at Oxford Circus, the two entertainment areas of Covent Garden and Soho (which should be similar but are very dissimilar), and the 'in between' area (in between the West End and the City) of Holborn, bounded on the west by the electronic and furniture offerings of Tottenham Court Road and, on the east, by the utterly different characters of the Temple and the studio warehouses of Clerkenwell. Seemingly, the only thing unifying such disparities is the fact that this is the historic heart of London, mostly developed during a boom period of 'Georgian' expansion during the late seventeenth to nineteenth centuries.

*View up Whitehall to Trafalgar Square*

The architectural interest of the West End is embedded in this history and the place's deep-rooted urban character. For example, it is difficult to appreciate Hopkins' Portcullis without addressing its context: Scotland Yard and the Palace of Westminster. Somerset House means more if one appreciates it as a riverside palace supplanting an earlier palace and at odds with a competing work of architecture (the Aldelphi) just upstream. (Similarly, Farrell's Embankment Place has less meaning when divorced from this series of large riverside works.) To the east, buildings in Clerkenwell have to be dealt with as the reinvention of what was once the backyard of Fleet Street newspapers, just as Fleet Street itself was partly appropriated by the City following the exodus to Docklands. And to the west, Knightsbridge and Notting Hill have become ever stronger bastions of affluence, resistant to significant architectural change.

*Downing Street gates*

Overall, almost without exception, important architectural work in the West End appears increasingly contextual and to engage a broad range of issues. The new British Library cannot be divorced from its relations with the British Museum and plans that go back to the 1960's. Foster's Great Court at the BM is very much a part of a pattern of expansion and alteration that has always characterised the BM. Venturi's Sainsbury Wing may be loaded with his North American, Post-Modern concerns, but it is literally locked into formal relations with a National Gallery architecture created more than 150 years previously.

*Bansky politically themed stencil*

This is hardly to claim that the area isn't changing. Even as we write about the West End in these terms, this book already acknowledges how its southern edge — the River Thames — has recently been redefined, at once breaking away whilst simultaneously linking the two banks of the river and thus extending the West End into southern parts from which it has long been divorced.

While 'improvement' in the ambitious Victorian sense has largely evolved into a tinkering with traffic schemes, the Mayor's ambitious decongestion charging and schemes for many central London squares (including the work realised at Trafalgar Square), a myriad of comparatively short-lived designs in the form of new retail outlets such as cafes, restaurants, shops and art galleries continue to inform the bigger picture and lend a vibrancy to London that it has not experienced in living memory (no, not even in the 'swinging '60's'). This is nowhere more evident than in the night life of the West End. Nothing lasts, but — in recent years — the joint has been jumping. One's conclusion is that an enjoyment of the West End's contemporary architecture can hardly be divorced from the totality of the area, its urban history and continued reinvention. It's as if — to paraphrase one London historian, Peter Ackroyd — the city has an underlying nature that quietly but adamantly insinuates new development, absorbing it all into a unified character that alters less than we sometimes presume. Whether that rumination is depressing or intriguing we leave to the reader. However, it touches upon a traditional architectural concept: the notion of a rational, 'natural beauty' with which an architect must be attuned (what is fundamental, lawful and 'structural') and a 'customary' (creaturely or modish) beauty to which they must also conform. The latter is certainly a key characteristic of parts of the West End — an area that City folk have traditionally sneered at.

More radical change is currently concentrated along the Paddington Basin / Kings Cross axis of Marylebone and Euston Roads, particularly around the latter (and working westward).

*St. Martin's in the Fields*

# Whitehall and the West End

In terms of London's architectural geography, the West End serves as the twin to the City. While the latter has traditionally been the home and focal point of trading powers, the West End has been its counter-balancing opposite pole where the monarch, the court, civil servants and the Houses of Parliament were to be found. The River Thames — London's historical life blood, both literally and symbolically — once served as a crucial highway link and, in recent years , has been 'rediscovered'. In between these two lay Holborn (including Fleet Street and the Temple, now also the home of London University) — traditionally an area of lawyers and journalists gossiping and benefiting by what was taking place on either side of them. The movement of the journalists to other locations (particularly to docklands and to Canary Wharf) has not altered the underlying pattern. This urban geography and its inherent social, economic and political patterns is still a fundamental part of London life. The annual speech of the Chancellor of the Exchequer (the principal finance minister) to City dignatories is an important event. Similarly, St Paul's Cathedral stands as  the major symbol of the presence of the church midst Mammon - and engenders London's most important ceremonial route, between the Cathedral and Buckingham Palace. The latter is hardly a significant work of architecture, but it and its location are hugely important. The same has to be said for Westminster Abbey, sitting opposite the Houses of Parliament, within the Palace of Westminster. The remainder of the West End is characterised by a development phase from about the late 1600's to the early 1800's, when many of its formal squares and terraces were laid out as speculative developments, most of them exploiting a tradition of royal patronage and aristocratic land ownership. In an enlarged sense that embraces the development of Belgravia, Knightsbridge, Kensington, etc., the West End and the City together can be considered to be bounded by the route of the Circle Line. However, above ground, the western urban boundary of the West End has natural edges along Edgware Road, Park Lane and Vauxhaul Bridge Road (also the boundary between Westminster and adjacent boroughs).

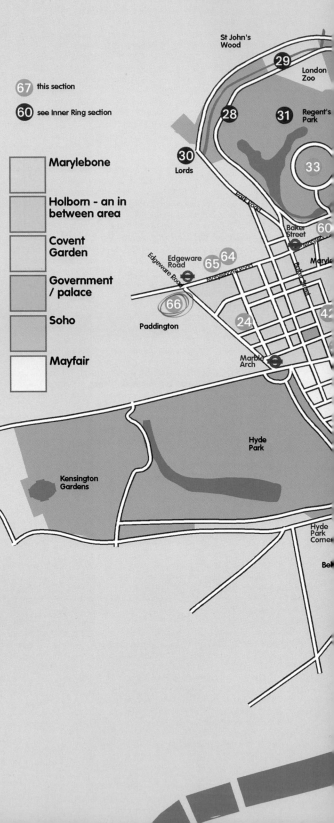

67 this section

60 see Inner Ring section

Marylebone

Holborn - an in between area

Covent Garden

Government / palace

Soho

Mayfair

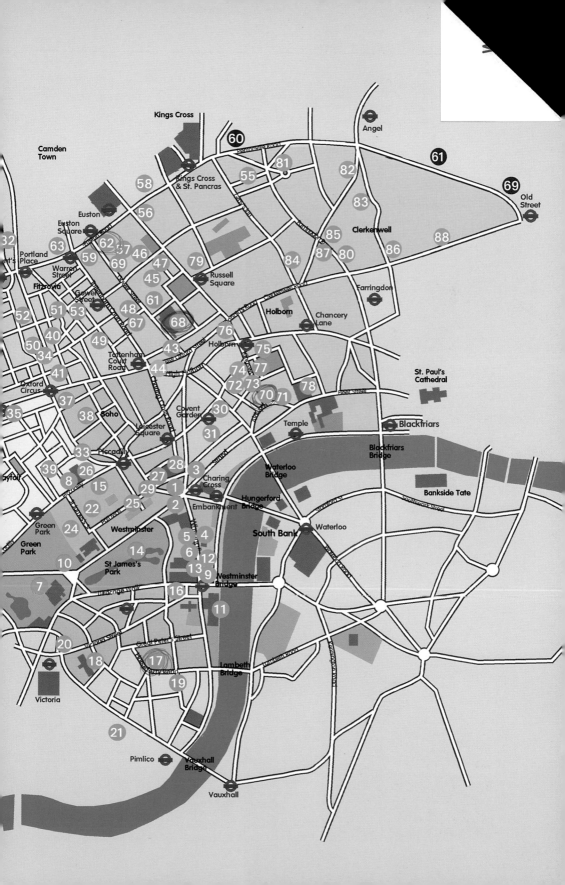

**1** ***Trafalgar Square*** *— especially as relaid out by the Foster team in order to ease pedestrian flows between the square itself and the National Gallery — sits as a strong termination to the north-south line of Whitehall, closing off a government area from the street-life realities of Leicester Square and similar places that lie immediately to the north, effectively turning its back upon them and orienting itself toward the Houses of Parliament and Westminster Abbey. Off to its right lies Pall Mall, leading up to Buckingham Palace; off to its east lies the Strand and Fleet Street, leading directly into the City. It is thus quite a symbolic place.*

*The history of the square dates back to John Nash and the urban developments and redevelopments of the C18th and early C19th. Apart from The National Gallery itself, the key features of the Square are the fountains and a Corinthian column topped by a statue of Nelson (raised in 1843). This column towers above a square that has always attracted political crowds and stirred paranoia in the minds of the establishment, engendering features such as the crowd-disrupting fountains placed there in 1845, later modified by Edwin Lutyens and now a feature of Foster's reclamation of the square (a 'world's square' project that excludes traffic from the northern side). The latter work transformed the square, returning it back to the people, but now as a place characterised by entertainment events (managed by the Mayor's office) rather than riotous behaviour.*

**2** ***Admiralty Arch*** *(1911, left), on the south-west side of Trafalgar Square, WC2, is a triumphal arch straddling the entrance to the Mall, its tapered plan attempting a formal transition designed to reconcile the dissimilar urban geometries comprising the cermonial route from Buckingham Palace, through the central Arch, along the Strand and Fleet Street to St. Paul's Cathedral in the City (a rather important aspect of London's architectural and urban geography). It was designed by Sir Aston Webb who (like Foster now) had, at that time, one of the largest practices in the country. The Deputy Prime Minister currently houses himself in the upper parts.*

**3** *James Gibbs'* ***St. Martin's-in-the-Fields*** *(1720–26) in Trafalgar Square is a much-copied, Roman-inspired design whose symbolism is almost Hollywood Gothic (take a pagan temple, complete with portico, and drive a Christian stake (i.e. the tower) through its heart). The interiors were amended by Reginald Blomfield, 1887, and there are current plans to make significant extensions. Nearby, at the Aldwych, you will find* ***St. Mary-le-Strand,*** *another fine church by Gibbs (1717), who was at one time involved at Burlington House (before Palladianism reigned supreme).*

**4** *In a London of half-timbered Tudorbethan buildings, Inigo Jones's* ***Banqueting House*** *(1619) in Whitehall, SW1, must have been horribly modern, foreign, erudite and shocking as well as ultra-fashionable among the aristocrats who held parties there. This alien from foreign parts was a message from on high to the Philistines below, as well as a play-palace for King Charles. Yet it was also a classic example of belief in what was later expressed as 'customary' and natural' beauty. The 'customary' (modish) part was the lavish banqueting; the 'natural' beauty was embodied in the geometries of the façade and the double-cube room at its heart which encapsulate the cosmological beliefs of the day in hierarchy, order, decorum and proportion: 'Untune the string and hark what discord follows', remarked one of Shakespeare's characters. No doubt the Banqueting House once experienced its share of untuned strings.*

**5** Whitehall is a fine place to walk and enjoy the **Cenotaph**, the Banqueting House (1619 - 22), **Horse Guards** (1750 - 9), **New Scotland Yard** (1890), and government buildings such as the **Foreign Office** (1862-75), the **Ministry of Defence** (1939 - 59), and **Portcullis House** (2001). But one of its better buildings sits as a hardly noticeable, quiet backdrop: **Dover House** (now Scotland office; the west facade appears in Horse Guards), designed by Richard Paine and constructed 1754 - 8, with significant parts (particularly the entrance areas behind the street screen) by Henry Holland. The screen wall itself is particularly elegant and a rare example of barely adorned rustication. (Sometimes open for Open House London.)

**6** One can't discuss Whitehall without mentioning **Downing Street** — a street dating from 1682. All that remains of it are the two most significant residences: that of the Prime Minister and of the Chancellor of the Exchequer. The former dates from a remodelling for the then Prime Minister, Sir Robert Walpole — not that you can see much from the IRA-proof gates that were placed there in 1989. No.10 is actually a marvellous piece of theatre — a massive and vastly reconstructed home / office concealed behind its relatively modest façade. A refacing took place in 1766 and Raymond Erith (the late partner of Quinlan Terry) effectively reconstructed the interiors in 1960-4. Other architectural names associated with the place include Sir Robert Taylor and Sir John Soane. Immediately to the south is Foreign & Commonwealth Office, by Sir George Gilbert Scott. The building on the north corner of Downing Street is the Old treasury building — a vast warren of a place usually open for London Open House.

**7** Within the depths of **Buckingham Palace** (1705 - 1913; Buckingham Gate, SW1, at the end of The Mall, laid out in 1660) are the remains of the original country house, which became the focus of the Prince Regent's attention in the 1820's. John Nash was the architect and neither he nor the Prince Regent came out of the reconstruction without scandal (the former overspending the budget by some 300%; the latter benefiting privately from the works and being replaced by Edward Blore). Other architects were later engaged, but the present frontage and 'rond point' (including the Victoria Memorial by Sir Thomas Brock, 1911) are by Aston Webb, 1913. Slowly, parts of the Palace are being opened up to the public (such as the 2002 Royal Collection galleries by the Prince of Wales' favourite architect, John Simpson) and Terry Farrell has undertaken a scheme to take this trend to a more radical conclusion (unlikely to be in the immediate future). Meanwhile, the true significance of the Palace concerns urban design issues rather than its heavily criticised and unloved architectural qualities, i.e. its role as the beginning of an impromptu royal, processional route from here, along the Mall, through Aston Webb's Admiralty Arch, down the old avenues of Strand and Fleet Street and on to St. Paul's Cathedral in the City itself.

**8** Modelled on Parisian precedents, **Burlington Arcade**, Piccadilly, W1 (right) was designed in 1815 by Samuel Ware. It remains one of the more pleasant (if expensive) shopping experiences in London. The less pleasant end facades were added in 1911. There are other arcades in this area, but neither are comparable with Burlington (across the road and west is **Prince's Arcade**; off Pall Mall at Waterloo Place is the **Royal Opera Arcade**).

9

# Portcullis House

Portcullis House, Victoria Embankment, SW1
Michael Hopkins & Partners, 2001
Tube: Westminster

When Norman Shaw's New Scotland Yard building was opened as a new home of the Metropolitan Police on the Victoria Embankment in 1890, it was popularly known as 'the jam factory' because of its horizontal bands of alternating red brick and Portland stone that were similar to a Crosse & Blackwell Pickle Factory in Charing Cross Road. Among its other peculiarities of this 'very constabulary' building, as it has been described, was the fact that the lower granite walls of Shaw's fortified, castle-like edifice were quarried by prisoners at Dartmoor and constructed upon the foundations of an incomplete national opera house. After 'the Met' moved out of Scotland Yard to a nearby building (of 1967), the 'Norman Shaw Building', as it had became known, became a useful adjunct to the Palace of Westminster, just across the road. In turn, the growing complex of parliamentary accommodation was recently added to with a new building on the corner of the Embankment, known appropriately as Portcullis House, providing additional and much-needed offices and meeting rooms for Members of Parliament.

Scotland Yard is square in plan, with a central courtyard; its roof is steep and dominated by huge brick chimneys — all of which served as motifs for the Portcullis design. However, Hopkins' design does more than pick up on a tradition of medieval and defensive references suggested by the building's name. It also tries hard to architecturally nestle into the historical tradition whilst remaining a contemporary act of design and construction, emulating many of Shaw's major architectural moves, particularly the general plan and roof forms. And make no bones about it: this is also a defensive design. Its cladding as surreptitiously bomb proof against today's terrorists as Shaw's had to be in its day (the original Scotland Yard buildings had been bombed in 1884).

**The Design**

*The design of Portcullis is basically a five-storey, rectangular donut with a 13.2m deep perimeter of offices off a double-loaded corridor, intended to accommodate 210 Members of Parliament and linked to Barry's splendid building across the road by an underground tunnel — all designed to a brief that required the building to last 200 years. And be terrorist-proof. And also to be aesthetically satisfactory. Most people are not entirely happy with how the last criterion has been meant, without being able to say why.*

The other contextual reference for Hopkins has been the Palace of Westminster itself. Dominated by the tower of Big Ben, the Charles Barry and Auguste Pugin design (completed in the 1850's) is surprisingly regular, and evenly modulated, and has a strong vertical character that fights against its horizontal massing. It is this regular vertical emphasis that Hopkins picks up on and applies to his own facades. In this way he strongly and positively responds to the two significant works of architecture that define a context for the Portcullis House design.

The outcome has been a contentious building that divides opinion. But as an example of architectural gamesmanship it is remarkable, offering two surprises to its contextual game: an amazing, neo-Piranesian Underground station beneath the building (Westminster station) and a timber-framed courtyard roof that is quite outstanding and a contrast with the rather comparatively dour exterior.

*Norman Shaw's **New Scotland Yard** building on Victoria Embankment (access from Parliament Street, SW1) is in two parts. The first and better half was designed and built between 1887–90 and the second between 1901 – 07. Both served the Metropolitan Police and are described by one historian as the nearest Shaw came to being serious (Baroque and Scottish Baronial). The base is made from granite quarried by convicts at Dartmoor. Above this rises a stout, square block in red brick with Portland stone stripes. The whole is topped by large gables and tall chimneys. At the corners, 'tourelles' are provided which help to give the building a stately castle air of the kind Shaw was familiar with from his Scottish background.*

## The Court

The ground floor of Portcullis provides shops and an entrance to the underground station on the street side and the building's main entrance along the river side. Internally, it is dealt with as one large room that reaches up two storeys and is covered by an arching laminated oak and glass roof studded with stainless steel fixings and bracing. The central part of this floor is a landscaped court with small trees and pools. On one side is a cafeteria and a waiter-service restaurant on the other, opposite the main doors. There is also an escalator that drops down to a tunnel leading under the road and links directly to the Palace of Westminster. A gallery runs around the space at first floor level, serving a series of committee and seminar rooms. This gallery runs behind six huge concrete arches that receive the building loads above and transfer them to pillars that penetrate through the lower structures beneath the building.

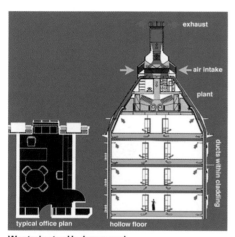

**Westminster Underground**

At the heart of the Portcullis House donut is a central courtyard and at each corner of the building there is a set of lifts and stairs. In principle, it's very simple. However, the building sits upon a massive structural zone that enables the relatively shallow District and Circle Lines to pass beneath it. In turn, this sits upon a deep 'escalator box' that drops down to the deep level of the Jubilee Line tubes. This 'box' is an outstanding experience, redolent with Piranesian references. You must go there.

## That roof and the cladding

The aluminium bronze alloy roof of Portcullis (three storeys high) is a ventilation system. The 'chimneys' draw foul air from the building, pulling it through huge pre-fabricated roof ducts (from secondary ducting built into the façade) up to where it is vented. And the roof form accommodates the machinery that draws the air out and pulls fresh air in (from the base of the chimneys), processing it and pumping it back into the building by means of other ducts in the façade that feed down and into deep floor voids, from where it gently enters the offices – and then leaves via the perimeter façade ducts. 13 chimneys extract and discharge air; the 14th chimney serves a generator and the boiler flues. Water for the air conditioning comes from two deep bore holes. This is fed through heat exchanges and provides cooling, thus obviating the need for refrigeration plant. (The same water is used as 'grey water' in the sanitary systems.) The roof, for example, includes three-storey, 700mm deep spine ducts cast from welded 6mm aluminium bronze plates assembled off site. Each duct assembly — weighing 3 tonnes and containing insulated air intake and extract ducts — is put together with an arching roof structure of steel and aluminium.

The roof arrangement for housing plant and processing air is merely one part of a complex servicing arrangement that provides the building with a rather sophisticated façade — one that is virtually bomb proof, making it rather expensive. Between the vertical rhythm of Derbyshire gritstone facings on the outside are pre-fabricated façade elements that comprise the ducting, windows, sun-shading and a 'light shelf'. The windows are triple-glazed, with cavity louvre blinds. The blinds help to heat air that is drawn upward to the air conditioning plant, where heat exchangers draw the heat away and provide it to the fresh air being supplied back to the rooms.

# Whitehall & the West End

**10** *This small demountable building (the summer **Buckingham Palace ticket office**) appears in the summer, camouflaged among the trees of Green Park, peeking out at the tourists visiting Buckingham Palace, like some stranded giant slug (located to the north of the Queen Victoria memorial that graces the area in front of the Palace. Its tensile roof and wooden structure serve to emphasise its temporary, summer nature as a ticket office for visitors to the Palace. Sited anywhere else, it might have aroused more architectural celebration, but one suspects this modest beast is too near royalty and throngs of tourists for most of the architectural profession. (Buckingham Palace, Birdcage Walk, SW1; Michael Hopkins & Partners, 1994; Tube: Green Park)*

**11** *The **Palace of Westminster** (SW1, 1835–60, right) is by Charles Barry and his assistant Augustus Pugin. The latter is the dominant figure – a precocious and talented man who was an impassioned convert to Catholicism, three times married and dying in the Bedlam Asylum for the insane by the age of 40 (in 1852). Barry carried on until he was 65, but was said to have died as a man worn out by the battle to realise Westminster Palace. Conditions of the original competition stated that the design had to be in the Gothic style to harmonise with Westminster Abbey. Barry held that regularity and symmetry were the main principles in design; Pugin, who was responsible for the decoration, commented that the design was, "All Grecian, sir; Tudor details on a classic body". Although tourist images appear to emphasise the Gothic decorative aspects of the design, it is Barry's ordered regularity which marches across the façades and gives the building its underlying strength.*

**12** *In this unfashionable striped, stone and brick façade sitting opposite Lutyens' Cenotaph, William Whitfield emphasises verticality against the natural horizontality of **Richmond House** (Parliament Street, SW1; William Whitfield and Partners, 1987) and gives street presence to a large government building behind a set-back facade that is rich in references to the C16th (e.g. the cloth-like, 'folded' quality of wood panelling and façades such as that at Burghley House in Northants) and to Norman Shaw's adjacent New Scotland Yard of 1890 (also the subject of reference by Michael Hopkins in his design for Portcullis House, the nearby facilities for Members of Parliament). Try going down the mews on the south side for a view of all three buildings.*

**13** *The **Cenotaph**, Whitehall, SW1, by Edwin Lutyens, 1919–20, is a small and dignified homage to those who died in the horrors of WWI (and is among many memorials by Lutyens including one at Tower Hill in the City - all of which are witness to the dictum of Adolf Loos that only such memorials are worthy of true architectural attention; all else should more properly be 'dumb building'). It remains a major site of ceremony and cultural memory and depends entirely upon its simple form and materiality for impact. Originally, it was intended to burn a gas flame – which would still be a nice symbolic touch.*

## St. James' Park restaurant

St James' Park, SW1
Michael Hopkins & Partners, 2004
Tube: Green Park

**14**

St. James' Park gets evermore popular and this simple Hopkins-designed St. James' restaurant is a welcome addition to the facilities there. The lake side comprises a verandah frontage to the restaurant and cafe, while the other side hides itself beneath a bunker that serves as an outdoor terrace, effectively disguising the presence of the building within the landscape. There aren't many similar buildings to compare it with; the pavilion in the Thames Barrier Park (by Patel & Taylor; p.171) comes to mind; the Mile End ecology centre (p.230) also bears similarities of strategy. *Note: the interior design is not by the Hopkins studio.*

**15** At the east end of Piccadilly sits what was Joseph Emberton's **Simpson** department store building (1935), now Waterstone's bookshop. Enough of the original remains to get a feeling for what it was like (try the upper level bar). Further along, adjacent to Wren's St. James' Church (1682-84; his only 'green field' church design) sits a small ex-Midland bank by Edwin Lutyens — an enjoyable 'Wrenaissance' piece of 1922. This has now been converted into an art gallery (symptomatic of their return to the Mayfair area after adventures in the east of London).

**16** The rationale for the **QEII Conference Centre** (Powell and Moya, 1986; Broad Sanctuary) derives from the context – the glass, lead and stone façades of the neighbours. The most dramatic feature is the employment of deep beams suspending the main conference floor (corresponding to the roofline of adjacent buildings). The stepped-back penthouse levels above hide an inner courtyard, delegates' bars, restaurants, etc., as well as secret parts even the architect is not entirely aware of. The overall aesthetic favoured by Powell & Moya is no longer fashionable, but that hardly detracts from the merits of the building (rather compromised by internal matters of scale).

## 17 Channel Four

124 Horseferry Road, SW1
Richard Rogers Partnership, 1994
Tube: St. James's Park

C4 has many of the brand features one has come to expect from this practice, especially a dramatic entrance area, complemented by scenic lifts, air conditioning towers and tall communications masts — features that were later developed in the City at Lloyd's Register and 88 Wood Street. Here, an axial geometry is 'hinged' upon the corner entrance. A bridge beneath the suspended canopy is another attempt at drama; however, behind this is a curiously constricted lobby whose acrobatic (sharp-intake-of-breath) suspended glazing only just manages to avoid a disastrous conflict of elements (e.g. ties and gallery brackets) — a rewarding experience that, inevitably, does not have the rigour and depth of resolution of Lloyd's. Beyond this again is an open landscaped area shared with a housing development that sits opposite. The two side wings hold offices and the studios are underground, their cladding is similar to that of the Rogers' design for Broadwick House (in Soho), K2 at St. Katherine's Dock, Lloyd's Register, and also 88 Wood Street.

There's a sense in which 80% of the architectural effort is concentrated in the 20% of C4 that constitutes its arrival area.

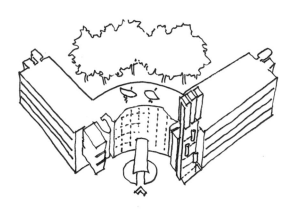

**18** Built upon the site of a former penitentiary, John Francis Bentley's **Westminster Cathedral** in Ashley Gardens, SW1, built 1895–1903, is striking enough on the outside (designed to be a different style to the Gothic of Westminster Abbey), but there is a real constructional impact on the inside: the unfinished recreation of an Italian Byzantine church, concrete domes and massive brick vaulting adorned at the lower levels with masses of glittering mosaic — all that and sculptures on the Stations of the Cross by Eric Gill (1913 - 18). Admittedly, this is a rather difficult building to deal with, but stay with it, give it attention and let its rewards come and meet with you.

The comparison to be made, of course, is with **Westminster Abbey** (the 'west minster') — a building too complex to anything on here except to note that it, too, is of course worthy of your attention (if you can cope with all the tourists). Note the two towers of the west front, which are by Nicholas Hawksmoor (1735 - 45).Its founding was apparently in the early C7th, but it had attracted royal notice by the C11th century and has remained one of London's major symbolic monuments ever since.

## Marsham Street

There are parallels between the site of the Marsham Street government offices and the career of its architect, Terry Farrell: both were formed in the 1960's, both became fashionably unfashionable, and both have managed to be latterly reinvented with some success. The building was an urban block-filler comprising a large podium and three towers (the 'Ugly Sisters' as they became known), occupied by a government department were considered to be an instance of urban blight. And Farrell, the UK's premier Post-Modern architect during the 1980's, was distinctly out of fashion when, in the early '90's, it was decided to demolish and replace the building. There followed a history of indecision about what to do with the site and whether or not the government would still be involved. But Farrell was already in there as an urban design master-planner – an area of architectonic expertise where he is able to exercise skills less subject to fashion. The outcome of this prolonged history was that Farrell was not only the master planner for the overall site but also the architect of a new building that the government had decided it did, after all, want to occupy (with about 3500 workers; the maximum capacity is nearer 4500). However, a major change over that period was that the government had instituted a policy of 'private initiatives', meaning that it preferred to lease rather than own. In this sense, the building is similar to many commercial ones and is, in fact, designed to be easily fragmented into separate parts that the government can divest itself of, leaving the owners to lease parts of the complex to other organisations.

Farrell's master-plan divides the site up into a residential strip and an office strip, with private gardens and courts in between, and two 'streets' that cut across these strips and attempt to enable pedestrians to penetrate the site from adjacent streets. This attempt at urban integration could have been particularly successful if not for terrorist threats which, inevitably, result in the 'streets' being closed off most of the time and otherwise subject to close monitoring. (A minor aspect of reality usually forgotten in the architectural 'spin'.)

The story along the site's more public and principal façade – Marsham Street – is more successful: a genuine urban place has been created that stretches all along the frontage of the building, providing water, grass, and seating for both workers and local residents to enjoy.

The offices themselves are made up of three blocks, each with a central atrium, bridge links and an internal 'street' that runs through all three buildings, lending some continuity to the interiors and providing meeting spaces, photocopying points, etc. Each building has a specific colour theme so give some differentiation. And, at basement level, there is a large cafeteria, a gymnasium and a conference suite.

It says a lot for Farrell's perseverance and design skills that both interiors and exteriors are successful, despite a government's preference for leasing the facilities from a commercial provider who has every interest in providing minimum standards of provision and finish, and not one iota more. But it is another sign of the times that his intention of providing an integral form of architectural pleasure was side-lined in a continuing policy of adding to the basic architecture with an art programme.

There are two aspects to this issue: on the one hand, clients feel that aesthetics are the province of artists, not architects, and that no self-respecting project should be without an architect-artist collaboration. On the other hand, there is the implicit presumption that the architecture is no longer capable of providing a sufficient kind of aesthetic delight – that the architect is a strategic planner and technician, but not an artist. This is now a theme running throughout British architecture. In this instance, artists were brought in to dictate both changes to the architecture (principally in the form of not unsuccessful, coloured glass panels) and a series of localised installations. The latter are a matter of taste; the former add to the architecture, but only by – depending on your viewpoint — appropriating it or losing the art within the architecture. Either way, it is still the artist that retains the kudos, and not the architects who flatter themselves that such collaborations fruitfully underscore their urbane status. But is this a dangerous game? Architects long ago lost control over any aspect of an architectural project with a numerate basis; then they lost out to project managers; and now court the possibility of losing out to artists. Apart from issues directly concerning the future of the profession, it is arguable that the architecture suffers by being transmogrified into an instrumental equation plus the palliative of some artful lipstick. This may suit the interests of governments and speculative capitalists, and – in the case of the Marsham Street building – the outcome is of benefit to all Londoners. But one wonders how far this trend is to go.

**19**

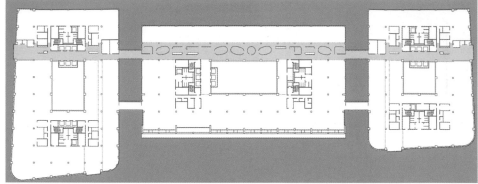

The Marsham building plan seeks to serve current Home Office needs whilst anticipating a future that might call for a fracturing of the accommodation into discrete buildings. Currently, the pink strip is intended as internal 'street', with meeting places, etc.

Note: the plan does not indicate the residential strip along the rear of the site (not designed by the Farrell office).

**20** **Cardinal Place** (opp. Victoria Station; EPR, 2005) is an interesting example of striving to locate a huge office and retail development (46,920 sq.m. of offices and 12,450 sq.m. retail) in such a way that it works in urban terms as well as architectural ones. The former aim is realised by views and links — particularly to the Cathedral. The architectural aim is dealt with by fragmenting the massing and lending the building's prominent 'nose' Foster-like gestural treatment. The overall strategy works well enough, the architecture is . . . well, interesting.

**21** The **Lillington Gardens** estate in Vauxhall Road, SW1, designed by Darbourne and Darke (1961 – 71), is a much admired piece of comprehensive redevelopment, although subsequent apartment sales have produced a strange crop of neo-Georgian doors and the like. A similar scheme in Islington (Marquess estate, opposite the Future Systems house, has undergone radical changes in order to reintegrate its courtyards back into the pattern of surrounding city streets. In the midst of Lillington Gardens you will find George Street's equally good church of **St. James-the-Less.**

**22** The **Economist** complex in St. James's Street, SW1, designed by Peter and Alison Smithson in 1962 – 64, ranks as an iconic example of urbanism — in part, the basis on which the Smithsons became architectural heroes. The development comprises three blocks (two offices and one apartment, together with a small window addition to the adjacent Boodles' club) arranged around a small, raised piazza – a mini Acropolis, all of it skilfully composed so as to terminate an urban block in the heart of establishment St. James'. A textured version of Portland stone infested with fossils lends an almost mannered air to a design born into an era of 'angry young men' and architectural 'brutalism', and more famous for rude, interventionist examples of ostensibly progressive 'comprehensive redevelopment' than anything so polite as this. The design was also coming from a generation looking across the Atlantic for inspiration and there is a neo-Miesian inspiration to the manner in which the columns are adorned. However, whilst the intention was to be progressive, the offices harked back to a previous era of the professional gentleman's facilities rather than the coming age of large

floor-plates and open planning. The corner (former bank) block, with its double height piano nobile, is occasionally reinvented as gallery or expensive bar. SOM have altered the lobby of the offices and added a gratuitous canopy signifying the location of the actual entrance door to that block.

## Urban School

**23**

This is a superb and under-rated building. The background is the usual story of lack of funds and aged premises, prompting this church school to sell off its playground and challenge its architects to come up with something special (which included the housing design that surrounds the school itself). The latter has an interior court area at the rear of the building that is straight out of Hitchcock's rear window, but it is the 3400 sq.m.. school itself that is special. The stacked playgrounds work especially well, enjoying daylight from a central light-well as well as from the street sides. Yes, the planning is extremely tight and space is at a premium. But it works and local parents are flocking to the place. If there is an Achilles heel, it is the occasional betrayal that this is — like most schools these days — a design & build job.

Hampden Gurney School, Nutford Place, W1
BDP, 2002
Tube: Edgeware Road, Marble Arch

**24** *Sir Denys Lasdun's **St. James'** apartment block at 26 St. James' Place, SW1, dates from 1958 – 60 and comprises split-level units (inspired by his former association with Wells-Coates' and the Tecton group's pre-war work) overlooking the park. It*

*was the first such private block of apartments after WWII and is a fine compositional exercise which helped to establish Lasdun's reputation. Now that the UK has enjoyed a massive change around from building houses to building apartments, this design exercise should be of great interest to those working in this field.*

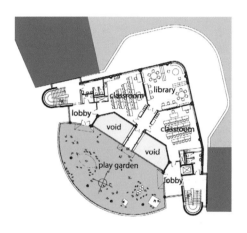

**25** *The **Traveller's Club** (1829–32) and the **Reform Club** (1841) sit adjacent to one another in Pall Mall, SW1 (the street deriving its name from 'pallo di maglio', a game, and once famous for its coffee houses and clubs). The two buildings are designed by Charles Barry as two Italian palazzo on the Roman model, thus introducing a new thematic note to London buildings. The central atria of both buildings are rather grand, the travellers as an open cortile and the reform as a glazed over space. The Reform — the more impressive of the two buildings — has a wide, slow staircase rising to a perimeter gallery (or cloister) and the grand rooms of its piano nobile (esp. the Library). The accommodational arrangement of the normal London house is reversed, with servants in the basement and overnight guest rooms at the top. It's a building worthy of detailed study, especially with regard to its services. Donald McMorran has a building on the Reform's west side (below, second from the left): typically stripped, daunting, but intriguing (also see the Wood Street police station in the City, and his extension to the Old Bailey). Also see the **Director's Club** (1817 - 19) and the **Athenaeum** (both by Decimus Burton; 1827 - 30), on Waterloo Place.*

## 26 Sackler Gallery: heart surgery

Royal Academy, Piccadilly, W1
Foster and Partners, 1991
Tube: Piccadilly, Green Park

At the core of the Royal Academy building lies the only surviving mansion from a bygone Piccadilly: Burlington House, designed by Sir John Denham, built in 1664 and, in 1714, inherited by the third Lord Burlington — a young aristocrat who included architecture among his enthusiasms and was to be described as 'the Apollo of the arts'. Boyle began to develop his estate in 1715 and — together with Colen Campell and the man who was to become his protégé, William Kent — he was to transform Burlington House into a showpiece of Italian Palladianism, based upon his experiences of Palladio's work on two Grand Tours and his studies of Palladio's Quattro Libri. Initially, however, significant architectural work began with a French-style screened and gated entry forecourt together with a double quadrant arcade, designed by the Italian-trained James Gibbs (later ousted during political machinations) and was later complemented by a host of trend-setting artists-in-residence. Burlington House came to epitomise Good Taste. Perhaps it still does.

One hundred years later, between 1815-19, came more remodelling, this time including Lord George Cavendish's relocation of the main stair to where it can be found now and a new garden façade, this time designed by Samuel Ware. In the meantime, London had changed enormously, the estate having to develop the Burlington shopping Arcade to capitalise upon the potential of a rapidly changing context. Then, almost two hundred years after the remodelled house had been originally constructed, the house was purchased by the government for the purposes of making a home for Royal academies — which involved selling the garden to London University, who, between 1866-69, had Sir James Pennethorne design what became The Museum of Mankind.

Between 1868 – 74 Charles Barry (son of the architect for the Palace of Westminster) and R.R. Banks were changing the forecourt to what one sees now, whilst Sydney Smirke set about providing a bridge from the landing of the old stair landing up to new gallery spaces located to the rear of the original Burlington House. In the process, two light-wells were generated between the old house and the new block. In addition, a third storey was added to the house in order to accommodate what

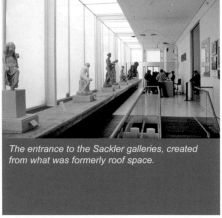

The entrance to the Sackler galleries, created from what was formerly roof space.

was called the Diploma Galleries and a new façade screen was layered onto Burlington's frontage.

Over the next century, yet more architectural amendments were introduced, including a new stair and restaurant by Norman Shaw (1883), a reworking of the front rooms and hall by Sir T.G. Jackson (1899), a remodelling of the library by Curtis Green (1927), and another reworking of the entrance hall by Raymond Erith (1962). Architectural action was piling upon architectural action. Burlington House was still somewhere in there, but by the late

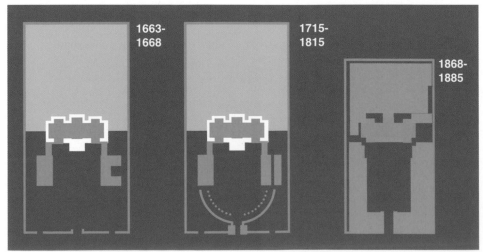

1663-1668

1715-1815

1868-1885

*The Sackler is experienced as the penetration of a series of screens and layers that draw the visitor deeper into the RA, beginning with the street screen, followed by the Burlington House frontages and the interior spaces that lead up to the Sackler Gallery lobby, and then into the galleries themselves.*

*Above: the gallery lobby area (a rather fine area when not cluttered up). Above top right: new glazing to the Victorian frontage. Above lower right: the staircase set within one of the former light-wells. Try arriving by the elevator and leaving via the stair.*

1980's it had become accepted that the building's arteries were seriously clogged. Strategic change was overdue and an opportunity arose with the need to replace the original, roof level Diploma Galleries. Norman Foster was appointed and his team (led by partner Spencer de Grey) subsequently instituted a remarkable piece of heart surgery to the aged pile, by then 325 years old.

In a dramatic and imaginary manner, the architects cleared out the two light-wells, roofed them over and transformed these formerly silted-up, redundant spaces into the most significant features of a new pattern of circulation. This includes a lift to one well and a stair to the other, straddling the old link between the old Burlington House and the Victorian block. These lead to entirely new gallery spaces on the upper level (where the Diploma Galleries had been), complete with their own cool and spacious entry lobby. The horizontal line of the Smirke's cornice — used as a shelf for classical and neo-classical sculptures — gives a unity to this space and is wrapped by a steel-framed enclosure holding white, translucent glass that admits daylight whilst obscuring the roof clutter outside (the current blinds on this glazing were a later addition).

Beam to column joints are carefully sweated over, air conditioning slots are neatly incorporated into the skirting, leading to ducts within hollow walls and artful strips of glass flooring carefully differentiate old from new whilst emphasising a vertical dimension that runs through the scheme and links the lower entry level to this new, easily accessible upper level. Similarly, inside the galleries themselves, the architects offer bald, vaulted and top-lit spaces with the minimum of distracting rhetoric or clutter.

However, there are difficulties with such a tight-fit, poised design which rationally disposes every element of the design. RA issues not anticipated or dealt with at the briefing stage and inevitably arising as needs and circumstances change have featured as a 'silting up': for example, the upper gallery lobby is often overloaded with miscellaneous furniture additions and the lower stair lobby sometimes accommodates heavy, Victorian pieces sitting upon the glass floor that contradict one's intuitive sense about its brittleness and load-bearing capacity. Despite such things, the design is still remarkable and it is a rewarding experience to walk an architectural promenade from Piccadilly, through Bank and Barry's gateway, on through Smirke's screen, into Burlington and Ware's hall, to then stand in the two light wells and experience Ware's pretentious garden façade on one side and Smirke's blind, utilitarian façade on the other, to then glide up in the glazed lift and sit in the upper lobby beneath Foster's frosted glazing and enjoy the work of the Ancients set upon the cornice. The architectural ghosts appear to be comfortable; no one being offended by Foster's interventions to keep old Burlington House alive and kicking.

National Gallery, Trafalgar Square, WC2
Venturi, Rauch, Scott-Brown & Partners, 1991
Tube: Charing Cross, Leicester Square.

## 27 Sainsbury Wing, National Gallery: Post-Modern manners

The controversial history of this project, which began as a commercially funded extension to William Wilkins' building of 1832, began when the competition winners, Ahrends Burton Koralek (ABK), had their scheme denounced by Prince Charles as 'a carbuncle on the face of an old friend' – a somewhat saccharine comment about a rather weak neo-classical building that forms the northern edge of Trafalgar Square and sits as the termination of an axis up Whitehall. Another competition was held (limited, this time, to keep out the riff-raff) and the eventual winner was Venturi, Rauch, Scott-Brown Architects, from the USA (now VSBA). The outcome was a controversial scheme, but one that is rich in intellectual gusto. No doubt you'll either engage and possibly respect that, or — like most of the English architectural profession — turn away in horror from the whole enterprise. (To gauge the tenor of the times look at the opposite, south east corner of Trafalgar Square, where there sits a multi-storey office building ostensibly at least 100 years old; it was constructed at the same time as the Sainsbury Wing, replacing an original building that looked exactly like this.)

The VSBA scheme almost literally hangs on a long transverse axis that passes through the main galleries of the Wilkins building, projected out into the new Sainsbury Wing building and terminated within (not by) a perspectival painting set within an arched frame (Cima's *The Incredulity of Saint Thomas*). The architects then bring the painting's architectural content out into their own architecture, so that the two blend together in a forced perspective play with a series of arched openings. This one gesture alone justifies a visit to the building and constitutes a powerful flourish of gamesmanship.

Visitors turn off this armature into a simple series of interlinked room settings with continual plays upon views of the unique and permanent collection of Medieval art, with carefully articulated diagonal views between rooms. Each of these enjoys well-engineered lighting (of

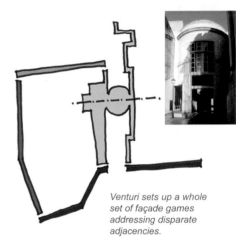

*Venturi sets up a whole set of façade games addressing disparate adjacencies.*

*Architectural Post-Modernism arrived in the UK as a transAtlantic import and quickly took over from moribund fashions of the '60's. Robert Venturi was one of its leading lights, strongly promoted over here by the historian Charles Jencks, who also befriended Terry Farrell, assisting the latter to become this country's premier Post-Modern architect. Whatever the term has meant in other cultural sectors, in architecture it mainly refers to those '70's and '80's conversations with a distinct pro-historical and classical inclination. Whatever other words, ideas and concepts filled the air, the principal ones were composition, hierarchy, layering, contexturalism; the principal game was historical quotation. (Although Venturi himself had originally informed the genere with a more erudite and complex employment of signage and symbol which blurred the boundaries between them botj.) Then came the 1990 recession, lasting until about '94. When we emerged, Post-Modernism no longer existed. It had evaporated. No one discussed it. Everyone pretended it hadn't happened. Late Modernism was back, but Hi-Tech — which had been Po-Mo's contrast — had also disappeared. And then everyone began to practise the kind of post-industrial, post-modernist practices of other cultural spheres. Even Farrell became a born-again Modernist. Now everyone is the genuine Po-Mo thing and even Foster designs parodies of '50's work, entirely without irony.*

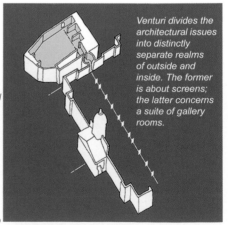

*Venturi divides the architectural issues into distinctly separate realms of outside and inside. The former is about screens; the latter concerns a suite of gallery rooms.*

*On the other hand it is interesting to note that there are again stirrings of the Po-Mo spirit among those 'younger' architects trained at that time (e.g. FAT). We could yet see some form of revival.*

which only a tiny proportion is real daylight) and makes reference to John Soane's rooms at the 1826 Dulwich Picture Gallery (England's first public gallery) whilst re-engineering the lantern to mask an upper service void and roof lights.

Outside, VSBA treats each facade as a set of discrete screens fronting a coherent internal suite of rooms, as if the two had little or nothing to do with one another — another move contradicting Modernist orthodoxy. The principal facade plays with the elements of the Wilkins' frontage and 'ghosts' them into (out of?) their screening extension along this northern side of Trafalgar Square. The opposite, rear facade plays with neo-Las Vegas billboard themes (it faces toward Leicester Square, to which it reaches out in implicit desperation) and the west side is utilitarian, plain and brick. The area between the new wing and the old building is more complicated: a clever inside / outside game that places the main stair in an ambiguous situation, at once outside (the solid internal walling, stone-faced and similar to the other facade screens) and a large glass screen that protects it from the elements whilst offering a view (a reminder) of the Wilkins building and the bridge link that features as a discrete tower. Because black glass and heavy framing was chosen it doesn't work and Venturi has admitted as much, but it's a game try at something complicated and ambitious. It adds up to erudite Post-Modernism, continually quoting precedents and employing recurring references to the original Wilkins building; gives a nod to Finland's great architectural hero, Alvar Aalto on the main stair, and the way a mezzanine landing is used; and even homage to Egyptian sources (small columns, the deeper meaning of which no one has yet uncovered and which Venturi claims is arbitrary). It's a design that exudes competence, is clever, ironic (as Post-Modernists used to say), playful and even witty. For example, the large arches above the grand staircase leading from the entrance lobby up to the gallery spaces enjoy a reverse perspective and are a reference to Bernini's famous Scala Regia at the Vatican. However, in this instance the ceiling arches deliberately float, touching nothing (they're plywood), playing the game and giving it away at the same time, enjoying participation in the history of architecture whilst asserting originality.

Perhaps the English profession is being overly dreary in dismissing all this. The validity of architecture arguably rests ultimately in its 'authentic' actions (admittedly a difficult concept) rather than mind games and an egocentric architectural mannerism that continually says, 'look at me being clever'. Aesthetics, as Terry Eagleton contends, is a discourse of the body, not the mind; on the other hand, Cassirer points in the direction of a mythical and symbolic awareness that most architects neglect. But, in the end, one has to ask: does the heart keep pace with the head's respectful applause of VSBA's erudite acrobatics? Is the essential immediacy and emotive quality of the building – fundamentally important to all architectural experience – forced into the background, prompting intuitive discomfort? Perhaps, in Venturi's own words, the Sainsbury remains 'almost all right' and is worthy of your attention. For, make no mistake: this is a level of architectural gamesmanship far too many architects are hardly capable of. Make a visit, but be prepared to stay awake.

1960's extension

National Portrait Gallery entrance

'Billboard' to Leicester Sq.

Entrance to the Sainsbury Wing

Entrance to the Wilkins building

*Like the NPG, the **National Gallery** is also undertaking a Dixon Jones transformation of its circulation spaces. Entry has traditionally been through a rather cramped portico. This is now being altered so that visitors can enter at ground floor level through paired entrances, either side of the portico steps (only one of which had been constructed in early 2006). People leaving can, of course, now walk straight across the road and into Trafalgar Square and this is a huge improvement.*

# Whitehall & the West End

## 28 National Portrait Gallery

The National Portrait Gallery sits discretely behind the National Gallery like some poor relation and, until recently, its lack of presence was exacerbated by access difficulties and a consequent reluctance of visitors to penetrate its depths (including a C20th room of glass screens designed by Piers Gough). But it has its own, splendid collection and the architectural changes implemented by Dixon Jones (the Ondaatje Wing) have entirely reinvented the place and lent the attractiveness it so desperately needed. Their key strategic move was to see the opportunity for a space swop with the National that benefited both organisations. This enabled the architects to introduce a new circulation system much in the manner that Foster had done at the Sackler. Visitors still have to penetrate E.M. Barry's older, but now short sequence, that brings them into a new, tall lobby with a long escalator that sweeps them up to the top floor, thus enabling a simple glide back down through the gallery spaces — or, if they want, they can enjoy the excellent views from the upper level cafe.

It looks easy and has transformed the NPG into a more enjoyable place. But realising the lobby space and its suspended mezzanine floor required some old fashioned acrobatic engineering (that Dixon Jones have discretely hidden away).

Other page, top left; photos of the older parts.

*Why not make a 'compare and contrast' tour of the major galleries that have been updated: the Wallace, the National, the National Portrait, the Royal Academy, Somerset House, Tate Britain, Tate Modern, the British Museum — even the V&A and, further afield, the Maritime Museum? Then try the smaller venues, including the Geffrye Museum — at which point the game slips into looking at art galleries and the like.*

## 29 New Zealand House

**29** ***New Zealand House*** *( Robert Matthew, Johnson-Marshall & Partners,1957 - 63; Haymarket, SW1) represents a fine example of the podium (with recessed ground floor) + tower (some 70m high) model that was once so fashionable. It was also one of the first buildings in London to be fully air-conditioned – a factor encouraging the architects and engineers to rather over-optimistically provide an all-glass façade. This produced so many problems that internal curtains were later added — which only adds to its character. The top level bar (not public) has a terraced perimeter with fine views. In early 2006 the building was being refurbished; let's hope the curtains are retained.*

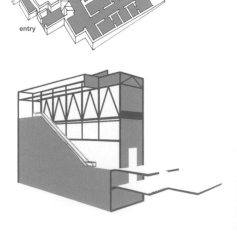

new lobby

C20 gallery

entry

(1) The Foster office's work at **Trafalgar Square** has resulted in a huge improvement. Despite the opposition of taxi drivers, the bus companies and car drivers, the establishment of strong and convenient links to the National Gallery and the engenderment of a new lease of life for the square itself has given Londoners a place that is now an entertainment venue managed by the office of the Mayor: a scenario of pigeons mixing with the traditions of political protest. This is to be seen in the context of the Mayor's '100 squares' programme and similar attempts to learn from places such as Barcelona and make London a more hospitable city whose reality matches its elevated reputation.

Photo: Nigel Young / Foster & Partners

## 30  Royal Opera House

Bow Street, WC2
Dixon Jones BDP, 2000
Tube: Covent Garden, Holborn

E.M. Barry's Royal Opera House of 1858, together with the adjacent Floral Hall (also by Barry) recently underwent a massive, long-winded, expensive and controversial renewal. At the root of the complex is a competition-winning scheme designed by Jeremy Dixon in the early 1980's, carried out in collaboration with BDP and Dixon's latter-day partner, Ed Jones. On the one hand it is an urban design exercise locked into historical and contextural issues concerning Inigo Jones and the original Covent Garden Piazza (hence the recreation of the arcade, extending the one built in 1877 which, in turn, recreated the Inigo Jones scheme of the 1630's). On the other hand, the design is concerned with programmatic issues concerning facilities for opera-lovers, dancers, administrative staff, storage, etc., together with the renovation of Barry's work. The outcome is not one building but four or five fighting for identity — a mix that discomforts many architects. Dixon Jones clearly attempted to have their cake and eat it, but it is the neo-historical parts that are surely the most successful.

 The future of the theatre was ensured by upgrading to three performance spaces. The auditorium was re-raked, re-seated, re-gilded and re-lit whilst retaining its familiar character (now seating 2262 people). Air conditioning was also added and sight-lines improved. The Floral Hall has been restored, reached by escalator and now with a mezzanine level restaurant bar, and serving as the focus of the new foyers. Escalators again take visitors up to the roof-level Amphitheatre Bar and terrace. Behind the scenes (literally and metaphorically) are vast areas of studio space and workshops, a new rehearsal room (underneath which is the new Linbury studio theatre with 446 seats) and four new ballet studios added to the two existing ones. The stage area has been rebuilt (effectively as another ground level across much of the site), given new stage lifts and a new fly-tower three times the height of the proscenium arch. More workshops and offices are in the southern-most wing and the Covent Garden Piazza side is colonnaded for retail units.

 To suggest this is a complex project would be an understatement. It required 150,000 documents and 80,000 drawings. The architectural outcome is another scheme which manages to blend old and new together (as with Bracken House, Lloyd's Register and Liverpool Street Station, for example), whilst utterly transforming backstage facilities (increasing the 'productivity' by a potential 50%, enabling three productions per day, instead of two) and giving the public hugely enhanced accommodation – including rooftop loggias overlooking the Covent Garden Piazza. And it is inside — literally behind the scenes — that the awesome scale of this project takes one's breath away. The refurbished, historical auditorium with all its trappings of history and class joins together with the stage to provide one larger stage behind which an army of people and a staggering amount of equipment and logistical capability service the performances of the players (whether singing, dancing or sitting in their seats playing out the role of audience).

 This is an outstanding building worthy of your attention. However, ironically, if there is an outstanding weakness it is the public access from the piazza, and the related foyer and restaurant spaces. Meanwhile, the formal Barry entrance on Bow Street feels secondary to what is going on. (The Lloyd's '86 building in the City suffers a not dissimilar problem.)

*A clever twisting bridge designed by Wilkinson Eyre links the main body of the upper level facilities to the ballet school across the road (north side of the building), attempting to make sense and enjoyment from the difficult relational geometries of the buildings being linked.*

*Above (from the left): a 'moderne' part; the old Barry entrance on Bow Street; a long view to the Wilkinson Eyre bridge; and the façade of the old Floral Hall, 1858-60 (behind which is a tall, decked gallery space with bars and café, accessible to the public and used at intervals between performances).*

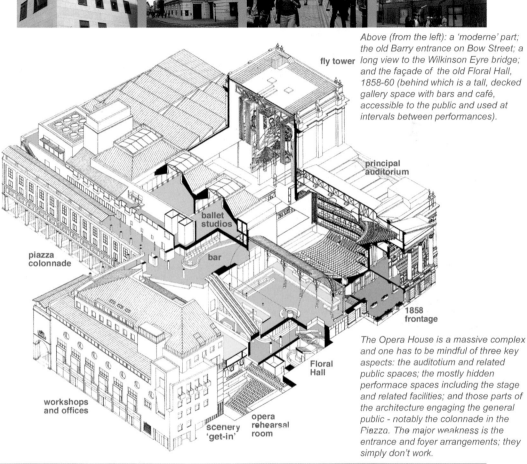

fly tower

principal auditorium

ballet studios

piazza colonnade

bar

1858 frontage

workshops and offices

Floral Hall

scenery 'get-in'

opera rehearsal room

The Opera House is a massive complex and one has to be mindful of three key aspects: the auditotium and related public spaces; the mostly hidden performace spaces including the stage and related facilities; and those parts of the architecture engaging the general public - notably the colonnade in the Piazza. The major weakness is the entrance and foyer arrangements; they simply don't work.

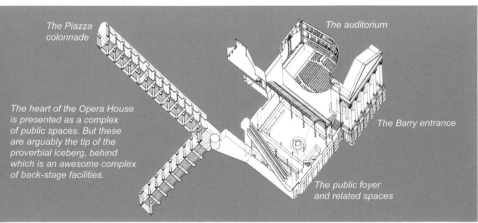

The Piazza colonnade

The auditorium

The Barry entrance

The heart of the Opera House is presented as a complex of public spaces. But these are arguably the tip of the proverbial iceberg, behind which is an awesome complex of back-stage facilities.

The public foyer and related spaces

# Whitehall & the West End

**31** *St. Paul's church Covent Garden, WC2 is a committed piece of architectural theatre finished in 1630. Its principal façade (which is, bizarrely, the blank east portico and not the west front) has become a theatrical proscenium and faces into what was once an open square and arcaded piazza — a part of what was an original design novelty in London streets called 'regularity'. The area's developer had to have permission of the King, who foisted the Royal Surveyor, the accomplished virtuoso Inigo Jones, onto the unfortunate man who,*

*asking for 'a mere barn of a building' met the response from Jones that he would have 'the finest barn in England'. The outcome was a fashionable area that slowly degraded as the West End developed, its piazza becoming a market and its arcades apparently becoming the resort of London's more debauched residents. However, much of what you see now is a restoration after a fire of 1795. Other London works by Jones include: the Banqueting House, 1622; the Queen's House, Greenwich, 1615 on; St. Mary's church; Lindsey House, Lincoln's Inn Fields, 1640.*

*The market was established as early as 1670 and the buildings themselves are early Victorian (Charles Fowler Snr., 1828 – 31) and served as London's main vegetable wholesale market until the early '70's, when a GLC scheme to move the market to a more accessible location and redevelop the area with new buildings, highways, pedways and lots of concrete prompted a popular unrest and effectively ended 'comprehensive redevelopment' in London. The Garden promptly became London's first trendy ad agency / studio precinct before retail values pushed most of them out in the '80's to other warehouses around Clerkenwell (then being vacated by support sectors to the newspapers of Fleet Street, themselves off to Docklands and new employment practices). Since then Covent Garden has remained a characterful retail and restaurant area focused upon the retained and restored central market buildings.*

**32** *Denys Lasdun's **Royal College of Physicians**, 1960 – 64, on the Outer Circle and St. Andrew's Place, NW1, is a design in the spirit of Le Corbusier married to the English Baroque. One has to imagine an*

*institution with medieval roots, small but hugely influential, dragged into the post-war National Health System and, by the late '50's, ready to attempt a move from a neo-Greek building in Trafalgar Square into a contemporary design. Professional, ceremonial and mundane functions are expertly conjoined into a pavilion terminating terraces along this side of Regent's Park whilst similarly acknowledging context on the eastern side, where administrative offices form part of an existing terrace. Most accommodation is ceremonial and highly symbolic (library as head and cultural memory, initiation room (Census) as heart, central tall hall with its central stair as lungs, dining areas as gut, roof top air intake as mouth and boiler exhaust as . . . (you guess); the auditorium to one side reads as a speech bubble on plan, etc. Bizarre. All of it self-evident in plan and section, but there is hardly a revealing word from Lasdun and an institution who will go no further than admit to the architect's interest in Harvey's concept of blood flows (equals architectural circulation). During the late 1990's, Lasdun was asked to add another 'pod-like' addition opposite the Census room and the College has been linked into nearby buildings to form a latter-day educational precinct for the profession. This includes a neo-classical building to the south by Nicholas Hare. Go here and then head north to the Nash terraces of Regent's Park (possibly on to Park Village and Camden Town).*

**33** *Regent's Street / Regent's Park (1811 – 30)*
*was designed as a via triumphalis (a 'royal mile')*
between Carlton House (on the south side of
the Mall), to a speculative development of aristocratic
villas and terraces on a crown property to the north (to
become Regent's Park). It was never used as such, but
its pragmatic, disjointed character says a lot about urban
design and large scale development in London, especially
during one of the city's most expansive and formative
periods.

It also says a lot about the skilled architectural
gamesmanship of its architect and planner, John Nash,
reputed to be a favourite of the Prince Regent following
a convenient marriage to the Prince's mistress (which
brought Nash instant career success as well as an instant
family). Cleverly, Nash proposed to follow a route along
the edge of a rather dense and crowded Soho in order to
make the new street a part of Mayfair and differentiate the
'nobility and gentry' from the 'mechanics and trading part
of the community'.

In a marvellously pragmatic manner, the street
winds its way north from **Waterloo Place** (where the ICA
is located) and the east end of the Mall via a necessary
curve which then avoided the better properties of St.
James's and prompted the idea of grand colonnades
(since demolished and replaced by the 'grand manner'
buildings we see today). It then sweeps north, through a
junction with Oxford Street to another difficulty: **Portland
Place**. This already existed, developed and designed by
the Adam Brothers, and aligned so that Langham House
(now replaced by the Langham Hotel; opposite it is the
BBC's **Broadcasting House**) could look to the fields due
north. At the crucial junction of new and existing, Nash
masterfully provided a church (**All Souls**) with a circular
colonnade at its west end to help us round the double
bend into Portland Place.

At the north end of this stretch, Nash faced
further formal difficulty and provided a crescent to allow
for an offset to the park itself. This was followed by a
series of splendid terraces within the park (especially
on the east side, e.g. **Chester Terrace**, 1825, and
**Cumberland Terrace**, 1826).

Only five of the intended villas were ever built in
the park, served by the Regent's Canal along its northern
edge, where there was also a market. In the 1980's,
Quinlan Terry was allowed to design three new villas
along the Regent's Canal, complementing the original
group (and these have more recently been added to).

At the north east corner of the development
sits **Park Village** East and West (now split by a Victorian
railway that characteristically charged its way through
the urban fabric), a delightful group of 'cottages in
the city', which set a keynote for future, anti-industrial
developments in London (e.g. the villas populating **St.
John's Wood**, immediately to the north) whilst continuing
a traditional theme in London's building mix.

Within Regent's Street itself, Nash had to
struggle to create order among disparate developers.
However, none of the original buildings now exist, most of
Regent's Street having being redeveloped between about
1913–28 to a scheme involving Norman Shaw, Aston
Webb, Ernest Newton, and Sir Reginald Blomfield (all
major architects of the day).

**34** John Nash's **All Souls Church** (Langham
Place, 1824), enjoys the overwhelming
significance of being a set piece in an urban
design scheme rather than especially interesting
as a church. Its architectural elements fit together
like some child's set of
building blocks — but
it works, especially as
the key feature of an
extremely difficult aspect
of Nash's scheme to
get from the Mall to the
new Regent's Park
with a semblance of
architectural coherence.
The building both
terminates long views
and facilitates us
easily rounding a bend
— an urban 'landmark'
demonstrative of an ease
of gamesmanship that
has become a lost art.
See the new parts of the
BBC building next door.

*Map labels: Views north · Regent's Canal · Regents Park · Cumberland Terrace · Hanover & Kent terraces · Canal basin · Chester Terrace · Park terrace hinterland · York Terrace · Park Crescent · Portland Place · Oxford Street · All Soul's church · Grosvenor Sq. · Hanover Sq. · Soho · Berkeley Sq. · Mayfair · Piccadilly · St James's Sq. · Green Park · St. James's Park*

## 35 Sedley Place

Sedley Place, W1
Fletcher Priest, 2004
Tube: Bond Street

Sedley used to be one of those seedy nondescript alleys that reached off behind Oxford Street into some strange backland — in fact, the place where Fletcher Priest set up their offices about thirty years ago. So there must have been a sentimental undertone somewhere within this design equation. The 'meat' of this scheme is the skilled Oxford Street frontage. However, this is a commercial building whose presence is somewhat lost midst the churn of 11m shoppers who apparently use this shopping venue each year (prompting one to long for someone to properly learn from the popularism of the strips and Google drive-ins of a 1950's USA, the contemporary Ginza architecture in Tokyo, and even the adjacent HMV store of 1939, by Joseph Emberton). It is Sedley Place itself that is the real architectural attraction. This can be approached directly off Oxford Street, down the alley that is all that remains of the old street (in truth a fairly bland scenario redolent with the kind of commercial values that probably thrill developers but almost no-one else, apart from shoppers for bling, cosmetics, new shoes and whatever else is being sold in the ground floor shop). However, the civic surprise is at the bottom of the alley, where the visitor will be surprised to find a small and very pleasant piazza, complete with a water feature, apartment balconies and the flavour of a hundred holiday visits made by the authors in the guise of architectural tourist (places from Navarra to New Orleans) — all of which translates into a welcoming backland that feels a million miles from the bustle of what is, in fact, merely a few metres away. Suddenly, one is exposed to that other London: the Georgian terraces, chimneys, small yards and the like that surprisingly characterise much of the in between areas, even in this part of London.

It is no mean achievement to pull this sort of thing off and one can imagine all kinds of heated debate that contrasted and yet sort to integrate the values of the street frontage with the more calm backland.

**36** *Selfridge's, Oxford Street, W1 remains one of the more impressive facades in London. Designed between 1907 – 28, its 'giant order' columns have a marvellous scale that brings the Chicago of Daniel Burnham to London (others involved included RF Atkinson and Sir John Burnet); 'the motif made history in England', commented Pevsner. In recent years the interior has been reinvented and the store transformed in status into one of London's premier shopping venues. Meanwhile, no one has challenged the stature of the façade.*

**37** *Raymond Hood's name – associated with skyscrapers in New York during the 1920's and 1930's – is an unsuspected one for the London scene. Palladium House (formerly for the National Radiator Company) was designed in 1928 for the corner of Great Marlborough and Argyll Streets, W1. Compare its black granite façade with the HMV shop in Oxford St. and the Daily Express frontage in Fleet St. Across the road is the half-timbered Liberty shop designed by E.T. and E.S. Hall (1922 - 3), and desperately attempting to be genuine arts & crafts. The Regent Street façade (by the same architects) was designed 1914 and constructed 1925 - 26.*

## Broadwick House

15 Broadwick Street, W1
Richard Rogers Partnership, 2002
Tube: Oxford Circus

This is a deceptively simple piece of architecture: a ground floor of retail units, offices above (used by Ford for its multi-brand design consultancy), and a double height + mezzanine office loft space at the top. But it's put together with panache and — whilst bearing all the Rogers' team hallmarks — neatly fits itself into this corner site in Soho, at the end of Berwick Street market. The entrance lobby leads to lift and services risers, toilets etc. that, as usual, terminate in the manner land-marking church spires once did. (We'll probably be able to scan the city skyline one day and easily spot all the Rogers' buildings!) The upper space with its curved roof and gallery is an especially pleasant space, with fine views. *See the building as part of a recent family: C4, Lloyd's Register, K2 and 88 Wood Street.*

**39** *Foster's refurbishment of the **Asprey** store in New Bond St. W1, is typical of the panache with which retailing has been developed by the practice (one remembers the Sloane Street Esprit and similar stores in London). The principal architectural event here is a large spiral stair set against a mirrored wall.*

**40** *Sanderson's Hotel (37, Berner Street, W1) is the conversion of the '58 Sanderson's wall paper shop into a 'hip hotel', designed by that trendiest (and talented) French designer, Philippe Starck (2000). Also see Starck's design for a similar 204 room hotel conversion (1999) for St. Martin's Lane Hotel (38; St. Martin's Lane). Both interiors are good; St. Martin's is probably the better one. (The developer for both was Ian Schrager.)*

**41** *All Saints, Margaret Street, WC1, north of Oxford Street (below), is a truly amazing design that you'll either love or hate for its 'constructional polychromatic' brickwork and shadowed, incense-laden, high-church interior. Apart from this, it is an immensely skilful piece of architectural organisation and gamesmanship — completely filling a 33 m.sq. site that is surrounded on three sides — whilst still offering an appropriate entry court as well as the church itself, a choir school and a priest's house. Designed by William Butterfield in 1858, it is a masterful work: architectural gamesmanship at its best.*

Manchester Square, W1
Rick Mather Architects, 2000
Tube: Bond Street, Marble Arch

## 42 Wallace Collection

The Wallace Collection has — like practically everything else — been 'discovered' in recent years and pulled out from its backlands existence into the limelight. And Rick Mather's conversion of its central court has significantly helped in making the place more attractive. Like the Soane Gallery, for example, it is now a popular venue. Since, however, these things are always relative, you will find the Wallace (and the Soane) relatively quiet compared with the national or similar places.

    The Collection was bequested to the nation in 1897 and forms a fine collections of French 18th c. paintings, old masters, furniture and china, including Frans Hals' *Laughing Cavalier*, all housed in a late C19 mansion in central London, formerly belonging to the Wallaces. Like most galleries, the Wallace was short of space and the kinds of facilities people now expect. But the building was without room for expansion. Mather came up with the idea of excavating the basement in order to create a new lecture theatre, educational facilities and gallery space. In addition he proposed to glaze over the house's central courtyard to create a new, top-lit café. The outcome is not a Sackler or National Portrait Gallery with their entirely reinvented circulation patterns, but is nevertheless a very good example of the quiet updating of an important (and rather pleasant) London museum gallery.

*The Manchester Square frontage.*

*The internal cafe / courtyard.*

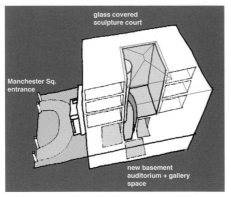

glass covered sculpture court

Manchester Sq. entrance

new basement auditorium + gallery space

**43** **St George, Bloomsbury** *is another fine Hawksmoor design, dating from 1716-31. During 2006 it was still undergoing renovation but this should be complete by the time you read this. Site constraints foprced hawksmoor to locate the grand entrance portico on the south, street side as a piece of theatre, with the real original entrances at the tower — a feature, with its references to descriptions of the mausoleum at Halicarnassus, that is worth your attentions.*

**44** *Colonel Seifert's* **Centre Point** *building on the corner of Tottenham Court Road and Oxford Street, W1, was in its day, notorious as an example of outrageous speculative greed. The ground level arrangements remain very unsatisfactory and await major urban renewal at this important road junction, but as memories fade and all architects acknowledge they are 'commercial', some have even started to enjoy Seifert's load-bearing building envelope and many of his other London buildings.*

## Brunei Gallery

University of London, Thornaugh Street, WC1
Nicholas Hare, 1995
Tube: Euston, Russell Square

**45**

Respectfully knitting in with one's neighbours has become a major architectural game (a legacy of Post-Modernist sentiments, contrasting with Modernism's instrumental penchant for contrast and, sometimes, a rejection of history). The Brunei attempts to relate to the materials, massing, organisation and careful geometry of late C18 neighbours (who employed an implied classical order); however, once around the corner, the design quickly changes mode and enjoys a new freedom not given in Russell Square, breaking away into a more free articulation around the entrance, where the brickwork now transforms itself into a veneer. Accommodation includes a cafeteria for students and an Islamic roof garden. The Gallery itself shows Islamic art and is worth your attention.

## Clore Centre

University of London, Torrington Square, WC1
Stanton Williams, 1998
Tube: Euston Square, Euston

**46**

Stanton Williams' design for the Clore Management Centre, close to the Brunei, adopts a different approach to contexturalism and terminates a Georgian terrace. Similar formal themes are adopted (base, piano nobile, attic storey), but their longer façade gives them the opportunity to carry through the geometry of the adjacent 7m. Georgian structural bay. However, when it comes to the key central section of the façade, they have rejected the windows-in-load-bearing-masonry approach in favour of large areas of hung glazing.

**47** *Two Denys Lasdun buildings are nearby: **SOAS** (1973), clad in white precast panels; and the **Institute of Education**, 1970, stretching along Bedford Way (both adjacent to Stanton Williams' Management Centre and the Brunei Gallery).*

**48** *This **Alfred Place** building is another speculative effort from the Richard Seifert office, this time dating from about 1972 — for my money one of the better of this under-rated architect's work (he is still vilified and unfashionable, largely for fashionable reasons).*

# Whitehall & the West End

20-21 Newman Street, W1
Buschow Henley, 2001
Tube: Tottenham Court Road

## 49 Talkback

Admin facilities for an independent TV production company that, we admit, are difficult to access. What is hidden behind the old street façade is a superb conversion that articulates the architect's determination to avoid the usual office stereotypes without resorting to gimmickry, i.e. a design informed by an appreciation of urban syntax, notions of the office as a place with domestic undertones, and self-conscious enthusiasms for a 1950's English architecture. Typologically similar to Ron Herron's Imagination, older inner and outer blocks are reinvented and unified into a new architectural whole by strap-on circulation routes and other devices. But there is an entire absence of intoxication with anything hi-tech — replaced by a joy in natural materials and 'accessible' detailing more likely to come from an Essex timber yard than some remote foreign factory.

Broadcasting House
MacCormac Jamieson Prichard (+ Sheppard Robson for P2), 2005-6
Tube: Oxford Street

## 50 Broadcasting House

This project will be either very good in spite of everything, or witness to how unfortunately things can go wrong these days. Externally, it looks very promising but, during mid-construction, the design architects were ejected from the project and replaced by Sheppard Robson. (The BBC has a deal with a developer: they provide the brief; the latter provides the building; the architect is novated to the contractor. Then the fun starts.) A two-phase programme for the 80,000 sq.m. building complex is not expected to be complete until mid-2006, but the 36 radio studios, 23 radio continuity studios, 6 TV studios, 2 control rooms and 60 edit / graphics suites fed by 10,000 miles of cabling should be worth a look! Art will, of course, have a presence and complement the Eric Gill on the original 1932 building (designed by Colonel Val Meyer). And we are told there will be extensive public access (as at White City?).

**51** The 186m high **British Telecom Tower** in Cleveland Street, WC1, in Fitzrovia, went up in 1964, suffered an IRA attack and then had its public deck and revolving restaurant closed to the public. Since then it has remained as an enigmatic landmark clouded in the kind of secrecy that surrounds a major urban microwave communications structure. Together with Centre Point, the new St. Mary Axe building, St. Paul's, the former NatWest Tower (Tower 42), and Canary Wharf it helps define the London skyline. Access can be arranged, but it isn't easy.

**52** The HQ of that architect's trades union, the **RIBA**, at 66 Portland Place, is well worth a visit: for a good façade, a fine staircase, library, bookshop and bar / cafe. It was erected as a celebratory building after decades had been spent fighting for state professional registration (monopoly protection to most people). And so, midst the continuing ravages of the Depression, Britain's architects strutted their stuff in the West End (Grey Wornum, 1932 - 4; Tube: Oxford Street).

## Arup offices

Designed by Sheppard Robson (why not Arup Associates, one wonders?), this studio building for a very large and prestigious engineering practice is itself a large conversion and recladding job that features a rather bizarre architectural event on its facade: what everyone characterises as a large alien beast clinging to the glazing. It really adds to the character of the streetscape, but if it was intended that way why isn't there more such stuff characterising a scheme that gets rather bland and corporate on the interior? Anyway, it's a good example of how world-class engineers design for themselves. (The external ducting etc. can be compared with Arup's building at Regent's Place.)

**Arups**
13 Fitzroy Street, W1
Sheppard Robson 2004
Tube: Warren Street / Great Portland Street

**54** *Congress House is the home of the Trades Union Council (1948-57; Great Russell Street, WC1) effectively the HQ of the trades union movement in the UK and dedicated as a grand monument to those trades unionists who died in two world wars — symbol of the power held by some 9 million trade unionists right up to the late 1980's. The Post-Modernism that brought Thatcherism and Blair's New Left government has placed a question mark over the movement and this institution, but the building David du R. Aberdeen designed for the unionists is a fine work of architectural gamesmanship worthy of attention. Aberdeen won a competition for the building in 1948; it was a grim, dire period in London's history, but among architects it was also a time of great optimism and hope for the future of post-war Britain. One has to imagine this work of bright, transparent Modernism arriving in a tightly urban street midst terraced, Georgian central London: a sooty, polluted place prone to the dense smogs contemporaneously romanticised by the likes of Frank Sinatra, many thousands of miles away from the reality. By the time the building was completed the country was well on the road to recovery, the Clean Air Act was two years old and Aberdeen's building was a significant social symbol. Rock 'n roll was at the door, a service economy was developing and an 'angry young man' syndrome had arrived upon the arts scene. However, the opening was to coincide with the beginning of a period of wretched union battles with governments of all political persuasions, reaching its finale with Margaret Thatcher's employer and MI5-assisted victory against the miners in the early 1980's. And David du Aberdeen was not to design another significant building.*

## Whitehall & the West End

## The Marylebone Road / Euston Road development corridor

This is another one Terry Farrell has his hands on and is a natural for his skills in attempting to lend a humane face to capitalism's speculative office developments — in fact, civilising the urban environment in general. With regard to the latter, for example, he has identified ways of pushing the traffic to the background and foregrounding pedestrian movements across this very busy highway that forms a northern boundary to the West End. If this can be achieved around the Tottenham Court Road / Euston Road junction the Regent's Place development would be more integrated into the heart of the city and residents immediately to the north would find their 'islanding' reduced. The same applies all along this stretch of road. At the time of writing Euston station is reporting ambitions to realise a commercial development on the scale of Canary Wharf. Barring a recession, it looks as if this route — and adjacent areas — is about to undergo massive change.

Paddington Basin

Regent's Park

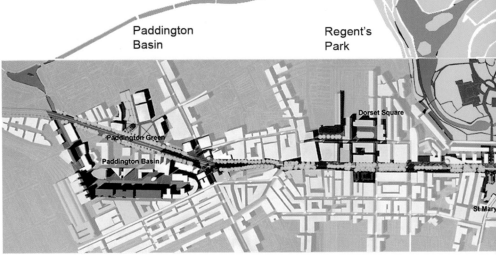

Dorset Square

Paddington Green

Paddington Basin

St Mary

*Drawing: Farrell & Partners*

*The corridor is lined with major stations: Paddington, Marylebone, Euston, St. Pancras and Kings Cross. In between these are interesting local, residential areas, often with an ethnic population bias (that, unfortunately, will inevitably change once redevelopment really gets going). These in between pockets need reinforcing and linking together across the highway so that a business presence and commuter traffic are balanced by the everyday lives of local inhabitants. Since the Paddington development and the start on the Kings Cross one, change has been quite tangible, rapidly spreading along the corridor and into adjacent areas. Whether other aspects of the Farrell scheme will be realised is a moot point, but the Mayor of London's Architecture & Urbanism Unit (led by Lord Richard Rogers) has slotted the corridor into its programme for redeveloping key parts of the metropolis, population growth, new housing and much more emphasis upon public transport.*

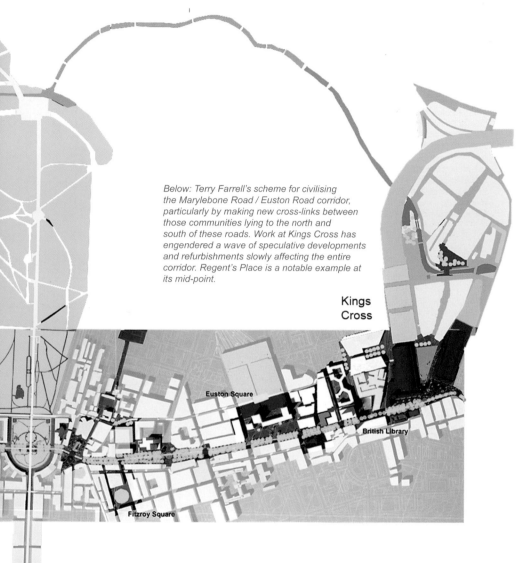

Below: Terry Farrell's scheme for civilising
the Marylebone Road / Euston Road corridor,
particularly by making new cross-links between
those communities lying to the north and
south of these roads. Work at Kings Cross has
engendered a wave of speculative developments
and refurbishments slowly affecting the entire
corridor. Regent's Place is a notable example at
its mid-point.

**Kings
Cross**

Euston Square

British Library

Fitzroy Square

*St. Pancras Station* and the Midland Grand Hotel in
Euston Road (immediately to the east of Kings Cross)
might one day become what they promise: the terminal
for the Eurostar fast link from the Channel Tunnel.
Meanwhile, this splendid and much loved pile is always
in danger of rotting away. The romantic
and picturesque hotel – sourced from
examples all over Europe – fronting the
station was originally opened in 1874
as one of the best in London, with 400
rooms. The architect was Sir George
Gilbert Scott, who between 1850–70 had
the largest practice in the country and
was a keen Gothicist. The station shed
was for many years the largest clear
span in the world, designed by W.H.
Barlow.

### 55 Gagosian Gallery

6-24 brittania Street, WC1
Caruso St John, 2004
Tube: Kings Cross

The Gagosian is about as up market as international galleries get: a fine one that evokes vague memories of the lost Saatchi in St. John's Wood (but not nearly as spacious). It is, as one might also expect from these architects, beautifully detailed — as much so as to flatter affluent buyers as provide a cool setting for art (don't even ask about prices: 'The art, my dear, has to go to the right buyers, not just to anyone — perhaps we could have a name and number and someone will call you at our convenience'). The concrete floor is immaculate; the white walls perfect; the lighting discrete and the reception arrangements suitably poised in a relaxed manner. But if you do come here (perhaps to enjoy famous and expensive art as well as the architecture), then also go to the Victoria Miro gallery for a similar blank box that throbs with a more gritty vitality of which the Gagosian is (possibly pleased to be) bereft.

### 56 The Place

16 Flaxman Terrace, WC1
Allies and Morrison, 2001
Tube: Euston

The Place is a major dance school and performance venue in mixed accommodation that stretches itself between two streets: an old entrance on Duke Street and a new one on Flaxman Street.
    The new entrance is the result of A&M's focus upon the identity of the institution, the performers' and students' facilities, and the dance studios, providing a new and dramatic entrance with a stretching area in front of the glazing to create a shop window-like effect for the School with passers-by viewing the dancers' silhouettes in motion. Other work increased the number of studios and improved the quality of existing ones, and improved the public areas.
    Also see this firm's better work at the City Lit and Chelsea School of Art. otherwise, as a successful practice, A&M are currently popping up all over London.

### 57 University College Institute of Cancer Studies

Huntley Street, W1
Nicholas Grimshaw & Partners, 2006
Tube: Warren Street / Goodge Street

At the time of writing, this building is still going up . . . but is already looking promising (hence the model shots, left). It's not my usual policy to point people toward buildings half-complete at the time of writing, but this will be complete by early 2006 and already looks promising. The scheme provides heavily serviced labs and teaching facilities as part of a scheme that adds the new to an old nursing home designed by an architect called Paul Waterhouse — the son of the more famous Alfred Waterhouse, retaining parts of the latter for offices, etc. and demolishing later extensions to the original, in order to provide the potential for the new labs, etc. (*Waterhouse did, among other things, the* **University College Hospital**, *the* **Natural History Museum** *in South Kensington, and the* **Prudential Insurance Company** *building in High Holborn, near the Foster-designed Sainsbury HQ.*)

## The British Library

St. Pancras, Euston Road/Melton Street, NW1
Colin St. John Wilson, 1964-98
Tube: Euston, St. Pancras

*The British Library forecourt area — which is slowly being inhabited, with cafes, etc., thus hugely improving an original bleakness.*

The British Library project began as a joint venture between 'Sandy' Wilson and Sir Leslie Martin (1908 - 99), then head of the Cambridge school of architecture and famous as the former head of the LCC architect's department and the key figure in the design of the Royal Festival Hall. At the time, Wilson was a one-man practice and a lecturer at Cambridge when, in 1962, the British Library competition came up. By the late '60's Martin had withdrawn into retirement and Wilson (together with his wife and other partners) was carrying on the project in the face of all kinds of political and sentimental opposition that transformed a job into a career. Their first design (1962-64) was for a site immediately in front of the Museum, in Bloomsbury, but the brief grew enormously and later designs had to accept that the site was too small. In 1973 another site was found at St. Pancras. By 1978 a new design had been completed and the building Wilson & Martin had started together was to be completed in three stages: the basement areas, entry hall (concourse), and Humanities reading rooms; the Science reading rooms; and an extension for a 'bindery' and more reading rooms. Construction was finally completed in stages between 1997 - 9. It had taken over 35 years.

Both the two early schemes to 1972 were low-rise, high density, mixed use schemes with housing and commercial uses, as well as a new library. (See the nearby Brunswick Centre.) The initial scheme also gave reference to a W.R. Lethaby proposal of 1891 for a 'Sacred Way' from the British Museum down to Waterloo Bridge. It was also at this time that Wilson made a proposal that, when the Library moved out, the Reading Room should be returned to public use and placed upon a north-south route — something Foster was later to return to with his Great Court scheme.

Wilson's original sketches for St. Pancras indicate the concept of two major parts to the design concept: an orthogonal part, to which more irregular parts are attached, much as ships at a quay. In reality, the actual designs appear to be more rigid and organised than this. The current plan, for example, clearly has a direct correspondence with the concept sketch (a rigid spine to which more informally arranged parts are connected), but the 'irregular' parts are arguably as formal and orthogonal as the principal spine. Nevertheless, there is a strong 'parti' to the scheme.

The section is as organised as the plan. The deepest floors are for book stacks and help to make the building a veritable 'iceberg'. Above this are mechanical plant areas. As we move above ground, a key criterion that enters the scene is an aspiration toward daylight and the layers of reading rooms vary in height according to what goes on within them. These upper parts offer a sensuous unfolding of the architecture, particularly within the central 'concourse' area (it would be difficult to call it a foyer or lobby), where the inspiration of Alvar Aalto's public spaces can be clearly read.

In Wilson's own words, there is a lot of 'icing' layered upon the raw, underlying concrete structure, but most of this derives from acoustic and maintenance criteria

### Homage to a stunning place

*Believe it or not, SOM were once the heroes of post-war Modernism to a generation of architects that included 'Sandy' Wilson. His King's Library at the heart of the British Library concourse is a straight homage to Gordon Bunshaft's design (while at SOM) for the Beinecke Rare Books Library in Yale (1963) — but without the 1.25 inch glowing marble panels (which have also become fashionable again, now sandwiched between sheets of glass; see the background to the image). But whereas the Wilson effort is rather lost, the SOM one stands forth as some enigmatic icon.*

that insinuated themselves into the design. It is worth comparing the building in these terms with Wilson's mid-'90's design in the East End for St. Mary's College, where the finishes of this library are much simpler and owe much to Lewerentz rather than Aalto (Wilson courageously dares to employ Lewerentz-style 'bagged brickwork' — a more rude and rustic treatment that literally uses a bag to spread the joint mortar).

British Library
concept model

above
ground

below
ground

### Books in 250 years time?

*"Those who would carry on great public schemes must be proof against the most fatiguing delays, the most mortifying disappointments, the most shocking insults and, worst of all the presumptuous judgement of the ignorant upon their designs".  Edmund Burke, quoted by CW.*

*• The BL was designed to last 250 years (i.e. more or less the period from its beginnings, projected into the future).
• It has over 12m books on 340km of shelving • The building goes 25m under ground and 48m above ground.
• The gross floor area of the Library is 112,643 sq.m. (1,212,039 sq.ft.)*

*There is something profoundly ironic within Wilson's stamina-loaded achievement of realising the British Library at St. Pancras, a building designed to last 250 years. The design was started in 1962 only four years after the integrated circuit was invented by Jack Kilby at Texas Instruments, at a time when the concepts of programming languages and programming software were well established. Perhaps this reality is somewhere in the background to the history of a project that underwent a 37 year gestation period and was finally allowed (by the then Prime Minister, John Major) to be finished in 1999 on the basis that it did not fulfil its ambition to a final phase of expansion — one of the very reasons it was located where it was. (A finish did not mean completion.) By that time every architectural practice took Computer Aided Design (CAD) for granted, an age of architectural 'blobs' had arrived and Wilson's great inspiration — the work of Alvar Aalto — self-evidently belonged to a previous era.
It had taken a long time and Wilson is fond of quoting the parallel period of gestation taken by St. Paul's Cathedral under Sir Christopher Wren ("on half pay for ten years and sacked before completion"). However, whilst we await the fates of books in a digitising era, it is hardly fair to criticise the British Library in terms of fashion. It's ambitions drew upon more profound sentiments. In the architect's mind, "the library and what it houses embodies and protects the freedom and diversity of the human spirit in a way that borders on the sacred". In a way, this notion of the sacredness of knowledge is embodied in Eduardo Paolozzi's piazza sculpture of Sir Isaac Newton, as inspired by William Blake's woodcut done in the 1790's.*

### Routes reinvented

*In a report of 1962-4 'Sandy' Wilson suggested opening up the old Round Reading Room to the public as part of a north-south route which incorporated a new Library on a site just south of the British Museum. This made reference to a 1891 scheme by W R Lethaby to create a 'Sacred Way' between the Museum and the old Waterloo Bridge. Norman Foster later reinvented the idea of a pedestrian route from the new British Library at St. Pancras, down through the heart of the British Museum (and its Great Court) and beyond to Trafalgar Square. As an idea this has never been realised; certainly, the BM Court will never be the central public space Foster envisaged. In fact, the real cross-town route rapidly effecting itself is east-west, from Kings Cross to Paddington.*

## University College Hospital

**59**

235 Euston Road, London NW1 2BU
Llewelyn Davies Yeang
Tube: Warren Street

It's not very popular, but this large hospital building on the corner of Tottenham Court Road and Euston Road plays a significant role in the transformation of this area. It looks as if it belongs to some Asian city rather than London, but perhaps that's a good thing. In fact, I like the colour; shame about the corner and entry features. And isn't it a lot more cheerful than the greyness of the Wellcome, next door? (But also compare it with the Hopkins building at St. Thomas' Hospital.) We're told the 669 bed unit goes 80m above ground and 17m below; it has 2000 rooms and 2400 PC's! The new building sits adjacent to a grand, red brick and terra-cotta 1896 - 1903 building by Alfred and Paul Waterhouse.

## Royal Academy of Music

**60**

Marylebone Road, NW1
John McAslan + Partners, 2002
Tube: Regent's Park, Baker Street

Another piece of architecture that is mostly subterranean, with a large roof with glazed ends popping up above ground on the Marylebone Road frontage. Beneath this is a new concert and recording hall, the focal part of a much larger remodelling and extension programme described as 'a living museum', archive, teaching and practice facility as part of the 1820's John Nash building occupied by the RAM.

**61** *Charles Holden's 1937 **Senate House** towers above Bloomsbury as the principal (admin and library) building of the University of London, having replaced some fine Georgian terraces that are now more to people's tastes. In fact, it represents only a part of a 1932 grand 'Gotham City' plan to sweep northward with such buildings, but only fragments of the scheme were realised. It is quite a beast ("a quiet insistence", as Holden put it), but does have quite a fine lobby area (try the approach off Malet Street) and is full of period details. The idea for a tower came from the client and, for many years, it was the tallest building in London apart from St. Paul's. However, one has to admit that a part of its interest derives simply from the status of its author as one of the notable architects of the period and designer for many fine Underground stations (e.g. Anros Grove, Boston Manor, Clapham South, Morden, Southgate, etc.).*

## 62   Gibbs Building, Wellcome Trust

Wellcome Trust
215 Euston Road, NW1
Michael Hopkins & Partners, 2005
Tube: Warren Street / Euston Sq. / Euston

Philip Johnson's infamous quip concerning 'turds in the plaza' reflects a not untypical attitude toward the problems of adorning architecture with art and, by inviting the artist Thomas Heatherwick to locate a gigantic suspended sculptural piece within the atrium of the Wellcome Gibbs Building, the architects of the Hopkins' team might have bitten off more than they bargained for. This rather delicious piece — a tall, sinuous form named 'Bleigiessen' that was entirely dependent upon digital technology for its realisation — shimmers and glows and, had it been more centrally located, would have dominated the architectural qualities of an atrium space that is otherwise quite splendid in itself. As it is, Heatherwick's sculpture is pushed to one end of the atrium, perhaps as a reminder of peripheral sentiments to those informing the Wellcome Trust and its charitable work in scientific research.

The piece metaphorically reworks a Germanic tradition in which molten lead would be poured into water and, from the resulting shape, the future predicted. But far from fatefully accepting the prognostications of lead shapes, the Wellcome Trust adopts a proactive stance that aims to influence what the future brings. And it is the expression of such a spirit that has been the hidden challenge to the Hopkins' design team: to bring together staff currently spread across numerous buildings and to express a spirit of informality, openness and exchange, modernity and optimism regarding the promises of the future. The aim to realise this aspiration on Euston Road has resulted in this large new building as a design twinned and internally linked to an original building of 1932 – the latter currently undergoing refurbishment as a new home for the Wellcome library and public exhibitions, etc.

It has to be said, however, that the grey exterior of the Gibbs building offers a dour promise and contrasts with the distinctly more upbeat brightness of its stylistically unfashionable neighbour, a new hospital. However, such issues are immediately forgotten upon entering the interior of the Gibbs building and exploring its ground floor meeting and conference rooms, the café within the atrium, the staff restaurant on an upper level (enjoying wonderful views across the London skyline), and its spacious banks of workstations, some of which enjoy open slots into the south-facing atrium (workers can hang out over the balustrading like residents populating some aged Hong Kong apartment block!).

Stylistically, this is classic Hi-tech: steel, glass and exposed structure tempered by refined detailing and the introduction of wood finishes. The inevitable contrast is with those corporate houses that are surely its equivalent in functional terms, but quite removed in terms of an expressed self-identity. It is the latter challenge that the Hopkins team have dealt with in a refreshingly commodious and (to pun) welcoming manner.

*Above top: the Euston Road façade.*
*Above: looking along the atrium.*
*Below: a part of the atrium façade cladding treatment.*

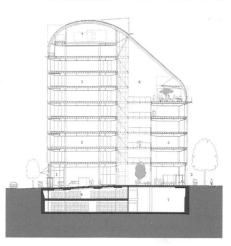

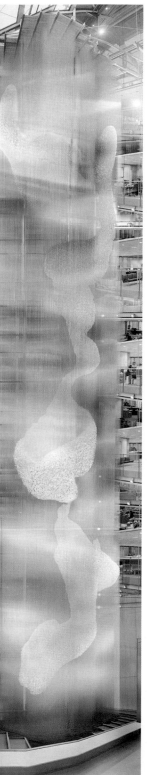

It is intriguing that scientific research and Hi-tech can so comfortably marry themselves with an artwork so thematically rooted in nostalgia and superstition. Perhaps this is as it should be — a reminder of all that is subjective and mysterious, and arouses a unique kind of wonder — so long, that is, that this does not fall into outright sentiment. Heatherwick's 'piece' (what on earth is art a 'piece' of?) is an outstanding work that, like the building and the nature of the work supported by the Wellcome Trust, is entirely dependent upon digital technologies. And wit. Apparently it was a rather late addition to the programme and the artist was called upon to do something that could get through the existing doors. He went all the way and designed something that could get through the letter-box and be assembled internally. Only the location — at one end of the atrium, behind galleries — is distinctly odd. Indeed, you will never see the object as this photo shows it!

## 63  Regent's Place

Tottenham Court Road has quietly experienced a change of character in recent years, shifting its activities northward, toward Euston Road. At the same time, Euston Road itself has undergone changes and Camden has proposals for a 'Euston Boulevard', designed in collaboration with Terry Farrell. A key part of this scenario is the redevelopment of the area around the old '60's Euston Tower building. This has been supplemented by a number of buildings, beginning with an Arup Associates' design and later added to by Sheppard Robson. The outcome has been a considerably enlarged employment and transport node nudging up against residential areas and cheered up by a rather large Michael Craig-Martin wall mural. But don't go there to see great buildings; go to see local urban change taking place (and how the contemporary face of speculative development works toward its healthy bottom-line). For example, the Arup Associates one is the best (1998), but now looking too small, even being adjacent to residential properties; have a look at Holmes Place on its ground level (designed by AHHM).

Behind the changes are programmes such as the Mayor's 100 Public Spaces and the reports of numerous consultants (among whom Terry Farrell — who did the Regent's Place master-plan — features large). It is claimed, for example, that the Euston Road / Marylebone Road corridor currently has about 25% of the development potential of the capital as well as having to cope with some 60,000 cars per day using this principal east-west route. And this is the context in which to view Regent's Place. Take your time and walk from Paddington Basin at one end to Kings Cross at the other, ranging off to the side streets and you begin to realise just how important and richly diversified a strip of central London this is.

The Arup Associates building (1998) at the rear of Regent's Place is still, by far, the best of the bunch, bearing touches of Stirling at Stuttgart. Also see the **Broadgate West Club** (a gym) on the ground floor, a design by AHMM (1998).

The 36 floor **Euston Tower** building (1972, designed by Sidney Kaye, Eric Firmin & Partners and recently refurbished and given podium level louvres etc., by Hawkins Brown Architects) was, for a long time, one of the most prominent buildings in London (at about 125m high). Like many other tall buildings of the period, it followed on the lifting of a 30m height restriction that had been in place in order to comply with fire regulations. The 17th floor was, apparently, once the home of MI5's telephone services. It's looking rather good (strange what time does).

The internal village-like assemblage of spaces and places beyond the entry gate.

**64** The thinness and transparency of these simple, Hi-Tech, prefabricated 'Patera' sheds (the studio of **Michael Hopkins & Partners**) sits incongruously, but not unpleasantly, within the brick fabric of Marylebone. However, dwelling on the technical aspects of the Hopkins' offices runs the danger of missing its key architectural quality: an informal grouping whose in between spaces are almost as important as the buildings themselves. Two sheds, an entry pavilion and an existing building to the rear of the site (used for workshops, stores, printing etc.) are linked by a fabric covered awning that runs down the length of one boundary. The spaces around and in between are dealt with as garden relaxation areas that have an almost Continental air about them, suggesting lazy summer meetings and vino stained table cloths. In other words: this is a very pleasant urban grouping concealed behind the gates. and in spite of conversations about Hi-tech, prefabricated architecture. The inevitable comparison is with the studios of Foster and Rogers. (27 Broadley Terrace, NW1; Michael Hopkins & Partners, 1986 on.) Tube: Marylebone, Edgware.)

**65** The **Lisson Gallery** appears to be one of the few galleries that has not moved to Hoxton and parts east, and is another example of Modernist contexturalism, managing to skilfully blend old and new. In this case, it's a two-stage minimalist conversion and extension to an art gallery which is L-shaped in plan, wrapping another, existing corner building. The first stage came through from Lisson Street; the second met it from Bell Street. The Bell Street façade attempts to reconcile disparate neighbours and, perhaps, does it so well that the game appears incidental to more interesting features. Huge sliding glass doors allow access for large art pieces and an upper loading door loans the facade an industrial overtone. The upper level is a studio. (Bell Street, NW8; Tony Fretton Architects, 1991.) Tube: Marylebone, Edgware)

    Also see **The Red House** (p.190) and **Camden Arts Centre** (p.206). For toher commercial galleries see the **Gagosian** (p. 98) and the **Victoria Miro Gallery** (p.217).

Paddington Basin, W2
various architects, 2002-2005
Tube: Paddington, Edgware Road

...n is a kind of mini-Canary Wharf, in west
...n former railway land and around a barge
...and Union Canal, just to the north and
...gton Station. In effect, the development
term... ...Marylebone / Euston Roads corridor
between Kings Cross and Paddington Stations whilst also
providing a northern boundary to the West End.

As master-planned by Terry Farrell, the site's
basin part (to the east) strives to link itself back into
surrounding areas (although there is little of the latter) and
the station is being re-oriented from the south to the north-
east, where the Heathrow link will terminate (this part to
be designed by his ex-partner and architect responsible
for the Eurostar building at Waterloo, Nicholas Grimshaw).

The overall development is four distinct parts:
the station; the Paddington Healthcare Campus, around
St. Mary's Hospital; Paddington Central (master-planned
by Sidell Gibson), to the north of the station and alongside
Westway, where office buildings are grouped around
Sheldon Square; and an area to the east, between the
Westway and the canal, called Waterside. The latter is
where there are two idiosyncratic bridges: one that is very
clever (above right) but badly located and without rhyme
or reason, by Thomas Heatherwick; and another bridge
which spans all of about 3m and acrobatically (and utterly
redundantly) spirals in order to make the link. One really
begins to wonder what is going on when creative and
engineering ingenuity is lent to such absurdities (brilliant
answers to stupid questions). But perhaps one carps: see
them as follies. (*In operation each Friday at 12 noon.*)

See Paddington Basin for issues of urban design
and the nature of London's current redevelopment. But be
warned: they don't like cameras (that familiar problem with
streets which look public but are, in fact, private).

*Paddington Central* has two parts: one by Sidel
Gibson and the other (on the west) by Sheppard
Robson and Kohn Pedersen Fox. Waterside has
office buildings from Terry Farrell and Richard
Rogers. Other buildings are planned. Alsop
Architects are lined up for a new CrossRail station to
the west of Paddington Station.

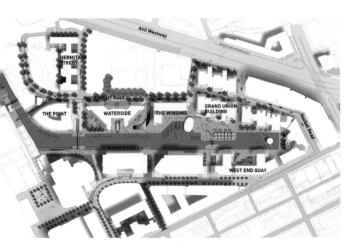

*The Rogers Waterside building is quite
fine, but loses something in a context
which has scale but lacks urbanity. Also
see his practice's City buildings.*

**67** *Imagination (Store Street, WC1; Ron Herron and Imagination Ltd.; 1989) was a project by an architect who built little but was highly acclaimed by others who have built lots (such as Richard Rogers and Norman Foster), a building designed as a home for creatives famed for developing 'brand experiences'. This was (and remains) their very own brand experience. Coincidentally, the building is also a fitting memorial to an architect one might characterise as an East Ender of vision, a man whose work repeatedly came back to themes that overlaid and reinvented the status quo, a man who grew up in a 1950's London enamoured with Pop Art and all things American, including Hollywood movies and the blue Gauloises cigarettes that probably helped kill him at a comparatively early age. His obsession with the idea of 'architectural sets' and private realms behind public façades (possibly an architectural reflection of Herron's private social and political concerns, as well as a homage to a famous 1949 scheme by Lubetkin) is amply demonstrated in this building.*

*At the heart of the scheme is a tented, central atrium, designed almost entirely without a defined, instrumental purpose: a 'cheerful' space that would suggest uses rather than serve anything specific in a brief, a space with open doors to potential, architecturally branding Imagination as an organisation with attitude. The hardware and the detailing of the atrium are delicious but, in essence, this is a design only superficially focused upon the stuff of things. It is the narratives acted out by people using the spaces that are really significant: this is Herron's own Hollywood set, awaiting its actors. Ironically, its owners have somewhat silted it up with a mix of physical additions and anecdotal myth. It was once a school. Or was it a hospital? And it was two buildings with an alleyway in between. Or was it one 'H' plan that Herron broke in two. It was the latter, but it hardly matters. What is possibly regretful is the manner in which the owners have slowly silted up the lower levels of the atrium. From another perspective this is simply life moving on — entailing acts of modification, obsolescence and replacement that Herron would probably have acknowledged (whilst moaning that it could have been done better).*

*Incidentally, Herron was the author of the famous 'Walking City' drawings done in the mid-1960's — the inspiration of the book and movie called Howl's Moving Castle (2005), in which the new, romanticised interpretation given to the concept makes a fascinating contrast within the Herron original.*

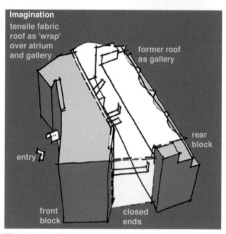

**Imagination**
tensile fabric roof as 'wrap' over atrium and gallery

former roof as gallery

rear block

entry

front block

closed ends

*The drama of the Imagination building is hidden behind the front block and wraps over the roof of the rear block of what was formerly an 'H' plan building.*

# British Museum Great Court: creation, obliteration, and reinvention

Gt Russell Street, WC1
Foster and Partners, 2000
Tube: Tottenham Court Road, Holborn

The British Museum's Great Court addresses 200 years of the building's history: from the Museum's 1808 scheme for extending the house occupying its site, through a history of rapid change and addition that closed off and built over the original landscaped court designed in 1823, obliterating the original concept of a central, public green space. Driven by the Museum's need for additional accommodation, the three sides of the original court were supplemented by a fourth and, at its centre, a large circular Reading Room was provided for the British Library. In turn, this was to become surrounded by storage rooms filling the interstitial spaces between the Reading Room and the quadrangle. The site was full; the Museum continued to expand its collections.

A 1960's plan to move the Library to other accommodation unleashed a new potential, finally enabling the central court to be rediscovered and reinvented – this time paved and covered, conceived as an indoor public space that simultaneously, provided a radical re-organisation of the Museum's circulation. However, none of this would have been possible without the Library moving out to St. Pancras (see British Library). By reinventing the Court as a covered, indoor space protected by a unique, domed glass roof, Foster's design returns this central area to public use, provides new facilities, reveals and opens the Reading Room, and entirely reforms the Museum's circulation.

The new roof to the Court, completed in 2001, is a tour de force. Ironically, it may prove to be the celebrated central design feature at the heart of a problematic situation which has the Museum bogged down in financial difficulties and falling attendance numbers (pulled off to London's other attractions, notably the Tate Modern). However, it remains a remarkable architectural achievement.

*It is arguable that the real heroes of the Great Court design and its realisation were Buro Happold. Given a brief to design a flat(ish) roof without cables they not only realised this in a deceptively simple manner, but also managed to get over the problem of welding the struts to the nodes — a difficulty that was, apparently, of critical importance and reliant upon Austrian engineering. Similarly, they were able to effect central supports to the roof embedded within the walls of the Reading Room and to do so in a manner that prevented the whole thing collapsing. Without this expert firm of engineers there wouldn't be a Great Court.*

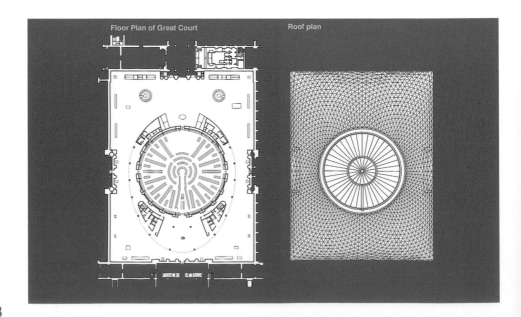

Floor Plan of Great Court                    Roof plan

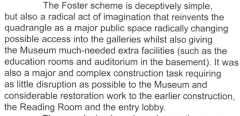

**68**

The Foster scheme is deceptively simple, but also a radical act of imagination that reinvents the quadrangle as a major public space radically changing possible access into the galleries whilst also giving the Museum much-needed extra facilities (such as the education rooms and auditorium in the basement). It was also a major and complex construction task requiring as little disruption as possible to the Museum and considerable restoration work to the earlier construction, the Reading Room and the entry lobby.

The new design has cleared away the areas around the Reading Room, initiated a major renovation of the surrounding quadrangle façades (including a controversial restoration of the south portico), given the Reading Room back to the general public, surrounded it with new shops, a restaurant and an exhibition space accessed by a symmetrical pair of grand stairs that sweep around the Room's curvature, and — above all — provided the Court with a spectacular glazed roof covering a quadrangle that is about 92 x 73m (larger than a football pitch). There are also extensive new facilities beneath the Great Court (galleries, the Clore Education Centre and the Ford Centre for Young Visitors).

Part of Foster's rationale for the scheme was that the new Great Court would offer itself as a covered public space featuring as a crucial component part of a pedestrian route from the new British Library at St. Pancras, down through the Great Court, and on to Trafalgar Square — an idea that has a history. 'Sandy' Wilson, architect of the new British Library, had proposed offering the central Reading Room to the public and opening up a north-south route in a report of 1962 - 4, associated with the first scheme to remove the Library to a site just south of the British Museum. In turn, this referenced a 1891 scheme by W.R. Lethaby to create a 'Sacred Way' between the Museum and the old Waterloo Bridge. Current financial problems (late 2002) at the Museum have rather curtailed this concept, reducing its opening hours in line with the galleries.

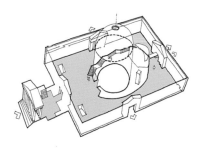

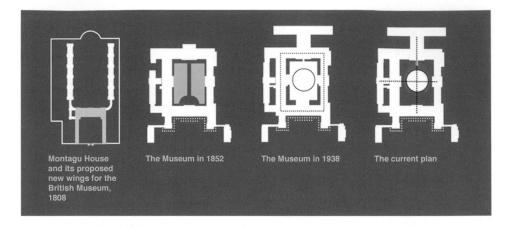

Montagu House and its proposed new wings for the British Museum, 1808

The Museum in 1852

The Museum in 1938

The current plan

### Background

*The BM has always occupied this site in Bloomsbury, formerly Montagu House and its gardens, originally built in 1675. It opened there in 1759 and grew rapidly, extending into the former garden in 1808. Robert Smirke came onto the scene in 1816 and again in 1821, suggesting new wings. His scheme was later amended to accommodate the King's library and became what was finally built: an initial stage providing new wings that formed an open, landscaped quadrangle, followed by the demolition and replacement of Montagu House itself. Smirke's splendid and proud neo-Grecian design was begun in 1823 and Montagu House was demolished in the 1840's; however the building had no sooner been completed in 1852 (together with a main entrance portico housing sculptures in its pediment symbolising the progress of civilisation from paganism to the sciences of the day) than further works were implemented to accommodate the expanding stock of the British Library. This was carried out by Robert's younger brother Sydney Smirke, who designed the domed, central Reading Room that is larger than that of St. Paul's and almost the size of the Pantheon in Rome. The need for additional space continued unabated and the interstitial spaces between the Reading Room and the Museum began to be filled by book stores. The pattern continued, notably in 1904 - 14, when the Edward VII galleries were added, designed by John Burnet, and then in 1936 - 8 when John Markham added mezzanine floors to the buildings along the north side of the quadrangle and also inserted new windows. The outcome of these layers of expansion and change were that the core of the donut plan housed the British Library, whilst the surrounding quadrangle of accommodation formed the Museum, accessible to visitors by a perambulatory, up and down route contrasting with a Reader's passage from the main entrance portico, through the entry lobby, into a tight low passage that led into the Reading Room (reserved for academics and researchers). When it was planned that the British Library – always hungry for extra space – would move to Colin St. John Wilson's St.*

*Pancras, the potential was released for a reinvention of the Reading Room and its relation to the Museum, whose visitor numbers appeared to be climbing towards 6.5m a year. Initially, proposals involved extensive demolitions and rebuilding within the areas around the Reading Room. This was amended in stages, slowly moving towards a more accessible concept. A competition was then held and Foster appointed with a scheme for a roofed central court and new accommodation surrounding the central Reading Room, leaving little space around it. However, funding from the Lottery Commission came with the requirement that the Court was open to the public for longer hours than the surrounding Museum, and the transition to the concept of a covered public space was complete.*

## The Roof

The 6700 sq.m. roof of the Great Court would have been impossible to either design, manufacture or construct until the advent of low-cost computing and the appropriate software. Every part of the 800 tonne lattice shell structure is different, designed so that the generalised geometry of the framing will fit to the disparate geometries of the quadrangle walls, the disparate heights of the portico pediments, and the location of the Reading Room (5m off-centre).

• The built design is a highly curved torus, described as a square doughnut with a central hole. Available double glazing sizes determined a grid that has 3312 panes of glass and 1800 welded steel nodes (requiring 5200 members).

• The outer supports are behind the stone parapets of the surrounding quad walls, resting on sliding Teflon bearings on 120mm stub steel columns that, in turn, rest upon a new concrete parapet beam; this allows for 50mm of thermal movement. The edges are actually louvred for natural ventilation.

• The central supports for the roof comprise twenty 457mm steel columns filled with concrete that surround the Reading Room, in turn encased in limestone, so that an in between space can be used for services.

• The roof is 26.3m. high above floor level at its highest point (which disturbed local planners, who argued this was somewhat above the planning permission given!). The tapering steel components were constructed in Vienna and then shipped to Derby and made into 152 prefabricated units totalling 478 tonnes of steel (with another 315 tonnes of double-glazing added to them). Ceramic surface 'fritting' on the glass copes with solar gain and covers 57% of the glass surface, but this is almost invisible to the naked eye.

• The 11kms of roof structure was built to an accuracy of 3mm's. Each outer pane of glass in the roof is covered in 50% green ceramic dots ('fritting') to reduce solar gain.

## The Reading Room

Based on the impressive results of using prefabricated cast-iron for the Great Exhibition of 1851, the original Reading Room structure was an impressive structure that used 2000 tons of cast-iron. The ribbed dome has a diameter of 42.6m (140 feet), only 61cm less than the Pantheon in Rome. The interior was a thick form of papier mâché, 1.27cm thick. Its shrinkage, together with constant movements of the cast-iron and timber framing, resulted in an extensive pattern of cracking. All of this cracking had to be dealt with in the restoration by filling the gaps with wadding and applying a flexible 'bandage'. This was then repainted in a manner matching the original materials, and new gold leaf applied. This restoration work to the internal linings and their decorative scheme was revealed by 'stratigraphic charting', scraping and using solvents to reveal the original decorations.

The Reading Room now houses the Walter and Leonore Annenberg Centre. This is a modern library that combines computer access screens with 25,000 volumes from the Paul Hamlyn collection of books.

## Façade Restorations

The internal façades of the Court have been substantially repaired and restored. In particular, this includes the controversial restoration of the south portico, entirely demolished in 1875. The stone used for the restoration (a Flemish limestone) was revealed to be self-evidently different from the older Portland stone used by Smirke. A lot of people got upset, wanted to know why this sleight of hand had been pulled, leading to calls for demolition and rebuilding. The Museum had to offer the rationale that, like the restoration of an old Greek vase that differentiates between old and new, the restored portico is quite properly different and not a pastiche (an attitude to 'honest restoration' that goes back to the likes of William Morris). This rationale proved difficult to fault and made a lot of sense, especially in the context of the British Museum and even more so when they — rather than the architects or contractors — provided it.

• There are 1000 tonnes of new stone in the great Court scheme. The flooring of the Court is a French limestone called 'Balzac'.

## 69 RADA

62 - 64 Gower Street, WC1
Avery Associates, 2001
Tube: Goodge Street, Warren Street

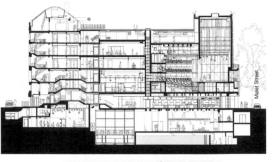

Playing the role of skilled theatre architect at the Royal Academy of Dramatic Art, Brian Avery has cleaned out one half of a long slice of building between Gower Street and Malet Street to provide an artful and compact linkage between old and new that manages to integrate and resolve a complex whole whilst maintaining a clear distinction between the parts. The newer parts of the complex include a new teaching theatre (the Jerwood Vanburgh) of 203 seats, together with production spaces, workshops and the like in a deep underground basement. The building is ten storeys high, three of them underground, and the fly tower of the new theatre forms the Malet Street frontage. But it is the gamesmanship that is noteworthy. One begins to take note within a foyer area that is ticket sales and cafe / bar all at once. Then one notices a distinctly Soanian note characterising the manner in which the rear end of the Vanburgh is separated from the John Gielgood studio theatre by a thin, full height void that reaches from the ground level foyer up to a skylight high above — through which, on the solstice, a shaft of sunlight can penetrate to the heart of the complex! Above here, the highly adaptable Vanburgh is intended to teach students at a small scale what they will have to practise at a large scale, and to add to that a variety of conditions and arrangements they will have to cope with. But this scale theme is deeply embedded in the architecture of the theatre and provides us with a hidden treasure hidden behind the façade — one that Avery has designed in total, including the rather comfortable and

simple seats. The theatre has four levels and appears tall, but the balconies are a mere 2.5m floor to floor, their fronts dissolved into wires so as to extend perceived volume to the outer walls ... and so on. It all adds up to a cleverly compact set of facilities that is both economic, functional and very enjoyable — a place that any educational institution would be proud of. Try to catch a public performance so that you can get right inside.

*Looking up the slot between old and new, with the Vanburgh on the left.*

## LSE Library

This 20,000 sq.m. library — sorry, learning resource centre — with 1200 study places is the conversion of a former book store (1916) on a site that has been a burial ground, a workhouse and a hospital. It's low budget and the Foster team offers a simple (almost utilitarian) solution that confronts the visitor with a splendid, full height space populated by earnest students and nearly 500 computer workstations. The building is served by a central circulation core (capped by a ventilating roof light and daylight reflector) comprising lifts and a large, spiralling, stepped ramp that feeds onto the gallery book-stacks (50km of shelving and 4m volumes), the 14 group study rooms and two training rooms. But penetrate the narrow banks of the latter and one comes to an almost secret perimeter study space. The 4th floor is the LSE Research Laboratory; the 5th is a new build extension. It's a busy place: sometimes open 24 hours.

*There is also a Student Services Centre here — a conversion by KPF in 2001.*

**70**

10 Portugal Street, WC2
Foster and Partners, 2001
Tube: Holborn, Temple

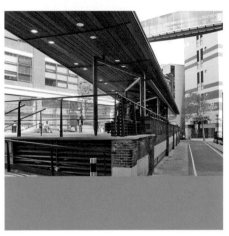

## Student piazza

Right outside the front door to Foster's library building sits a piazza with a single-storey coffee bar catering for the thousands of students who throng the LSE. It's a simple but well-designed building that makes a significant contribution to changing the character of the area and making it more urbane.

**71**

10 Portugal Street WC2
MacCormack Jamieson Pritchard. 2003
Tube: Holborn, Temple

**72** Ashley & Newman's **Freemason's Hall** of 1927 - 33 (in Queen Mary Street) has to be one of London's more pompous buildings, but is not without its points of interest, particularly on the inside (usually open during Open House London). Externally this — the third Freemason's hall in the street — is topped by an over-scaled tower that appears to owe a lot to the old Port of London Authority building in the City (opposite the Tower, 1912, by Sir Edwin Cooper, designer of the first Lloyd's building of about the same date as the Freemason's Hall).

**73** Colonel Seifert's 1962 **Space House** is very similar to Centre Point — not only in construction, but in suffering a ground floor area desperately in need of renovation. A&M even enjoy the vision that, one day, this will become the buzzing resort of cappuccino drinkers (although that drink might be well out of fashion by the time that happens). The building can be also compared with the hotel in central Knightsbridge (also circular) and other Seifert work such as the sleek office building in Percy Street. They are all 'almost all right' but not quite; however, why people persist in villifying the man (who, apparently, had little to do with actual designs but whose name attaches to them) is beyond me.

## 74 City Lit

Keeley Street, WC1
Allies & Morrison, 2005
Tube: Holborn / Covent Garden

As a now established and well known London practice, Allies & Morrison do all kinds of work that stretches them from comparatively small-scale developments to massive speculative office developments. In between, are educational projects such as this one. This building sits directly opposite one of Col. Seifert's circular towers (similar to his hotel building in the heart of Knightsbridge; now occupied by CABE) Given you can distract yourself from Seifert, you can turn around to enjoy this beige brick design from A&M, a scheme bearing all their usual signature marks: the windows, in particular, suggest an obsessive degree of nuanced attention; then there is the accompanying metalwork; finally, the end wobbles to the building plan that declares this is a practice that knows their Alvar Aalto. In fact, one suspects even the brickwork is Aalto influenced.

The City Lit hosts about 2700 adult education courses and originally appointed A&M in 1997 — when they had a much larger budget. This ended up as significantly lower, prompting a radical redesign. And the building has some notable architectural neighbours to contend with — not only the Seifert building, but also the 1933 Freemason's Hall and 1880's Peabody social housing that sits opposite. The City Lit's parapet level match's that of the Peabody and the Wild Street Aalto playfulness attempts to counter the neo-baroque massiveness of the Freemason's building. The screened-off colonnade on Keeley Street no doubt gives security when the cafe windows are open and probably hopes for the future removal of the screening so as to enjoy a future renovation of the area under the Seifert building. Meanwhile it is a bit of an oddity.

As a public building, the City Lit is readily accessible; however, beyond the ground floor reception and long cafe area it is hardly interesting — exhibiting disappointing qualities after the promises of the exterior: double loaded, bland corridors bearing a singular absence of character. This is the latter-day educational world of 'generic' spaces and facilities. (Are these educational spaces? offices? Perhaps someone should have looked at even second rate hotels and stolen a few ideas.) Emphasis upon the exterior is also demonstrated by a curious architectural conceit at the ground floor, where the cafe is fronted by a long, 'blind' colonnade without access. While there is possibly some concealed rationale for its existence, the arrangement reads as an architectural conceit underscoring the disappointments of the interiors, where there is little of such playfulness. But perhaps one carps: let anyone try and achieve this level of quality at such a low budget. In fact, it could all be another example of the architect dealing with imposed constraint philosophically and exercising freedoms where they can.

And if the Lit leaves you hungry for more architectural experiences, there is always the contrast of Seifert across the road, even if that building does suffer the deplorably unsatisfactory ground floor areas also characterising Centre Point.

*Compare with this same practice's work at the BBC White City Media Centre, Chelsea College of Art, etc..*

*The well-considered principal façade.*

*View down the narrow, gated Keeley Street colonnade (which you normally can't get into).*

*The Wild Street façade is comparatively that: a curvy, Aalto-esque piece of playfulness that nevertheless introduces a scale addressing the adjacent Freemason's Hall. Purists may object to the tectonics of 'floating' brickwork without lintels.*

## 75 An Original Cabinet of Curiosities

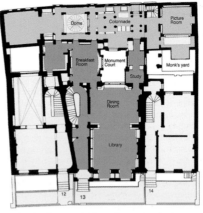

*No serious architectural enthusiast can visit London without taking in the **Soane Museum**, Lincoln's Inn, WC2, the remarkable house, office and private museum of Sir John Soane, built between 1731 and 1833 (at which time the houses were left to the nation).*

*The Museum is actually three, adjacent Georgian terrace houses (nos. 12, 13 & 14) that the architect secured and carefully developed stage by stage, typically slicing off the rear end of the last of the three to benefit the central house, then selling off the remaining property. The central part that forms the core of the scheme and the present Museum (since extended into the first of the three houses, on the west side, and fitted with a small display room designed by Eva Jiricna) is almost sufficient in itself and filled with architectural delights that marked Soane's aspiration toward urbane living. But behind the horizontal layers of this splendid but otherwise not untypical Georgian house Soane blossoms into another kind of game that exploits the vertical possibilities and links a series of architectural devices together into a (ostensibly) complex enfilade of top-lit spaces.*

*From the stone and brick arches of the basement, the construction reaches up in lighter construction layers toward the daylight, adorned at every step with plundered classical antiquities to delight the architect and educate the staff of the practice. It is difficult to understate the inventiveness and civility of it all, including such delights as the picture room with its layered walls and connecting views.*

*And there, in the heart of it all, in the vaulted basement, Soane secured a home for an invented, alter ego figure redolent with the romance of the late C18: a monk living amongst Gothic architectural features 'borrowed' from works at Westminster Cathedral. This Monk's Parlour is rather mischievous, perhaps humorous, yet underscored by personal bitterness and even cynicism that reveals Soane as a real person as well as a distant architect of huge ability. Few works of architecture have such a strong voice, dissolving the underlying formalities and concerns of its places and spaces as it speaks to us about making and inhabiting an architecture.*

*Soane's plan is wrought from three standard Georgian terrace houses, with some of the key parts ranged across the rear of all three.*

*Below: a typical piece of architectural gamesmanship from Soane — layered panels for hanging paintings, opening into a light well and giving views down in to the basement.*

*Below left: the splendid Beakfast Room. Centre: a basement view through the Colonnade. Bottom right: the Monument Court, with daylight coming from above. All such places, spaces and features are filled with a celebratory delight in architectural gamesmanship.*

# 76 Victoria House

Southampton Row, WC1
Alsop Architects, 2003
Tube: Holborn

This conversion of a 1922 - 32 'grand manner' building in Holborn started as a bid proposal to house the GLA (see City Hall) which was located at More London instead. But Alsop got a conversion job anyway, being commissioned to strip out its heart and convert the former insurance offices into 20,000 sq.m. of new office accommodation together with a health club and retail spaces at ground level. The 'kerb appeal' of it all is hidden away within two new atria of unusual section, inhabited by double storey 'blob' meeting spaces propped on legs like some mini version of Herron's 'Walking City'. It's Peckham, Mecanoo's Budapest bank, and Gehry in Berlin — quite cheerful and uplifting the dreary architecture of the average speculative office. But to see this kind of thing at its best (admitedly with less fashionable, '80's Scandinavian styling) one still has to look at the interior of Erskine's much under-rated Ark in Hammersmith.

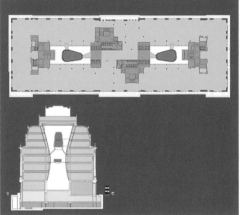

**77** **Lindsey House** on the west side of Lincoln's Inn Fields (Inigo Jones, 1640) was divided into two in 1751 and is without surviving interiors, but the outside gives a good idea of what was happening at the time, when such a façade was a novelty in London. Strip it back and you have the basis of the Georgian London house front embodied in the building regulations of the C18. The key point about such designs is not only their intrinsic neo-Palladianism, but the very novelty of the idea of order and regularity that was meant to spread along the street façade and sweep away the remnants of medieval London. See it when you go to the Soane Museum.

**78** George Street's **Royal Courts of Justice** (in the Strand, at its Fleet Street east end; 1871 - 82) are a familiar media image and a marvellous architectonic pile. As a project following a 'thorny and troublesome' path (as Wagner characterised architectural endeavour), the project was similar to St. Paul's, the Palace of Westminster, the current British Library, etc., exhausting Street (who drew most details himself and died in 1881).

**79** Plonked down into the heart of Georgian Bloomsbury, Patrick Hodgkinson's **Brunswick Centre** project arrived in 1972 like an alien ship (Marchmont Street / Brunswick Street, WC1): complete, almost fully formed and demanding its own 'living space'. Conceived by Patrick Hodgkinson with Sir Leslie Martin, 1959–72, the complex was intended to stride further north, to have private tenants, and to have other features such as glazed covering to the pedestrian deck. Intended as a demonstration, high density / low-rise urban block, it is rather flawed, but will always have an important place in London's architecture.But whatever merits the scheme had, they did not include respect for what existed or any attempt to 'knit into' the existing urban fabric. In fact, one is reminded of Hans Hollein's contemporaneous drawing of an aircraft carrier nestled in a hilly landscape. Born in a climate of progressive thinking by angry young men who preferred buildings to impose their own infrastructure rather than accommodate themselves to an existing one, Brunswick was truly a Modernist manifesto preoccupied with new ways of living as opposed to the hierarchical values believed to be implicit in the Georgian terrace. This was especially true with regard to the most fundamental point that Hodgkinson was attempting to make: that low-rise / high-density could work as an alternative to tower schemes set in a parkland (as occasionally happened) or an urban wilderness (the usual reality). He was also attempting a mixed use/mixed classes scheme that flew in the face of a current planning orthodoxy and its concerns to separate and zone. Unusually, the project started off as a (then) rare example of mixed-use, speculative development. It ended up as another complex of single-class social housing and a not entirely successful project that has posed difficulties and problems to this day. However, the scheme made Hodgkinson's name and he has been respected for it ever since. It's worth comparing with the Alexander Road complex at Swiss Cottage (London Borough of Camden Architects, under Neave Brown, 1969–79).

**80** The idea of a **Visitors Centre and Archive Centre** for both Guardian and Observer newspapers began with the need to house all original documentation from the papers' histories, dating back to 1821 and 1791 respectively. A colonnade has been formed behind the existing brick façade by removing and rationalising the jumbled assortment of openings. The key architectural elements occur in the three successive zones of the building, which become progressively more private on the main route through the building: the entrance area and a public café, which can be opened independently of the Newsroom; a permanent exhibition space bordered by a temporary space (which can be converted into a lecture theatre via a series of moveable partitions and a retractable seating unit); and highly environmentally controlled archive vaults which hold the original photos and paper documents. The third band of accommodation houses the more private education rooms, a study relating to the archive and ancillary areas. It's worth a visit. This is Allies & Morrison at their best: when not swamped by commercial and instrumental values. (60 Farringdon Road, EC1; Allies and Morrison, 2002; Tube: Farringdon)

**81** **Bevin Court** (1952 - 5) is a classic Skinner, Bailey and Lubetkin job (formerly part of Tecton): a 'Y" shaped plan of 130 units, with splendid central staircase giving onto external access balconies. The façade is of the kind that has become highly fashionable (an alternating pattern). There is also an unexpected entrance mural by Peter Yates

## 82 Sadler's Wells

Rosebery Avenue, EC1
RHWL and Nicholas Hare Architects, 1998
Tube: Angel

This reinvention of a 1931 theatre is aimed at providing an intimate performance space with links to the local community. Its accommodation includes a new, large auditorium designed for watching dance performances and the refurbishment of the small, Lilian Baylis Theatre, together with an education centre, rehearsal rooms, etc.: a veritable community of facilities packed into the site. Internally, the designs are direct and functional, with an emphasis on simple finishes, glass and steel. Nicholas Hare Architects were involved as advisors on the exteriors.

## 83 School of Social Sciences

School of Social Sciences, City University
St. John Street, EC1
Stanton Williams Architects, 2004
Tube: Angel

You can guarantee cool, refined work from STA and this 7000sq.m. university building is no exception. It is very energy efficient and, as one might expect, internally flexible, with its accommodation centred around a central atrium or 'hub' feature which aims to serve as the focus of movements, meetings etc. Externally, the cladding is a well-designed and rather sleek glass rain-screen.

*The building is adjacent to the three blocks of Tecton's **Spa Green Estate** (1946 - 50). The engineer (as at Highpoint) was Ove Arup.*

## 84 Independent Television News

**84** *Independent Television News (200 Gray's Inn; Foster & Partners, 1989; Tube: Chancery Lane) is a 10 storey, heavily serviced, 37,000 sq.m. building, with two of the floors underground. Its architectural interest principally resides in three features: the central atrium; the elegant double-glazed cladding with its 300 mm gap; and the set-back entrance area sporting an extremely tall revolving door once intended to lead to a more lively space, where the public could experience the news broadcasting. Unfortunately the construction timing hit the recession and the possibility of low rental incomes, cutting back the budget. The entrance works well, the atrium has a dramatic hanging mobile by Ben Johnson, and the openness of the building is engaging, but there is a certain blandness about the place.*

**85** *Finsbury Health Centre, designed by Tecton, 1935–38, Pine Street, EC1, belongs to a beginnings of a former age of Modernism when architects and their patrons were overtly socialist and humanist and there was a belief in the power of architecture to contribute to the well-being of others, especially the deprived and disadvantaged. They believed in a different future, mediated by a design that would throw away the past and embrace a new, egalitarian future of well-being. The key designer among the architects was Berthold Lubetkin (his partners were well connected ex-Architectural Association students he had teamed up with in 1932, after coming from Russia via Warsaw and Paris). As a young practice, they had managed to design and exhibit a clinic design seen by people from Finsbury — then one of London's poorest boroughs, with appalling health problems. English social connections, left-wing politics and European inspiration with a mix of impeccable sources (Russian Constructivists to Perrault and Le Corbusier) had made an unlikely meeting. The outcome was a remarkable Modernist exercise in the tradition of 'art leading the facts of science'. Two wings (exhibiting with self-evident beaux arts symmetries) house administration and consultation rooms, and a central mass houses reception, waiting areas and an upper lecture hall — all designed so that services, accessible from outside, could rise at the blank ends and run along the façades, into the accommodation. The framed construction and the way it is serviced and organised is a model of rational design, an example to the profession of how architecture could be at once modern, instrumental, at the service of the people, and beautiful. And yet there is an odd note indicative of the period: the basement was designed as a processing and delousing unit into which coach-loads of children would be driven, mattresses brought and burned — a concept with undertones reminiscent of the functionalist, ethnic cleansing machines of National Socialism!*

*Sadly, FHC is a rather neglected building but, together with Tecton's Highpoint buildings and the Penguin Pool at London Zoo, it is a rare example of a European-inspired modernism intruding into a London scene otherwise preoccupied. It was a design that married instrumentalism and aesthetics into a model architectural configuration that remains as a bench-mark for contemporary architects.*

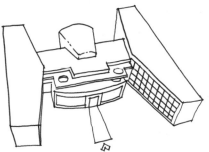

**85** *Brewery Square (north St. John Street, EC1; 2004) started off as a design from Eric von Egeraat, the Dutch architect, and ended up by Hamilton Associates (run by former Denys Lasdun people and better known as a production outfit hidden in the background). Take a look: this is a fine scheme, with novel projecting elements that still lend the whole a rather un-English character. (BDP have their offices in a warehouse behind here.)*

## 86  Gazzano House

Farringdon Road EC1
Amin Taha Architects, 2005
Tube: Farringdon

This apartment block is a refreshing infill, with both a materiality and a character that copes well with urban grittiness, offering us Corten steel cladding in that currently fashionable 'cookie-cut-out' style beginning to crop up all over in 2005 (see, for example, the Feilden & Clegg school at Chalk Farm). The (fashionable) layered / cookie cutout façade is well handled and the Corten steel (OK, also fashionable) manages to offer itself as at once gritty and elegant: a proverbial metaphor of authenticity.

*See John Winter's house in Highgate for the only other notable example of using Cor-Ten steel in London.*

Photo: Amin Taha Architects

## 87  St. Luke's / LSO

Old Street, EC1
Levitt Berstein Architects, 2003
Tube: Old Street

St. Luke's Church was a derelict shell without a soul: broody, romantic (John James; wonderful obelisk spire by Hawksmoor; 1728). But now it has been revitalised as a music education centre (serving a programme called LSO Discovery) and at the heart of the new body is the Jerwood Hall: a large, galleried rehearsal and recording facility for the London Symphony Orchestra, able to accommodate an audience of 350p. A new steel structure of internal 'trees' props and frames the new roof and underground excavations to either side of the church (in the crypt and former graveyards) provide ancillary accommodation. Acoustics, of course, were a prime concern and a silent (as the grave) heating and ventilating system utilises 100m deep undergound bore pipes and the stable conditions at that depth. It's impressively done, but also a polite English interplay with an important old building that avoids real dialogue across time. For example, the interior is impressive, but externally, the new work is almost entirely suffocated by the coffin of the old shell.

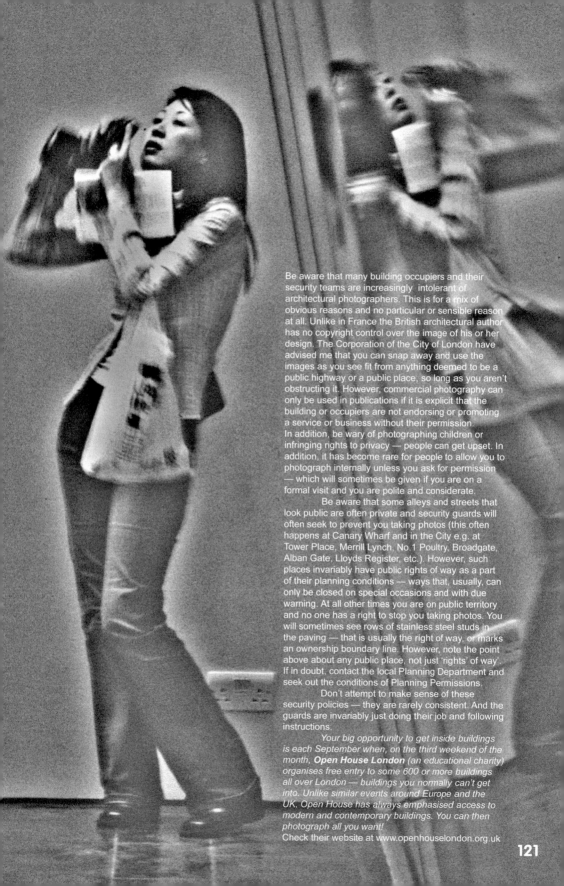

Be aware that many building occupiers and their security teams are increasingly intolerant of architectural photographers. This is for a mix of obvious reasons and no particular or sensible reason at all. Unlike in France the British architectural author has no copyright control over the image of his or her design. The Corporation of the City of London have advised me that you can snap away and use the images as you see fit from anything deemed to be a public highway or a public place, so long as you aren't obstructing it. However, commercial photography can only be used in publications if it is explicit that the building or occupiers are not endorsing or promoting a service or business without their permission. In addition, be wary of photographing children or infringing rights to privacy — people can get upset. In addition, it has become rare for people to allow you to photograph internally unless you ask for permission — which will sometimes be given if you are on a formal visit and you are polite and considerate.

Be aware that some alleys and streets that look public are often private and security guards will often seek to prevent you taking photos (this often happens at Canary Wharf and in the City e.g. at Tower Place, Merrill Lynch, No.1 Poultry, Broadgate, Alban Gate, Lloyds Register, etc.). However, such places invariably have public rights of way as a part of their planning conditions — ways that, usually, can only be closed on special occasions and with due warning. At all other times you are on public territory and no one has a right to stop you taking photos. You will sometimes see rows of stainless steel studs in the paving — that is usually the right of way, or marks an ownership boundary line. However, note the point above about any public place, not just 'rights' of way. If in doubt, contact the local Planning Department and seek out the conditions of Planning Permissions.

Don't attempt to make sense of these security policies — they are rarely consistent. And the guards are invariably just doing their job and following instructions.

*Your big opportunity to get inside buildings is each September when, on the third weekend of the month, **Open House London** (an educational charity) organises free entry to some 600 or more buildings all over London — buildings you normally can't get into. Unlike similar events around Europe and the UK, Open House has always emphasised access to modern and contemporary buildings. You can then photograph all you want!*
Check their website at www.openhouselondon.org.uk

# London Riverside: Vauxhall to the Tower

The Thames has always been London's life-blood: a quietly serving, much abused artery that in the Middle Ages provided fresh water and fish, and by the middle of the C19 was a stinking open sewer spurned by all except those river workers — the East End dockers and sailors and the like — to whom it gave a living. By the 1950's the river was still a very sad, grey, cold thing known for its poisonous waters, tides, vicious currents and hot weather smells — a sister to the infamous London fogs. In 1957 only eels could survive in its waters and it was declared dead. And then the closure of the docks in the late 1960's quietly coincided with a period initiating a massive rehabilitation, but hardly anyone noticed and most Londoners continued to turn their back upon the Thames. Bankside, for example, where the Tate Modern is located, was until very recently a lost backland in a borough where the planners were desperate to regenerate the area.

Then something remarkable happened: around the Millennium, London's citizens rediscovered the Thames and its embankments. It became not only possible but desirable to walk from Vauxhall Bridge all the way to Butlers Wharf and beyond. The riverside — especially the south side — had become a major leisure route. Parisian-style glass topped tourist boats plied the river and offered new prospects and camera opportunities to tourists. Commuter boat services to Canary — an off/on affair at the best of times — were now viable and reliable. London had apparently rediscovered its historic artery.

Of course, with hindsight, one could see the improvements slowly coming into place. But it is still remarkable how a vast re-orientation took place triggered by a few significant events such as the London Eye, the Tate Modern, the Dome, the Millennium Bridge, and the Somerset House works. Places that had invariably been accessed from the landside suddenly became features of a new riverside promenade. Older sights such as the Southbank, the Design Museum and the Globe Theatre attained a new significance midst a brotherhood of riverside friends from whom they had previously been divorced. Two new bridges (the formerly-wobbly Millennium and the additions to Hungerford) were opened. A new City Hall appeared. Farrell's much criticised MI6 and Embankment Place buildings were suddenly respectable riverside ornaments.

Fishermen watched by tourists now patiently awaited the nibbling attention of live fish whilst older Londoners smiled in bemusement. Web sites on the Thames proliferated. The tourist authority promoted the river experience as a major London event and weekends saw the southern embankment from Westminster to the Tower thick with curious crowds. Even the more disjointed northern embankment enjoyed new attention. And our third edition of this guidebook had to rejig its content.

Of course, it's not all so rosy. London still has major problems in dealing with a combined rainwater run-off / sewage system that periodically gives anything living in the Thames the fright of its life. It may seem like a fun idea to play on its low-tide beaches and waddle in its waters, but it's not to be recommended as the most healthy of past-times.

*This section covers buildings along the river, from Vauxhall Bridge to Butlers Wharf, principally on the southern side, especially after Blackfriars' Bridge.*

*Left: **Embankment Gardens**, below Charing Cross Station, with the 17th water-gate now left stranded by the C19th creation of the Embankment.*

# London Riverside

*Above: summer tourists on the Millennium Bridge, with St. Paul's in the background. Right: people enjoying the river near the OXO building.*

## A riverside perambulation

The southern embankment of the Thames has become a promenade. Most people are likely to begin using that promenade at **Westminster Bridge** (using Westminster Underground Station) but we begin this section at **Vauxhall Bridge** (at MI6), where the Embankment walk logically begins and where the **Tate Britain** is located (best accessible from Pimlico Underground Station). You could start here and walk all the way to **Tower Bridge** and beyond (or vice versa).

Vauxhall will offer you Terry Farrell's **MI6** building (on the south side) — which has always suffered the fate of huge unfashionability (possibly a good reason to look more closely at this latter-day spy fortress disguised as an ordinary office building) and has been joined by an equally odd **housing** group by EPR and **Vauxhall** tube / bus interchange designed by Arup Associates. Your more likely attraction will be on the northern side, at Stirling's **Clore Gallery** extension to the old Tate and the more recent John Miller work (at **Tate Britain**), adjacent to which is Allies & Morrison's **Chelsea Art College** building (a rather nice conversion). You might then find yourself wandering down to **Lambeth Bridge**, perhaps darting into the backlands to visit **Channel Four** where the nearby street market makes an interesting lunchtime diversion), Farrell's **Marsham Street** government buildings, Edwin **Lutyens'** housing at Page Street (not his best, unfortunately), and the under-rated **Westminster Cathedral**, etc. Your aim should be to cross the river again at Lambeth or **Westminster** bridges, back to the south side. Westminster will offer you the **Palace of Westminster**, **Westminster Abbey** and **Portcullis House** (all on the north side and in the West End section because they are equally and perhaps more properly a part of Whitehall).

Starting at **Westminster**, you are likley to come through Hopkins' remarkable **Jubilee** station and crossing the bridge will provide some fine views that naturally draw you toward the **London Eye**. Beyond that is the revamped **Hungerford Bridge** and the **Southbank** cultural centre, together with Denys Lasdun's **National Theatre** and **IBM** building. The choice here is to go across Hungerford Bridge to explore Farrell's **Embankment Place** and the adjacent **Embankment Gardens** (with Inigo Jones' riverside gateway). You could then return down the other side of the Bridge to the Southbank.

From this point on you are likely to be keeping to the south side all the way to Tower Bridge. This neglects some fine attractions on the northern side such as **Somerset House** and the **Temple**, but you could make a diversion across **Waterloo Bridge** for some of the best views in London.

The southside embankment is particularly pleasant just east of Waterloo and after this it will take you past the **Oxo** Building, refurbished by Lifschutz Davidson, who also did the recent work at Hungerford Bridge. Another diversion around here is to **Coin Street** itself, where there is interesting housing by Lifschutz Davidson and Haworth Tompkins.

Winding along the river and under bridges is interesting enough at this point, but your next major attraction is the new **Tate Modern**, the **Millennium (foot) Bridge** and the thatched reconstruction of the **Globe Theatre** (possibly as unfashionable among architects as Farrell's buildings, but well worth a visit if you are capable of standing for a two hour performance).

As you move east toward London Bridge the attractions become rather touristy (the Clink, Vinopolis, etc.), but scratch the surface and there is genuine historical interest here. But the best attractions are **Southwark Cathedral** and **Borough Market** — the latter beginning in the late '90's as a 'farmers' market' and quickly blossoming into a major weekend venue for (delicious but somewhat overpriced) organic foodstuffs.

Like a similar 'spontaneous' eruption at Spitalfield, Borough Market is continually under threat but its success appears to have saved it for the moment (although the 'farming' content becomes increasingly questionable). The Fish restaurant here is an inventive design by Julyan Whickham (no longer in its original ownership).

Walk under London Bridge toward **Hays Galleria** — a former barge inlet serving warehouses, now infilled and covered over. On the opposite side of the river, on the axis of Hays' central mall, are principal City buildings such as old Billingsgate Market and Lloyd's of London.

Walking east from here brings you to London's new **City Hall**, designed by the Foster office. The adjacent office development around City Hall is also by Foster.

Now you are at **Tower Bridge** (the alternative starting point for this perambulation) and the next attraction is an area that is technically a part of Docklands: **Butlers Wharf**. You will now walk along **Shad Thames** — once a street serving the adjacent warehouses that have now been converted (many by Terence Conran) into apartments and restaurants. This leads you past a large Julyan Whickham development redolent with Dutch overtones (his father-in-law is Aldo van Eyck) to the **Design Museum** and a small building by Hopkins. It's an interesting area, solidly defined, once all warehousing, and worth wandering around.

From here you can cross **St. Saviour Dock** on a recent footbridge designed by Nicholas Lacey and you can see two buildings designed by Piers Gough (**China Wharf** and a small housing block, both hanging over the river). You can now return or continue through new riverside housing on to **Rotherhithe** and beyond. If you do want to go on, you can get to Cherry Garden and **Hope (Sufferance) Wharf**, where there is a small 'village' including recent work by Hawkins Brown. The energetic among you can get to **Surrey Quays** (which feels like a 'new town'; Canada Water Jubilee Station is here), to rapidly changing Deptford (also served by the DLR and where the **Laban Centre** is located) and even on to **Greenwich Peninsula** (again served by the Jubilee Line).

*Left: street sellers on Hungerford Bridge.*

## The bridges:

• **Westminster Bridge**: *1739 - 50, original by Charles Labelye, who raised clouds of jealously and he left for Paris (no dogs allowed and death to anyone defacing the walls); closed 1846; replaced 1854-62 by Charles Page with Sir Charles Barry as consultant. This was the first bridge after the historic London Bridge.*

• **Hungerford Bridge**: *originally 1841- 45 — a suspended footbridge by Isamabard Brunel (then with the largest span in Britain); replaced 1863 by John Hawkshaw (who also did Charing Cross Station; until then trains stopped at London Bridge station), 1860-4. Current pedestrian additions by Lifschutz Davidson, 2002.*

• **Waterloo Bridge**: *1811 - 17, as private toll bridge, by John Rennie, demolished 1937 - 38 (after settlement of the piers — a fairly common occurence to Thames bridges) and replaced by a design from Rendell, Palmer & Tritton, with Sir Giles Gilbert Scott's as consultant, 1937 - 44 (which engineers tell me is utterly theatrical and not what it pretends to be — the structure is actually box girders, not arches).*

• **Blackfriars Bridge**: *1760 - 9, Robert Mylne; replaced by Joseph Cubitt and H. Carr, 1860 - 9 when a then unpopular Queen Victoria opened the bridge to the hissing of the crowd. The bridge opened up Southwark for development. It was widened in 1907 - 10.*

• **Blackfriars rail bridge**: *1862 - 4 by Joseph Cubitt and FT Turner. Now disused; only the piers remain.*

• **Southwark Bridge**: *original by John Rennie (as Vauxhall and Waterloo bridges), 1814 - 19, in three arches in cast-iron, the largest attempted in cast-iron. Replaced 1912 - 21 by present five-arch bridge by Mott & Hay with Ernest George as consultant architect.*

• **Cannon St Railway Bridge**: *1863 36 by Hawkshaw and J Wofe-Barry; widened 1886 - 93 and remodelled in 1979 - 81.*

• **London Bridge**: *AD100-400; timber crossing restored 1000; stone by 1176 - 1209 (lined with houses, with nineteen arches, a drawbridge at one end and an overhanging chapel at the centre); houses along the bridge pulled down in 1758 by George Dance the elder (who designed the Mansion House) and Sir Robert Taylor; structure replaced 1823-31 by John Rennie (elder did the design; his son built it); widened 1903 - 4; replaced 1967 - 72 by Mott Hay & Anderson (Rennie's went to Arizona where the facing stone was cut up and stuck onto a concrete substructure.*

• **Tower Bridge**: *1886 - 94, by John Wolfe-Barry as engineer and Horace Jones as architect. The opening span was designed to cope with the dense shipping traffic of the period. The styling is meant to be sympathetic to the Tower. The Visitor Centre at the middle of the bridge is by Michael Squire, 1992.*

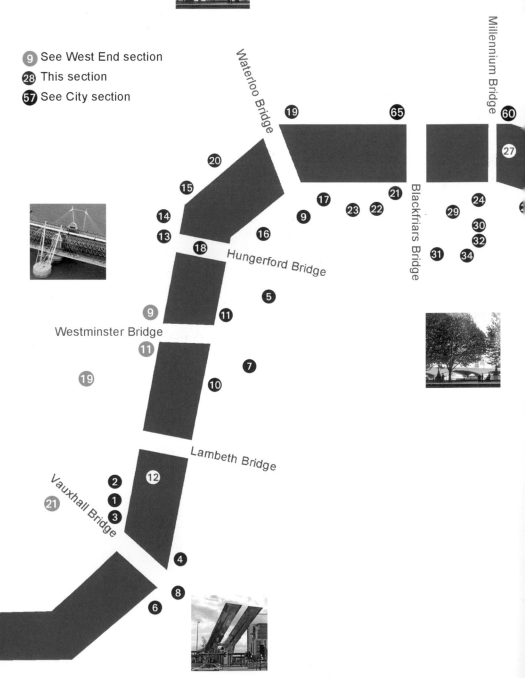

⑨ See West End section
❷❽ This section
❺❼ See City section

Waterloo Bridge

Millennium Bridge

Blackfriars Bridge

Hungerford Bridge

Westminster Bridge

Lambeth Bridge

Vauxhall Bridge

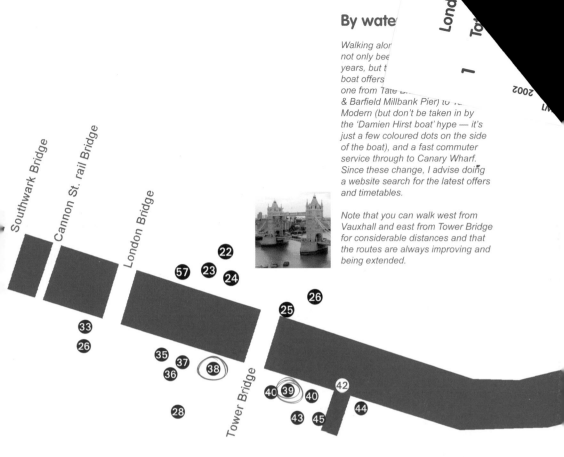

By wate_

*Walking alor_
not only bee_
years, but t_
boat offers_
one from Tate _.
& Barfield Millbank Pier) to _.
Modern (but don't be taken in by
the 'Damien Hirst boat' hype — it's
just a few coloured dots on the side
of the boat), and a fast commuter
service through to Canary Wharf.
Since these change, I advise doing
a website search for the latest offers
and timetables.*

*Note that you can walk west from
Vauxhall and east from Tower Bridge
for considerable distances and that
the routes are always improving and
being extended.*

## South & North

It is worth remembering that, for some 700 years,
London only had **London Bridge** as its sole river
crossing. However, because the stone bridge of 1209
had nineteen arches that were each some 8 - 10m
thick, the river conditions upstream and downstream
were quite different. In fact, there was almost a 2m
difference between one side of the bridge and the
other, making passage under it a rather challenging
exercise. Upstream, the waters were calm and
relatively stable, facilitating the ease of movement
up and down, and back and forth; downstream, they
were more turbulent. This was the situation until the
bridge's centre spans were opened in 1759 and the
whole bridge was then demolished and replaced by
a Sir Charles Rennie design in 1831. A faster flowing
river now became a barrier between north and south
in a way it had never been before. The original London
Bridge was also a shopping and residential bridge
with, at its northern end, Wren's church of St. Magnus
Martyr having its porch on the bridge pavement. Thus
continuity was given between the two sides of the
river.

In contrast, the need determined for a
new bridge at the eastern edge of the City, at St.
Katherine's Dock (now **Tower Bridge**), addressed
a metropolis not only divided between north and
south, but also between the bulk of shipping traffic

on the east side of London Bridge (in 'the Pool')
and the upstream parts leading into Westminster.
Sitting across the midst of the Pool that held so much
shipping, the new bridge had to have some means of
allowing passage — hence the opening 'bascules' of
the winning proposal by Sir Horace Jones for a new
crossing finally approved by Parliament in 1885. A
complicating consideration was a height difference
between the northern and southern banks — an issue
that engendered a design from Sir Joseph Bazelgette
proposing a 450m spiral ramp on the southern side.

It is worth taking the time to overcome tourist
instincts and actually look closely at the way the bridge
is put together: a swan-song of nineteenth century
daring among London's monuments. The real author
of everything we see now — including the architectural
dressing up — was the engineer, John Wolfe-Barry
(Jones died in 1887) and his assitant architect, George
D. Stevenson.

Improved transportation links and the
creation of walkways along the river banks have done
much to lend the Thames a more positive significance
and also to link north and south. However, there
remains a failure to make the radical step of going
back to inhabited links. It has been discussed and
there has been an idea competition. Perhaps one day
it will happen and the river will once again serve as
London's most significant artery to an extent that is still
hardly imaginable.

Millbank, Atterbury Street, SW
John Miller / Allies and Morrison
Tube: Pimlico

Since the opening of Tate Modern at Bankside, the old Tate (Sidney Smith, 1897, with additional 1937 Duveen sculpture galleries by Romaine Walker and John Russell Pope; Llewellyn Davies et al's 1979 galleries; and the Stirling Wilford Clore Gallery) has reinvented itself as the Tate Britain and has been provided with new galleries and a new west side entrance designed by John Miller (whilst Allies and Morrison handled the external landscaping).

The Miller design adds about one third to the gallery accommodation (the refurbishment of five galleries and the addition of nine new ones), but this has been seamlessly handled so as to blend in with the old building. The heart of the work is a new, spacious entrance hall with a grand staircase. In all, it's an interesting and finely crafted mix of gallery motifs, taking from Smith, from Stirling and possibly a variety of other sources. Oddly, this almost detracts from the merits, identity and potential uniqueness of Miller's work. Nevertheless, it all adds up to a reinvigorated Millbank Tate that has won a lot of converts favouring this building rather than the Herzog & de Meuron building.

*From here it is easy to visit the Chelsea Art College, the Millbank estate, Darbourne & Darke's Lillington estate, and George Street's St. James the Less — continuing up to Victoria as an option. Alternatively, continuing the river walk, you can cross Vauxhall Bridge to MI6, EPR's housing and the Arup interchange, continuing east to Lambeth.*

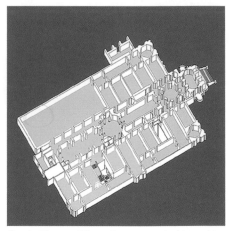

Top: inside one of the gallery spaces, looking out to the new entry stair
Above: axonometric of the area of Miller's additions and alterations.
Below: the new main entry stair leading up to the gallery floor from the lobby. Left: old and new gallery spaces.

There is a skill to the understated landscaping design of the Clore's (much neglected) entry forecourt which is important to one's arrival at the building's gaping mouth.

Part of the fun of the Clore is Stirling's gamesmanship, played out externally in relation to the classical features of the original building; and played out internally in the manner in which the visitor enters the building. It is as if the architect had sought out areas of a tight brief in which he could play, away from the burden of debate and controversy characterising the internals.

**1**

The **Clore Gallery** (Stirling Wilford Associates, 1986 ) is a skilled 3200 sq.m. addition to Sidney Smith's 1897 edifice funded by the sugar magnate, Henry Tate, and designed to house the Gallery's Turner collection. The building sits quietly in a corner of the Tate entrance garden, looking somewhat forlorn and out of fashion — but this does not take away from the interest it holds — much of it based on the fact that Stirling was highly constrained. The budget was tight and the client's brief very specific (room layouts, their sequence, a principal level as the existing galleries, etc.). Perhaps as a consequence, one feels Stirling searching out room to manoeuvre that could engage his penchant for architectural gamesmanship without encroaching into areas of performative contention — a classic case of the architect reframing a project and posing his own problems.

Much of this begins on the pavement as an understated approach through a landscaped forecourt. We then find that the façade quietly integrates itself with other buildings on the site by picking up their key formal features (the classical language, red brick and Portland stone), incorporating them and then quickly abstracting and intruding upon their influences. Characteristic Stirling trademarks include notes of irreverence which delight, for example, in using an acid-green he must have known most people dislike. He plays a mild joke with what is ostensibly the structural grid of the façade and then gives the deceit away at the corner and even attempts a joke with corner windows which thinly refer back to 'missing' stonework in his Stuttgart art gallery (1984).

The internal organisation includes an arrival axis at 90 degrees to a series of events (a minor, compressed architectural promenade) which includes a brightly coloured, top lit staircase and a proscenium arch leading into the gallery rooms. Sadly, the latter have now been altered to remove the carpet, change the controversial beige fabric wall colouring and remove a screened seating area formerly overlooking the understated landscaped forecourt.

Recent improvements to the landscaping around the Tate (by Allies & Morrison) have made quite a difference to the setting of the Clore. However, there have succeeded in rearranging the garden so that the original, formal arrival and approach axis promoted by Stirling has been rudely overlaid by a new axis between his façade and the main road. For the garden in general, this is an improvement; for the Stirling schema it is not.

**2**

The **Millbank Estate** that sits behind the Tate Britain (right), was completed by the London County Council (LCC) Architect's Department in 1903, following its very first estate in Shoreditch (the Boundary estate). Further north, in Page Street and Vincent Street, SW1, there is a large estate designed by Sir Edwin Lutyens (1928–30). It's a curious design, the façades being patterned with a now fashionable off-set motif. Apart from that, both schemes are worth looking at if you are interested in housing and apartment blocks for families.

## 3 Chelsea College of Art

University of the Arts, Chelsea College of Art
Atterbury Street, SW1
Allies & Morrison, 2005
Tube: Pimlico

Art is, of course, (paradoxically) big business. And its educational institutions are very much a part of the UK business sector: in competition and churning out artists by the hundred. That's the background to this conversion job from A&M that sees them back in good form after all that speculative office stuff which appears to be distinctly confusing to them (they do it well, but not as their most interesting work). The keynote of this conversion is a schematic clarity to the architectonic mix of old and new that leaves the massive central forecourt as a void pregnant with possibilities as yet unrevealed, and a more detailed and qualitatively characterised mix that (one hates to say it) artfully blends old and new together with a surprising degree of what (rather appropriately) verges on crudity. Old hospital and new building work, insinuated additions, extensions and links happily intermix as a comfortable coupling that seems tonally on target for an art school: the new flatters but is without preciousness; a

proverbial 'commodity, firmness and delight' hang loose in a disarmingly casual manner that in no way looses a tight effectiveness of organisation and facility. It is work that won't take your breath away but nevertheless subsists as an architecture of pertinence and sufficient sharpness to draw one's admiration. Now, if this practice could handle the instrumentality of their speculative office building commissions in this way . . . (There has actually been a suggestion that the architectural character of this scheme is more to do with the client's insistence than the architect's enthusiasms. We'll never knoiw.)

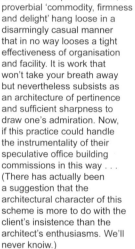

*Above: the College's triangular exhibition area.*

*Above: the main staircase between the old buildings and the new workshops.*

**4** **MI6:** *Once upon a time . . . There was a competition-winning residential scheme which evolved into offices to suit market changes (see nr.6 below). Such things often happen in architecture. During scheme design, the telephone rang. It was the Prime Minister. She — the lady with the handbag — wanted a large building for a secret service that, one had to understand, didn't exist. And so the design was reinvented as an impenetrable river palace for the mysterious figures of MI6, with the most expensive concrete cladding in Europe*

and a fit-out costing more than the shell: a sculptural, striking green glass and cream concrete construction, appropriately defying easy interpretation of its inner organisation (the massing derives from origins in a competition-winning design by Farrell for apartments; the idea was that everyone would have a river view). The outer garb was inspired by the New York of the 1920s and 1930s, when Captains of Capitalism wore broad shoulder pads, posed in Moderne guise, and sported stepped-back buildings designed by the likes of Holabird and Root, Raymond Hood, Betram Goodhue and Hugh Ferri. There was even a hint of early Frank Lloyd Wright in Mayan mood in the HVAC housings on the top of the building, and spikey features incongruously reminiscent of the crown on the Statue of Liberty. And James Bond moved in and everyone lived happily ever. You can even walk in front of the building on the riverside walkway and enjoy a close view of where the MI6 spies live. But they might be nine floors underground, deep below, where a secret world subsists in contradistinction to the open offices above.

**5** The brand game at **Waterloo Eurostar** (Nicholas Grimshaw & Partners, 1993) was to provide akin to the airport experience: arrival, checking-in, waiting areas, shops, etc. But the tectonic challenge was to provide a design integrated into an existing Victorian station, its structure rooted into the brick vaults supporting the rail lines. The roof is the upper, most visible part of what is described as a 'five-layer sandwich' comprising roof, platforms, departure level, arrivals level, and basement car park. It comprises a 400 m long series of three-pin arches with off-set central pins to cope with the eccentricity of five rail tracks and constraints such as underground tunnels. The eastern side is mostly opaque, with an internal structure, reversed on the west side so daylight can be admitted. Standard parts fit the varying, difficult geometry and take the shock-waves generated by long, heavy trains arriving from France (the glazing has to accommodate an 80 mm horizontal movement and a 6 mm vertical movement as the trains impact the station) e.g. all the glazing would normally have been thousands of special cuts, but Grimshaw has used flexible gaskets and standard, rectangular sheets of overlapping glass. However, no matter how clever it all is, Eurostar is moving to St. Pancras by 2007.

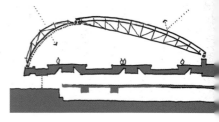

**6** Immediately to the north of the Vauxhall tube station sits a row of apartment block towers (designed by Broadway Malyan) that, at the lower levels, merge their podium base into a terrace forming a river edge. The schema (derived from an earlier Terry Farrell scheme) is fine; shame about its detailed handling, particularly at the top, where the towers break out into the most bizarre roof shapes imaginable. Close up, it's not as bad as from a distance and the scheme does extend the riverside walkway westward.

What is it about Vauxhall? On the east side of Farrell's MI6 buildings is an access point to the river used by a tourist company who specialise in using ex-WWII 'ducks' — or wet / dry vehicles equally at home on the road or in the river — a bizarre but alternative way to travel on the river. The tall building immediately behind this strange vehicle is the Millbank Tower, Ronald Ward & Partners, 1960 - 3 (recently remodelled by GMW).

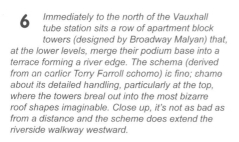

# London Riverside

## 7   Centaur Street House

London is full of very localised architectural initiatives these days, often hidden away in strange locations. This is one of the better examples — a fine design from a small practice with a growing reputation. The site (and the house) are bang up against the rail lines that bring the Eurostar trains into Waterloo Station, in one of those curious inner London locations that mixes facts like that with the realities of local communities who live there, use the nearby public park, etc. The principal attraction of the design is simple: a refreshing attitude to cladding issues that is simple and distinctive and without preciousness. Obviously, there is more to the architecture. But this is a major contribution of this simple insert (please don't call it an 'intervention') into London's fabric. The architects describe the building as "a hybrid of the European horizontal apartment and the English vertical terrace house. Each apartment enjoys a Raumplan interior organised as a large, open double-height living space, interpenetrated by adjacent enclosed bedrooms and stairs, which form a concrete buffer to the railway. Construction consists internally of high exposed concrete economically over clad externally with insulated rain screen. Other than in site concrete, all components are prefabricated, specified from international sources according to dRMM's catalogue design methodology."

*There is a rather un-English quality to the character of this small building, although its blunt conjunction with a main railway line is typically London. Architecturally, small buildings like this make the metropolis a considerably more exciting city.*

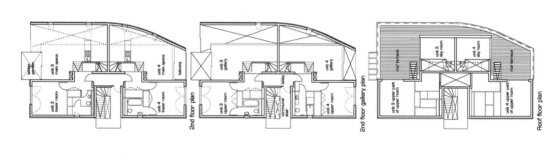

**8**   *Arup's dramatic exercise at **Vauxhall** Underground station and bus interchange (Arup Associates, 2005) strives for iconic exuberance, almost literally waving, "Hey, I'm here . . .!" It is very simple: a control building set above the underground station itself and an axial run of bus stops that run down the road for a considerable length, all of it in bright stainless steel. To the immediate south is the rail tracks coming into Waterloo; to the north-west is EPR's exercise in tall apartment blocks; and to the north-east is Farrell's MI6 fortress. So, the Vauxhall station completes a trio of peculiarities. Whether it's wonderful or ridiculous is hardly for this bemused author to say . . Pay it a visit and make up your own mind.*

**9**   *This **IMAX** 500 seat cinema (Waterloo Station / Bridge; Brian Avery Associates, 1999) is a comparatively simple and clean statement. It takes the form of a glass drum sat within the centre of a large traffic roundabout (but accessed at a lower level, from the Southbank) and has thus become an instant, self-advertising land-mark of the kind that is still quite rare in London. It is also an important part of proposals to renew and revitalise the whole of the South Bank cultural area. The photo shows the building in context (Farrell's Embankment Place can be seen across the river, at the top left). Unfortunately, they clothe the outer face of the drum in art, as if this were somehow better than plain architecture, a celebration of cinema, or even advertising. (See photo bottom right for what it was like when just constructed.)*

# Evelina Children's Hospital

**10**

This is the first purpose-made children's hospital in London for more than a century: a 140 bed facility, operating theatres, intensive care units and a variety of specialist services centred around a large atrium which provides a cafe, performance space and children's school.

Lambeth Palace Road, SE11
Michael Hopkins & Partners, 2005
Tube: Westminster / Waterloo

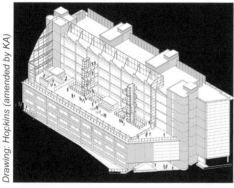

*Drawing: Hopkins (amended by KA)*

*Photo: St Thomas' Hospital*

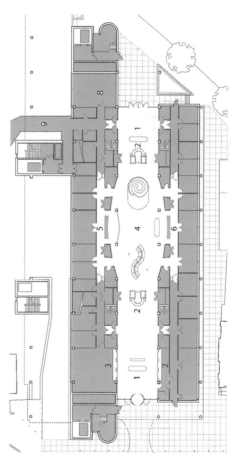

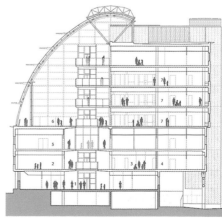

# London Riverside

Jubilee Gardens, Belvedere Road, SE1
David Marks & Julia Barfield Architects, 2000
Tube: Waterloo, Embankment

## 11 London Eye

The 135 m diameter London Eye was the swan amongst the Millennium ducklings, in effect being a private enterprise initiative the government would not support, prompting the architects to become entrepreneurs. In itself, this giant rotating bicycle wheel is dramatic, spectacular and entertaining. But it has also shifted the nature and pattern of tourist attractions in the area, helping to revitalise Westminster Bridge and the South Bank.

The Eye was conceived by its authors as a Millennium scheme, in response to the then Conservative government's call for appropriately whacky ideas. They didn't see this (sitting opposite the Palace of Westminster) as a suitable one and, unable to win Lottery funding, the architects resorted to commercial interests. British Airways saw the publicity opportunity and backed the scheme (with part ownership and at an enormous 29% APR interest rate on the capital loan). Planning permission was granted — initially a temporary five years — and the Eye's spectacular success had soon won everyone over.

The structure (erected by a Dutch company accomplished in such things and possessing a floating crane) hangs the wheel over the Thames and triangulates and stabilises it in one axis where the motors are located. The other axis has gigantic steel legs holding the wheel in place (tied back onto a tiny piece of land owned by the Southbank authority, who — in 2005 — attempted to exploit this by threatening not to renew the lease!). Each of the 32 glazed capsules slowly rotates on bearings as the wheel turns on a flight (sic) that takes about 35 minutes, providing superb views (on a clear day), but try to book before turning up.

To the upset of the ownership-sharing architects, Madame Taussaud's (the third partner in the enterprise) took a controlling share in late 2005 (later buying out the architects) and one awaits with horror what possible changes they might bring to something whose joyful simplicity is a key part of the attraction. Get your ride before it becomes accompanied by some waxworks historical figure in the corner of the capsule.

**12** *Marks Barfield also designed the Tate Britain jetty that provides rapid boat links to the Tate Modern. It is located in the river Thames, immediately outside the Tate Britain*

## Embankment Place

Charing Cross, WC2
Terry Farrell Partnership, 1991
Tube: Embankment, Charing Cross

One usually finds a variety of functional, urban and historical themes in Farrell's work. In this instance – one of the few buildings which positively addresses the Thames – they include employing the air rights over the 1863 rail station; external service cores (as at Lloyds, as Farrell points out); historical references to the large houses and palaces once lining the Thames between the City and Whitehall; references to Ledoux in the water feature of the lobby, to the Moscow Kurskaya station on the station platforms and, near the Embankment, to Otto Wagner's Vienna stations. Nevertheless, the building does have its own identity.

The new work sits upon the old station undercroft of brick vaults (a feature that is comparable with the work of Farrell's ex-partner, Nick Grimshaw, at Waterloo), making it reminiscent of conquering cultures building new temples upon the foundations of the existing ones, literally absorbing history into what is contemporary (and, in this case, simultaneously regurgitating other historical themes). Strong features and contrasts characterise one's experience of the building. For example, there is the massive scale and character of structural acrobatics involved in spanning the rail tracks (best appreciated from the South Bank, from where one can also see how the service towers straddle the sides of the upper offices and the station itself). There is also a (not unsuccessful) contrast between the building's Baroque presence and the scale of older buildings, especially in Villiers Street, on the east side.

*The **Station Hotel** (Strand side,1863–64), is by E.M. Barry, (1830 - 80), third son of Sir Charles (1975 - 1860), who designed the Houses of Parliament; it is one of the first buildings to use artificial stone. Barry was also involved in work at the Royal Academy and the Royal Opera House.*

**14** *Once reputed to be designed by Inigo Jones, **York Watergate** (1626), within Embankment Gardens, SW3, was built by Nicholas Stone (master mason for George Villiers, 1st Duke of Buckingham), as the gate to York House and marks the bank of the Thames before the Victorian Embankments were built. One's imagination might bring back the ghosts of river travellers, mounting steps such as these in order to get to York House and, later, to the streets immediately behind. The latter included Villiers and Buckingham Streets – some of the first speculative developments in London (1670's on), founded on the novel and modern idea of order and regularity, and developed by the notorious speculator, Dr Nicholas Barbon. (Execution usually produced an appealing form of irregularity resulting from the development of individual plots by separate builders.)*

**15** *The **Thames Embankment** is a tremendous 3.5 mile engineering feat of health engineering and was constructed — against all the odds — in 1868–74, by Sir Joseph Bazalgette. Major parts of London's rain-water run-off and sewage is taken by the tunnels of the Embankment to east London, where pump houses change its level and discharge it to sewage works and the river. One of the Embankment's key features, **Cleopatra's Needle,** is a plundered Egyptian obelisk dating from 1500 BC. Strangely, no one seems to notice it very much.*

# London Riverside

**16** The **Royal Festival Hall**, SE1, was built as a 'people's palace' for the celebratory Festival of Britain in 1951 and remains its lone survivor (the rest having been demolished by a disgruntled and reactionary Winston Churchill). It was principally designed by Leslie Martin, Peter Moro and Edwin Williams at the LCC Architects Department as an inner 'egg' (the 2600 seat auditorium) surrounded by foyers and other accommodation, including a remarkable 'flowing' staircase concept and as much transparency as possible. The building is a monument to when post-war architects believed in socialism, progress and the notion that 'art should lead the facts of science' and experts were closely involved from the very beginning in the design of its auditorium. But the constraints of time and budget meant that it was never completed as intended and, by the early '60's, its neo-Scandinavian aesthetics were being dismissed as 'nautical whimsy' (Warren Chalk) and the building overlaid by more robust neo-Corbusian enthusiasms that included extensions, refronting and relocating the main entrances from the side to the river front. By then the building was a firm feature of new masterplans for the Southbank and its lost 'small hall' became the seed for the Queen Elizabeth Hall — added to by the Purcell Room, a gallery idea (now the Hayward) originating with an ICA scheme to move here and the National Film Theatre (a reinvention of the Festival's 'Telekinema'). Much of this became the 'brutalist' concrete buildings and surrounding decks created by London County Council architects (who included the Warren Chalk, Ron Herron, Denis Crompton trio of Archigram).The RFH remains a splendid building, now more easily accessible because of the new Hungerford Bridge. The restaurant was refurbished a few years ago by Allies and Morrison, who are currently architects for a larger refurbishment and master-plan scheme aiming to restore some of the original features and cope with the deck issues. Some of this work was being realised in the summer of 2005.

**17** The **National Theatre**, Upper Ground, SE1, designed by Sir Denys Lasdun & Partners (1967–77; petulantly denounced by Prince Charles as something akin to a nuclear power station) makes a superb contrast with the RFH. Where the latter's spaces are open and filled with light, people 'pouring' down its grand staircases, the National offers a different aesthetic agenda more enthused by (a Japanese-like) enthusiasm for shadows and contrasts between dark, light, for huge cantilevering horizontal planes, and embodying an underlying obession with castles (surely the major clue to the whole place?).

The plan configures three halls into a more or less square plan cut across by a diagonal axis that focuses upon the north-west corner, adjacent to Waterloo Bridge, emphasising this entry corner and locating service and support areas to the south and east sides (in different circumstances, the back end of the building). The scheme is simple but the experience is complex and dramatic: in-situ concrete finishes, enclosed staircases, views between floors, a plush purple carpet and wonderful views toward St. Paul's. Well, it was that way until generations of managers silted up the place in order to provide the layers of before, between, and after performance servicing that theatre-goers now demand (the airport equation that is more about the incidental, in between opportunities to milk the wallets of customers than the principal, dramatic reasons for visiting the place). The outcome was late '90's revisions to the lobby area by Stanton Williams that deeply troubled Lasdun and compromised his architecture (they were completed in '98; Lasdun died in 2001). Alternatives from the original architect that might have improved access — especially car drop-offs and other vehicular servicing, together with proposals for tented structures populating the rather underused terraces and providing cafes and the like — were rejected, although he did manage to prevent 'pollarding' the terracing and having the SW proposals approved on the basis that everything could be easily reinstated. However, this is a robust building and well worth exploring. Go to the Lyttleton for a performance. But also go some sunny day when the National is empty and quiet, and you can explore its castle-like spaces and search out the ghost of its architect: some little boy probably still excitedly rooting around what he finds to be the most interesting place in the world.

Photo: Donald Cooper

## Hungerford Bridge

Victoria Embankment, WC2
Lifschutz Davidson & WSP Group Engineers, 2002
Tube: Embankment / Waterloo

I am told I fail to appreciate anything about engineering when I say that, despite this bridge's faults, I prefer it to the Millennium Bridge. My point is that the latter is engineering before it is a passage for people; the Hungerford is flat, wider and more of a boulevard-bridge that seems to put people first (whatever the intentions of its designers). The Millennium may be prettier and more structurally daring and elegant, but I still prefer this bridge. So: *damn your instrumental mind-set and abstracted aesthetic inclinations!* In any case, I confess: the manner in which this structure appropriates the old railway bridge by grasping onto it is dear to my heart; a veritable symbol of London's regenrative endeavours. Structurally, the new work straps itself onto the old like the beast in 'Alien' locked onto the face of an unlucky astronaut.

The proposal for the new bridge was rooted in an early '90's consultancy about Waterloo Station, calling for improved access across the river. The problem was

that generations of Londoners had suffered a ludicrously uncomfortable pedestrian way strapped onto the northern side of the Hungerford Railway Bridge — a principal means of getting from Charing Cross to the Southbank cultural centre and to Waterloo. Years later, having dealt with an unexploded WWII bomb, the consequent delays and extra costs involved (requiring Mayor Livingstone to bail out the scheme), Londoners were able to enjoy a hugely improved bridge with two new pedestrian walkways strapped onto the old railway structure.

Bizarrely, the architects talk of the suspension structure as 'angel's wings' and such like, but one has little need for this sort of promotional rationale now that the bridge is complete. The white steelwork of the new grabs a hold of the old Hungerford Bridge stanchions and sends tall suspension masts into the air on either side. What the river crossing pedestrian experiences is transformed: what was ugly has become a stroll across a (comparatively broad) river boulevard that comes complete with entrepreneurial street sellers quick to recognise the opportunities that other bridges fail to provide. Meanwhile, commuter trains rattle by. And at night the lighting reveals it as a thing of beauty. Principally for urbanistic rather than tectonic reasons, I much prefer it to the Millennium Bridge.

Ironically the project suffered many problems and the architect's scheme ended as a design & build exercise from which they resigned, leaving all sorts of contention regarding value engineering, details, cross-links between the walkways, end terminations, etc. Sad, but the reality of the thing is sufficient.

*Drawing: Lifshutz Davidson (amended by KA)*

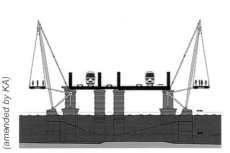

# 19  Somerset House

Strand, WC2
Dixon Jones / Inskip & Jenkins / Feilden & Mawson, 2001
Tube: Temple, Embankment, Covent Garden

As you find it now, Somerset House is an exercise in reclamation from a government bureaucracy that filled its interiors with dreary offices and its courtyard with dozens of parked cars. Without the Parisian *grand projet* as examplars, it might never have happened.

Somerset House was originally designed by William Chambers (1766), built to house the learned societies, government offices and the Navy Board. As the reinvention of a former Tudor palace on the site it was effectively London's first major public office building and paralleled the quite different Adelphi exercise by the Adam Brothers, just upstream (begun 8 years before). Both schemes straddled a wider River Thames before the Embankments were constructed and enjoyed direct boat access to vaults at the lower level. Access from the Strand was at a much higher level and the difference is still a key part of the experience (e.g. moving from the entry lobby down the flights of stairs to the basement cafe).

The building's reinvention in the late '90's cleared out the Inland Revenue and its less-than-imaginative use of the central court as a car park, giving the buildings a long overdue *grands projet* treatment. Dixon Jones were responsible for the excellent fountain court (shades of Parc Citroen in Paris) and the more tentative river terrace (which includes a footbridge link onto Waterloo Bridge). Other parts include the Courtauld Gallery, Hermitage Rooms, and Gilbert Collection (of decorative arts). However, it is regrettable to see much of it sinking back into a stereotypical English mish-mash of half-resolved gestures, situations, and services. The building fabric was handled by Feilden Mawson. Inskip & Jenkins did the Gilbert.

But even if the museums fail to interest you, and the cafes could be hugely improved, the outer river terrace is a fine place to sit and view London; and the inner court is a wonderful place to simply sit and think about space, and classicism and the fine gamesmanship of Chambers. (Each December, the central court hosts an ice-skating rink.)

**20**  *The Adelphi that the (three) Adams Brothers designed as a speculative venture between 1768 - 74 is apparently lost apart from a few remaining terrace parts. Certainly, the central block which formed what the Pevsner guides call 'the first great Georgian riverside composition' is long gone (now an office block from 1936). But the Royal Society for the Arts, Manufacture and Commerce (RSA; John Adams Street) gives us some semblance of what it was all about — particularly if you enter from the Strand side and go down to the lower, vaulted levels of this labryrinthian building.*

## OXO Development

Another Coin Street development by the same architects as for Broadwall, this time as a redevelopment of the old OXO building (whose idiosyncratic tower remains). The cherry of this 15,000 sq.m. mixed-use development is the riverside restaurant, bar and brasserie on the top floor of this reinvented 1928 building. It's rather 'late 1990's yuppie' (managed by Harvey Nichols), but the views from the terrace are superb, even if its north-facing aspect makes it less than the warmest place in town. The ambience of the restaurant is affected by overhead motorised fins which change the ceiling colour and alter both lighting and acoustics. Other floors include 78 apartments designed for the Coin Street Housing Association.

OXO Development, South Bank, SE1
Lifschutz Davidson, 1997
Tube: Waterloo

## Broadwall

**22**

Coin Street Community Builders are the non-profit making developer behind this scheme of 27 units, now in the hands of a housing cooperative. Eleven of the homes are for families, in 3 storey units; walk-up flats are at the southern end of the row in a 4 storey block (no lift); other small flats are concentrated in the 9 storey northern tower. The street side has well-handled access and nominal buffering from passers-by. The garden side is stridently articulated with flues (additional winter heating) and the whole thing has an evident Danish inspiration that is refreshing on the British scene. The scheme is worth comparing with the Barcelona-cum-Georgian enthusiasms of the more recent Haworth Thompkins scheme (see below). The mix of family terrace units and towered apartments is comparatively rare in an era when we are told that the white middle-classes with children are deserting central London in droves (a Richard Rogers alarm call).

Bernie Spain Gardens, Belvedere Road, SE1
Lifschutz Davidson, 1994
Tube: Waterloo

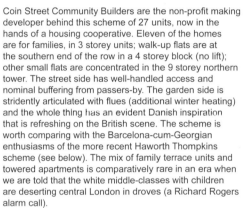

## Iroko housing

**23**

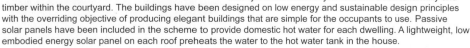

This Coin Street community scheme sits above an underground car park and bounds the block with tight terracing that forms (or will do when the fourth side is complete) a private inner sanctum for tenants. The model is vaguely Holland Park from the early C19, as reinvented at Milton Keynes, now translated and tightened up for this urban setting, and given a rather Spanish-inspired aesthetic. The project provides 59 dwellings and includes 32 family houses which can each accommodate up to 8 persons; the balance of accommodation is made up of a mix of flats and maisonettes. All dwellings are for rent and are managed by a housing co-op formed by the residents. Access is via a common balcony. A simple series of planning principles have been established: all houses have street level entrances and private gardens opening on to the communal courtyard; all flats and maisonettes have large balconies and each of the bedrooms overlooking the courtyard has a balcony. Bricks are used externally and timber within the courtyard. The buildings have been designed on low energy and sustainable design principles with the overriding objective of producing elegant buildings that are simple for the occupants to use. Passive solar panels have been included in the scheme to provide domestic hot water for each dwelling. A lightweight, low embodied energy solar panel on each roof preheats the water to the hot water tank in the house.

Belvedere Road, SE1
Haworth Tompkins, 2001
Tube: Waterloo

# London Riverside

## 24 Tate Modern

Bankside, SE1
Herzog & de Meuron, 2000
Tube: Blackfriars, Southwark, St. Paul's

The English appear to suffer the need to house their new institutions in buildings formerly intended for something else (perhaps as reassuring remembrance of the past). Banking halls become wine bars, pumping stations become restaurants and, in this instance, a not very old power station made from 4.2m bricks has been transformed from utilitarian purpose into an edifice devoted to the consumption of art. As such, the Tate Modern — perhaps more than any other London building — embodies the transformation of our economy from manufacturing goods to manufacturing sources of entertainment (as well as a recent and novel propensity among the English to patronise foreign architects — a fact the Swiss architects were aware of and, apparently, not an experience they are keen to repeat).

Bankside was designed in 1947 by Sir Giles Gilbert Scott (1880-1960) and completed in 1963. Being oil powered it was closed in the late 1970's after the 1974 oil crisis and the ensuing economic crisis. It was then quickly forgotten and ignored, despite its scale and location. In part, this was because the Thames itself had been forgotten and partly because the local area was on the wrong side of the river — self-evidently a poor cousin to the City on the opposite, northern bank.

In its present guise the building has been hollowed out internally whilst retaining the massive brick walls and chimney (some parts still await future funding and conversion). The massive Turbine Hall has been reinvented as a monumental, top-lit lobby space accessed by an equally generous ramp sliding down into the sunken ticket, information and educational areas, adjacent to which is one of London's largest bookshops. Access escalators, lifts, new gallery floors and other accommodation — including cafes, restaurant, an auditorium, a members room, etc. — are stacked along the adjacent, northern side of the building, overlooking the Hall.

*Below: The Turbine Hall is impressive, but you'll often find that the Tate turns off the light boxes during the day (rather missing the architectural point of it all).*

All of this is terminated by the two floors of a 'light beam' that sits upon the brick stack and serves as the principal external device signalling the changes; within it is air conditioning plant, restaurants, etc. New entrances on the north and west sides lead visitors into the vastness of the Turbine Hall, itself dominated by projecting 'light-boxes'. Escalators then lead to a sequence of upper level gallery spaces of varied dimensions and characterized by a daring (but subdued) palette of architectural materials and finishes (including raw oak flooring). The success of the whole experience is mixed but always unique, making this an exhilarating scheme equal of the Parisian *grand projets* that are its precedents, but possibly less than the architectural wonder the media would have us believe. Having said that, it has been hugely successful.

Externally, public areas are concentrated around the northern (shaded) side and the Millennium Bridge termination on the riverside walkway that now runs along the Thames. This has always been unsatisfactory, but the completion of a new shop designed by the architects within the northern entrance has immensely cheered it up and made it more attractive. However, there is still an unresolved problem of access.

Is it good? I confess to a fluctuating opinion. Parts are easy to hugely enjoy; but the galleries, for example, are less than wonderful spaces (the Tate Britain offers, on the whole, more pleasant spaces). And why are the Friends' (and related) spaces so dreary? Interestingly, however, what stays in one's memory are some of the most simple and basic features. For example, the daring raw oak floor that appears to wear so remarkably well. And then those brown painted stair handrails that are now suffering wear and tear. Together, these two features alone manage to lend this building a warm, welcoming feeling: it is ageing and distressing well. Of how many other buildings can one say the same? Let's hope the management understands such points of identification and lovingly protects and nurtures them.

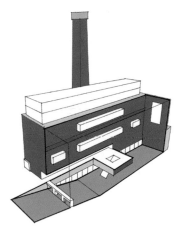

**25** The **Globe Theatre** (Pentagram Design, 1995), just east of the Tate Modern, is a London peculiarity not without attractions: an ostensible re-creation of the 1599 theatre near to where Shakespeare's plays were performed, complete with oak timbers, an open air pit, and a thatched roof (with water sprinklers in case of fire, of course). But, make no mistake, this is serious architecture as well as theatre; it's not Disney. Architecturally, it strives to fill a gap between medievalism and the regularised Palladianism of Inigo Jones as a public architecture rooted in Vitruvius' descriptions of Roman theatres. Toward the end of the C16th and beginning of the C17th, this was providing London with a stock of radical public venues and building types. One has to imagine such a Renaissance period as at once looking back to antiquity and simultaneously

radical — a mix we now find difficult to appreciate. In these terms, the attempted recreation of the Globe ('attempted' because the records are so parsimonious) is a parallel to the recreation of the Barcelona Pavilion. But while the theatre itself is worthy of attention, the associated contemporary designs hardly are — and that is unfortunate (a missed opportunity). But if architectural history fails to arouse your enthusiasms, simply try attending a play at the Globe — it's a novel experience.

**26** **Borough Market**, beneath London Bridge, is not so much a work of architecture as an urban place architecture that marries old and new and manifests a popular spirit that transformed the potential of an area that was to be demolished and lost. The former wholesale market was saved by going retail and an architectural competition (won by Greig + Stephenson) which has resulted in all kinds of careful restoration work and subtle interventions. Best Friday and Saturday.

# 27 Millennium Bridge

River Thames
Foster and Partners; Arup; Anthony Caro, 2002
Tube: Blackfriars, St. Paul's

I can recall sitting at dinner with an engineer who remarked, "Not dangerous! Don't you believe it for a moment!" A remarkably daring design from Arups had no sooner opened than it was immediately closed again, and stayed that way for some twelve months while engineering ingenuity, considerable computer analysis and long talks with insurers sorted out the problem. And the bridge was opened again — plus a few large dampening struts that nobody (apart from engineers) notices very much — and its reputation for wobbliness was quickly forgotten. (But, just in case, the Arup web site gives pages of reassurance.)

Arup explain the bridge as follows: "In 1996 the Financial Times held an international competition . . . to design a footbridge crossing the Thames between Southwark and Blackfriars bridges. A long span bridge, as needed to cross the Thames at this point, is a pure expression of engineering structure. A city centre footbridge, however, is equally about people and the environment — a piece of public architecture. When considering a link between Tate Modern and St. Paul's Cathedral another element is vital: the pure sense of physical form that drives a sculptor" They continue: "A unique collaboration was formed . . . [The competition had asked for a collaborative exercise between an engineer, an architect, and a sculptor] creating a minimal design that gives pedestrians unrivalled views of London . . . The 4m wide aluminium deck is flanked by stainless steel balustrades and is supported by cables to each side. These cables dip below the deck at midspan enabling unimpeded views of London. The bridge is a very shallow suspension bridge where the highly tensioned cables sag 2.3m. over the 144m of the central span, a span to dip ratio of 63:1. This is around 6 times shallower than a conventional suspension bridge."

But was this design also a case of rather clever answers to less than intelligent questions (i.e. self-imposed problems)? Clearly, the competition-winning architect (Foster) and collaborating artist (Anthony Caro) — intent upon the concept of a low-profile 'blade of light' — had landed the engineering team with quite a problem. They handled this brilliantly and elegantly. But one can't help feeling that certain cultural dimensions other than abstracted aesthetics and engineering acrobatics had been eclipsed — considerations that Lifschutz Davidson's almost contemporaneous bridge upstream at Hungerford offers in bundles (if even as a flawed default). Whereas the latter strives to welcome a stroll across the bridge as an urban boulevard upon which a person can interact with street sellers, the 4m wide metal-decked Millennium Bridge succeeds in being merely a device for crossing rather than a place to stop and enjoy the river.

But it is an elegant device. And, of course, what a brilliant piece of engineering: aspirations and hi-tech skills married together in a consoling and inspiring manner

*Crowds at the southern end of the bridge, turning around on themselves to access the embankment.*

bridge section

Drawing: Arup
(amended by KA)

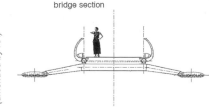

*The Millennium Bridge is definitely in the category of self-evidently (elegant and acrobatic) suspended structures that contrast with the likes of Hungerford Bridge's boulevard aspirations.*

that leaves Hungerford as a cobbled together Cinderella.

The most notable flaws are at the ends. The northern termination flows easily into the street pattern and runs out near St. Paul's (passing the Salvation Army building), although this passage is cut across by a major highway. On the other hand, the southern end suffers a difficulty in terminating itself within the short space allowed between the river and the Tate. Height problems force a return that plonks bridge users right on top of people flows along the river's edge — a crude aspect of the bridge that was (amusingly) a point of serious TV broadcast controversy between Foster and Herzog & de Meuron, designers of the Tate. However, overall, in linking St. Paul's to the Tate Modern and Globe Theatre on the other side of the river – the bridge (the first new one across the Thames in one hundred years) — has undoubtedly become a popular route across the river, enlivening two river banks that have been blighted by poor access.

Photo: Martin Hartmann

**28** The **Fashion Museum** *(Bermondsey Street, SE1; Ricardo Legoretta, 2002; Tube: London Bridge) is a hot Mexican number plonked down in a street of small warehouses in Bermondsey, designed by an AIA Gold Medal winner, and a museum claimed to 'be the first of its kind to showcase the talent of local and international fashion and textile', and to be a venue for exhibitions, shows, etc. The upper floors are apartments, helping to fund the project at the two lower levels.*

*In reality, this colourful number (as eccentric as its sponsor, Zandra Rhodes) is a proverbial 'black box' that gives little away about its programme. It's a blank building that looks as if it could truly be fighting off the heat of a Mexican summer. Or is that its defensiveness? On the one hand it's wonderful and colourful, and has done wonders for this street near London Bridge station. On the other hand, it's possibly as bizarre as a Rhodes outfit and raises all kinds of (topical and) old-fashioned questions about appropriateness of style, local traditions, cross-cultural mixes and the like — as if the English weren't capable of an authentic architectural cheerfulness. Are they?*

**29** *CZWG long ago established a reputation for combining a throwaway, irreverent wit (of the 'gonna die before I get old' variety) and (a developer driven) commercial opportunism. Their buildings usually have character and maintain an upbeat note, but the practice's output is hugely variable. These 130 apartments (**Bankside Lofts**, Hopton Street/Castle Yard, SE1, 1998), offices and a cafe adjacent to the new Tate Gallery (photo near right) combine old and new buildings and are a more complex and Modernist design than the practice usually offers and it is possibly one of their more successful designs, especially in the way variations in construction and materials are mixed and employed to culminate in a yellow, spiralling tower overlooking this part of London. There is a more recent CZWG building nearby, on the Southwark Street / Gt. Guildford corner (photo far right), which cants out at the top — not quite as successful.*

## 30 Bankside 123

Bankside 123, Southwark Street SE1
Allies & Morrison, 2005
Tube: Southwark

This development epitomises the challenges A&M have faced as growth pushed them into the mainstream as servants of instrumentally-minded clients and the architects of large, speculative office buildings — in this instance, a large development trading off the kudos of the Tate as a neighbour and the convenience of a Jubilee Line station around the corner (Southwark Station), intended to serve as a link between art (sitting on the Thames) and the prosaic depths of Southwark as defined by the realities of Southwark Street (where, incidentally, A&M have their own offices). It attempts to create three blocks that leave two 'fingers' (somewaht as at Foster's More Place) facilitating a greater permeability between the star attraction to the north and the highway along the site's southern boundary. By implication, this also primes the urban space in between the Tate and these massive office blocks, preparing it for future work on refurbishment of the southern side of the Gallery building. Thus the success of the masterplan ultimately depends on the Tate extension and some degree of reorientation away from the river and toward the inner parts of Southwark. Also like the More development — which included City Hall as a prestigious feature — Bankside is intended to include a juicy morsel in the form of Zaha Hadid's design for the Architecture Foundation. The 10-12 storey office buildings themselves comprise 85,000 sq.m. of space in three similar blocks offering the usual large floor plates on a 1.5m grid — meaning most of the 'architecture' is the external skin and public areas. (Building One, completed 2006, is about 46,000 sq.m.; the other, smaller, two buildings should be complete in 2007). Externally, A&M demonstrate a familiar obsessive attention to detail and compositional issues, but their floating blue fins give the impression of an anxious striving to cheer up a bland glass skin and introduce gratuitous modulation (justified on solar shading grounds) to a thin facade and what unavoidably subsists as a massive corporate lump of deep office space maximising its internal dimensions. *Compare with Palestra, below.*

## 31 Palestra

Palestra, Blackfriars Road,
Alsop Architects, 2005
Tube: Southwark

This 38,000 sq.m. gross office building is quite a beast, taking the instrumental demands characterising the standard speculative office block and wilfully distorting a comparatively narrow zone of design freedom into a presence to be reckoned with. This district has, of course, been rapidly changing since the successes of the Tate Modern and the Millennium Bridge, both supported by the fine character of Southwark Station and Palestra — together with Allies & Morrison's Bankside 123. Given its generally forlorn status, this part of Southwark invites strong gestures. And this is exactly what Alsop has provided.

The inevitable comparison one makes is with A&M's similar efforts around the corner. Whereas they strive to be polite, Alsop is straight in there with arbitrary projections and canted columns, offset grids and coloured glass panels — rather like the difference between a twinset and pearls, and some dude strutting his bling. Having said that, Alsop treads a path that makes him vulnerable to the vicissitudes of fashion. As both buildings near completion one has the suspicion, presuming the interiors will be more or less similar (as they invariably are these days), that it is the Alsop design that will win applause. A key difference, of course is their respective relations to street

and, of course, to the Tate. Palestra will be without two runs of retailing arcading to enliven the ground floor. On the other hand, A&M don't strike one as the natural choice for a design to provide popularist places (see, for example, the BBC's Media Village, at White City).

## A & M Studio

This A&M studio (sitting directly opposite Bankside 123) is a welcome addition to this rather dreary street — especially at night, when the façade becomes more lively. The interior is a clever accomodation to a difficult site and is redolent with Tadao Ando undertones and a generally civilised air that befits this practice. The ground floor not only serves as entry lobby, but also provides a rather nice public cafe and a lobby area for seminars and for model displays.

**32**

Southwark Street, SE1
Allies & Morrison, 2004
Tube: London Bridge

**33** *Southwark Cathedral. As it now stands, one experiences a largely C19th restoration, ranging from 1818-1897 and the Cherry / Pevsner guide suggests the need for serious 'architective' work to deconstruct the Cathedral's fabric into latter day and C12th parts (the guide devotes eleven pages to this). The north side has been added to with recent work completed in 2001 (Richard Griffiths Associates), forming a quadrangle and providing the always necessary shop, cafe ('refrectory' to you), library rooms and exhibition spaces in materials striving to harmonise with the Cathedral fabric (e.g. limestone, flint, copper, etc.). Architecturally, these parts are not without interest, although they are wholly in some non-descript historical style. However, a glazed passage between these buildings and the Cathedral itself draws one's attention away from issues of styling to the underlying architectural in the sense of a strategic, dispositional and configurational set of issues. This is claimed to be an ancient alley that has been recovered and repackaged as — wait for it — Lancelot's Link! As ever, such theming merely belies the real architecture, of whatever merits or demerits and in no way assists visitors in realising an authentic meeting with the thing itself. Perhaps visitors should all be given a simple guide that says, 'Damn the history — open your eyes and look! Find the architecture — it's waiting there to enter into a dialogue with you.'*

**34** *The **Jerwood Gallery** (Paxton Locher, 1998; 171 Union Street, SE1) and studios is a scheme refurbishing existing school buildings, providing rehearsal spaces for theatre and dance, offices, apartments, and a strip of gallery space (converted from the old bicycle sheds) together with an adjacent outdoor sculpture court and an adjacent cafe. It is the kind of scheme they are good at: a development equation that balances the client's core 'wants' with the necessary developmental 'needs' which make such projects viable. The spaces to visit are the gallery and cafe since the rest of it is effectively private. The Tate Modern is minutes away.*

**35** *Hays Galleria, Battlebridge Lane, SE1, is a 'U' shaped arrangement of refurbished Victorian warehouses that once grandly formed the surrounds to an inlet into which river barges come in for loading and unloading. Much of this has been retained in the design of Michael Twig-Brown & Partners (1986), except the water has infilled to form a mall and the buildings are now offices for a bank. The scheme has a naturally-ventilated, open-ended, roof structure enclosing the central area, and the ground floor periphery is shops and cafes that have become quite popular. Views to the City, across the river, are also very good. In fact, overall, this has proven to be a fine development, despite the Po-Mo undertones (compare it, for example, with Foster's More London, next door). From here, you can easily walk west to the South Bank, or east to More London, the GLA, the Tower Bridge, and Butler's Wharf.*

# 36 Unicorn Theatre

Tooley Street, SE1
Keith Williams Architects, 2005
Tube: London Bridge

The Unicorn Children's Theatre is a welcome addition to this area and, especially, to More London, neatly twinning with City Hall to make up three utterly disparate building types within this development (all dominated, of course, by the railway station, not to mention sundry venues such as the 'London Dungeon' across the road in the viaducts). Williams' brief was to make the theatre 'rough but beautiful'. He tells us that, "The new building is an asymmetric pavilion. Its elevations are open and transparent where they need to be, revealing the heart of the building to the public, yet elsewhere deliberately solid and cliff like, punctuated by carefully controlled window openings and toplight". Whether you consider ordered formality to be appropriate or not for a children's world is a thorny issue I shall leave up to you, the visitor, to decide.

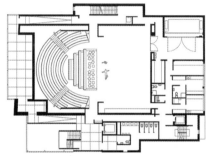

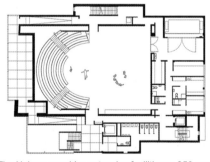

The Unicorn provides extensive facilities: a 350 seat auditorium (the Weston Theatre); a 120 seat studio theatre; a rehearsal theatre, and the usual back-up facilities, including an education room and a multi-purpose meeting room (to the left of the plan). The Weston's geometry uses the 'golden mean' and has distinct Vitruvian undertones.

View down Tooley Street (toward London Bridge Station), with the 'green room' glazed balcony projecting into the street. (More London to the right).

# More London

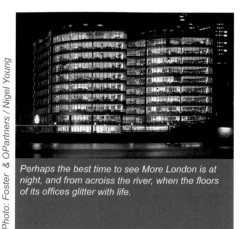

Photo: Foster & OPartners / Nigel Young

*Perhaps the best time to see More London is at night, and from acroiss the river, when the floors of its offices glitter with life.*

This site had been empty for too long, and its regeneration and integration into the urban fabric of Southwark has to be welcomed. The development is also symbolic of the City expanding beyond its traditional boundaries and also of the Thames becoming a unifying feature rather than something divisive between north and south London.

As an urban speculative business park (of 195,000 sq.m.), More London employs the Canary concept of an undercroft service area beneath the buildings. Above ground, its strongest feature is a diagonal pedestrian route that represents a desire line from London Bridge Station toward Tower Bridge, terminating within the development at City Hall — the 'strawberry' of the scheme, as the Japanese used to call such things (very appropriately in this case). This strategic organising principle is quite successful; however, as a main artery of the scheme it deliberately seeks to bypass Hays Galleria and to provide an alternative set of retail attractions at ground level on the basis of an 'It's us or them . . .' argument. It is difficult to see what the alternative might have been, but it is the quality of the architecture that is questionable: the Foster office improvising arguably bland and undistinguished glass boxes (the largest of which holds about 4500 people). These office buildings (plus a hotel, shops, etc.) are mostly large floor-plate structures, sometimes with a central atrium. However, while the architectural equation is competent enough, most of it relies on the novelty of such devices as sliced off and curved ends to unremitting glass façades oriented and engineered to persuade planners that they follow historical precedent and the riverside walkway is not excessively over-shadowed (they are described as 'fingers', in between which light can penetrate). The reality, in some parts, is more akin to desolate alleys. Or did we miss something? Perhaps, when the buildings on the southern side are complete, the development will feel stronger and socially more 'organic'.

*One has to compare More London with Merrill Lynch, the BBC Media Village at White City, Canary Wharf, Paternoster, Broadgate, Regent's Place and Paddington Basin. All represent a now familiar pattern in the contemporary redeveloping of London: large islands of single site ownership posing as a public realm populated by a diversity of building and tenant types. In the background is the instrumental rationale that believes 'if it can't be measured it can't be managed', that every value can have a number assigned to it and that the only thing that counts is the bottom line. This is hardly new, but is a mind-set having an unprecedented impact on London's urban fabric. The indications are that, eventually, any particular equation will mature and begin a second phase, if only because twenty years is a long time in current office design — at which point all kinds of issues arise. Perhaps the most difficult of these is how a dinosaur of a design can age gracefully. Do we simply pull it down and begin again? Or is it more likely that such developments will remain valuable investments but rated as second-class?*

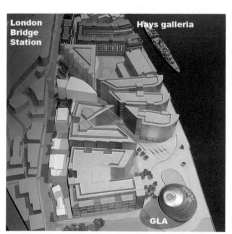

*The site plan of More London slices a strong diagonal desire route from London Bridge Station toward City Hall and Tower Bridge, by-passing Hays Galleria.*

## 38 City Hall

Tooley Street, SE1
Foster and Partners, 2001-2003
Tube: London Bridge

Dubbed by one newspaper as 'Foster's testicle', the City Hall that serves the Greater London Authority and the Greater London Assembly stands in apparent, grand isolation until one realises that the sunken facilities adjacent to the 'blob' tap into an underground service road that caters to the surrounding set of office buildings also designed by Foster for a commercial client who provided the Hall and clearly saw it as the 'strawberry' (as the Japanese would call it) in the development equation. It adds to values but, cannily, only on the basis of a 25 year lease. (One wonders what will happen then; such is the Public Finance Initiative.)

The building was commissioned on a design and build basis from the Civil Service some two years before the electoral elections brought Mayor Ken Livingstone into power. And then — half-way through completion — the client (the GLA) arrived on the scene, with its own interpretation of need. That Fosters were able to adapt such an extremely difficult design on the run, and in such circumstances, is a serious compliment to the practice and the partner in charge, Ken Shuttleworth.

Since it employs the kind of difficult circular geometry that First Year architecture students are told to avoid like the plague, the Hall would have been impossible to imagine, represent or construct without digital technologies and inventive architects. On the one hand, the design is rooted in what the practice achieved at the Reichstag in Berlin: the concept of a glazed assembly chamber acting as an ostensible symbol of transparent democracy. On the other, it pursues a very 'green' agenda, seeking to consume only a quarter of the energy needed by a conventional office building. For example, the exterior spherical form results from the Buckminster Fuller equation of minimum surface area: maximum internal volume. In addition the sphere is distorted to the south, so that its slices of office floors provide some degree of self-shading.

*Figures released in 2005 suggested that City Hall is, in fact, somewhat less 'green' than intended. Whereas a highly 'sustainable' pretension might claim around 120Wh/sqm, City Hall is actually consuming 376kWh/sqm. Its design target was 236kWh/sqm. Whilst this fact engendered much huffing and puffing in the media, it is not a bad performance (although 8% above current guides for best practice even as it is 34% typical practices). Plans are to add solar energy panels to the roof.*

*Above left: the ground floor entrance areas.*
*Above centre; the ramp from the lobby up to the Chamber.*
*Above right: the view northward from the terrace around the 'London Living Room'.*

Access is into a ground floor lobby (which boasts a rather bizarre chromed ceiling) from which there is no choice but to spiral around: either down to a lower floor of cafe, meeting rooms, etc., around to the lift core; or up and around to the public areas giving access into the central Chamber that sits at the very heart of the building.

Around this latter central space is a wrap of offices that takes up some two-thirds of the circular plan. And, on top, sits what is called the 'London Living Room' — an assembly space with surrounding terraces and fine views. Given the building's geometry one might expect tthe offices to be rather difficult but, since opening, the facility managers have managed to stretch their accommodative capacity from about 400 to 650 workers, and it all appears to work reasonably well. (However, that is it: the nature of the Hall's form hardly allows for extensions.And there are the usual complaints about open plan.)

Above the central Chamber soars a spiralling, stepped ramp. However, this is not normally accessible to visitors for rather obvious reasons of security and noise. Instead, visitors normally take a lift to the Living Room and are sometimes allowed (when the Assembly is not sitting, of course) to walk back down the ramp — an exhilarating experience, especially at night. This enables the visitor to see clearly into the office areas and obtain a better idea of how the building functions. In fact, this is the ramp's most useful function: to enable staff to focus upon it and see everyone who comes and goes between floors. Having said that, its varied, stepped spiralling induces the most peculiar gait. And there are fine views across the river to the City.

But one inevitably has to ask: is this compound of glamour and symbol in the public sphere (no pun intended) a clever resolution of a not so clever framing of the design problem? The idea that democracy equates with metaphorical material transparency is absurd. And it has been associated with a difficult circulation system severely compromised by the security issues that have over-run the design. To be fair, the latter could hardly have been forseen and, despite such flaws, the building still bears within it a spirit one has to admire.

**39** *Not so many years ago, **Shad Thames** (Butlers Wharf, SE1; Conran Roche, 1990; Tube: London Bridge / Tower Hill) was grotty and crowded, bearing marks of the questionable romance of East End working class history. Now it is pristine and literally sweet smelling – pleasant and gentrified, especially in the form of the renovated and refurbished Butlers Wharf warehouse, now a large apartment block facing the river. The street has been expertly reinvented, complete with some of the many bridges that once linked the outboard to the inboard warehouses and this small stretch of narrow space between former warehouses from the late C19 has been restored to include a ghetto of Conran restaurants (he lives around the corner, at the top of the former **David Mellor Building** designed by Michael Hopkins). Is it old? new? real? Whatever, it's quite pleasant.*

# London Riverside

**40** *Julyan Wickham's late father-in-law was Aldo van Eyck and one detects vaguely Dutch motifs at* **Horselydown Square** — *a fine development of apartments with shops and offices on the ground floor (Wickham & Associates, 1989; Tube: Tower Hill / Bermondsey). The forms and their detailing are inventive, and unconventional, offering us an unusual English building with some superb compositional plays. Having said that, the piazza at the development's heart is less than successful, being devoid of the vegetation that would have made such a huge difference in this part of London (there is a car park underneath). The scheme may be ageing, but it holds up well.*

**41** *It used to be among the dreariest of river warehouses and then Conran Roche drastically transformed it — the* **Design Museum** — *into a piece of pseudo-Gropius, circa 1930, complete with white render, horizontal windows, etc.; no doubt Pevsner would have loved it (Butlers Wharf, SE1; Conran Roche 1989; Tube: Tower Hill / Bermondsey / London Bridge). One doubts if historic theming was anywhere near the minds of these forthright Modernist architects designing a museum dedicated to mythologising that C20 invention called the design professions, but it might have been. Perhaps the museum takes itself too seriously? Perhaps it should have gone all the way and invented some ostensibly forgotten Modernist author from that era, faking the whole thing: background, associations, etc. . .Why not? The ground floor has a shop and cafe; the permanent museum and the gallery are (somewhat concealed) upstairs and the Blueprint restaurant fronts the first floor. At the time of writing the Museum, is looking for a new (and better located) home.*

**42** *Apparently people steal the parts off this intricate, swivelling, pedestrian bridge called* **St. Saviour Dock Bridge** *(Nicholas Lacey, 1997). Perhaps it's a way of saying it is rather overdone and needs pruning back. Nevertheless, it is a virtuoso example of stainless steel design, especially pleasant when the tide is low, mud is revealed, and boats in the inlet (once berthing a dense pack of barges nestling up to the warehouses) sit at odd angles whilst they await the return of the tide and the heavy timbers which stop boats crashing into the bridge are fully exposed. (It is easy not to see these as a part of the design.)* **New Concordia Wharf**, *on the east side, was one of the first warehouse conversions in the area (Pollard Thomas Edwards, 1981–83).*

**New Concordia Wharf** *and similar warehouses here were among the first to be converted and become desirable residential buildings. However, this did not last and, whilst the focus of activity shifted westward again (e.g. to Butlers Wharf), the eastern stretch between Butlers and Rotherhithe remained derelict until about 2000 on, when the dynamic returned and there was an evident push from the east end of Butlers onward — all of which is indicative of just how long it takes to regenerate such areas, despite closeness to Tower Bridge. (There is a tendency to think the relevant period of Docklands regeneration has been short; in truth, the docks closed in 1970.)*

**43** **The Circle** is typical CZWG's Po-Mo inventiveness: a concoction of throwaway pieces rooted in a single idea and put together with panache: in this instance a blue forecourt feature of glazed bricks at the heart of this 302 unit apartment complex, created out of the notion of a huge glazed jar, broken into pieces (in reality, more reminiscent of towering and threatening owls!) The other key feature is a series of balconies ostensibly propped by large timbers. It's all very serious in attempting not to be conventionally serious, but even if the informing meanings are inconsequential and loaded with contradictions, they are at least entertaining. However, inside, the apartment plans are ordinary and the corridor-access unpleasant, betraying the facade as quick-fix, one-liner architecture. And for that there is no excuse but to blame the developer. Interestingly, even though stylistically dated, the development appears to hold its own. (Queen Elizabeth Street, SE1; CZWG, 1989; Tube: London Bridge / Bermondsey.)

**44** This now ageing Po-Mo apartment and office building (**China Wharf**; Mill Street, SE1; CZWG, 1988; Tube: Tower Hill ) still presents a strong river facade whose red, cut-out and profiled frontality wilfully adds to the scenic qualities of the river edge. Its vaguely Chinese (?) quality is striking, but the most bizarre touch is the rear end of a boat, set cantilevering from the building and acting as a balcony at about the right height for it to float on a (very) high spring tide – probably among the more genuinely witty touches CZWG has offered because it is rooted in context rather than being a throwaway feature. The land-side, responding to different conditions, is simpler but equally characterful: white concrete and deeply fluted (apparently a reference to long-gone silos), with inset windows angled to catch views and any available sunlight.

Immediately to the east of China wharf is another Gough design on the river's edge: a riverside house complete with cantilevering stairs and well worth a look — not the greatest design in the world but one that clearly enjoys the location and strives to make the most of it (2000; photo right).

**45** Thie Mellor Building (Shad Thames Street, opp. New Concordia; Michael Hopkins & Partners, 1990) started off as a building for the kitchen utensil man, David Mellor, and ended up with Terence Conran's penthouse on the top. Ever since construction it has stood out as a fine, simple building (exposed concrete frame, with lead side panels) in contrast to most other buildings within Butlers Wharf.

A similar white block next door is by Conran Roche, 1998; designed as offices, never occupied and bastardised into apartments.

# Docklands & Greenwich

*Right: the tidal Deptford Creek, adjacent to the Laban Centre*

## Docklands Notes

The area downstream of London Bridge, around the Tower of London, used to be known as The Pool: a densely packed scene of ships, boats, warehouses, every imaginable kind of associated trade and not a little criminal activity. In a boom-time London of the late C18 congestion became so bad that the idea formed of developing the flat, marshy areas to the east and in a period between 1790 and 1830 a remarkable series of engineering undertakings gave London an array of tidal docks and new, secure warehouses, many protected by high walls and defensive moats. Beyond these arose the East End – an area of housing for the workers who toiled in the docks and the sometimes foul industries which made the place into a backyard for London, its pollution removed from the rich merchants in the City and the politicians of Westminster by the prevailing south-westerly winds.

Managerially, the docks were never a success. Even at the height of the British Empire, after the Port of London Authority had been formed to administer the wealth imported from this, the world's first global empire, the docks remained problematic. And so matters remained until well after WWII, even after awesome wartime damage. However, change was coming. Whilst traffic was at its historical peak, in the 1960's, the revolution of mechanisation and containerisation was about to change everything. By 1970 most of the docks had closed, traffic was going through new container docks at Tilbury, at the mouth of the Thames, and London was confronted by a vast area of derelict land. (In 1980, Dockland was described as, "a tip: 8000 acres of forgotten, and to be forgotten, wasteland".)

*Above: the rear end of boat cantilevered out from China Wharf — a welcome o]piece of fun and a rare example of an architectural joke that actually works.*

*Below left: the Millennium Dome Centre: the view west from one of Canary's tall buildings.*
*Right: the escalators at Canary Wharf Jubilee Line station.*

What to do? The first ideas were mixed. Mysterious fires burned down some fine warehouses and well meaning managers and politicians infilled many of the docks, hoping to create large, flat areas of land suited to industrial sheds and a tradition of manufacturing that was almost over in the London area (the service economy was about to be dominant). An autonomous 'development area' was formed, free from what was seen as a sentiment of reactionary, left-wing instincts within local boroughs suffering an obsession with traditional forms of employment. Backed by tax breaks, newspapers were attracted from their historic location in Fleet Street to decant into new facilities, taking the opportunity to reform outmoded labour practices — in the process engendering serious riots. Such was the character of Margaret Thatcher's regime of change in labour practices during the early 1980's, but — with hindsight — its was during this period that (for better or worse) the foundations were laid for later periods of economic and urban change.

*Comparisons are currently being made between the 36 sq.km. of Docklands and the 518 sq.km. of proposed development area called The **Thames Gateway**, that area to the east of London, around the mouth of the River Thames. Here, it is propsed to provide some 200,000 new homes and controversy currently rages between visionary plans that positively anticipate rising sea levels, and others oriented entirely toward 'build-it-quick' instrumentality.*

Slowly but surely a vision of what was possible became more optimistic and more ambitious. In the 'bubble economy' of the mid-1980's Docklands became a minor boom town in itself, making and breaking developers' fortunes. Industrial workshop schemes turned into proposals for offices and studios. Housing opportunities were eagerly grasped, particularly by the newly enriched 'yuppies' desirous to live adjacent to the City, by the river, and in warehouses now lent romantic overtones (the loft phenomenon had arrived from New York, even as graffitti went up in Wapping encouraging the locals to 'mug a yuppie').

At the heart of it all was the Canary Wharf scheme that had lifted the stakes as high as they could go – presuming that is, that the government could be persuaded to support the kind of infrastructural changes that could get commuters in and out. However, by 2002 the capacity of the Docklands Light Railway (initially a rather toy-train effort routed on formerly disused tracks) had been substantially extended (and continues to be pushed further out), the Jubilee Line Extension had been constructed (just in time for the Millennium and the opening of the Dome), the London Docklands Development Corporation had handed everything back to the local boroughs, and housing developments were everywhere. There was much to criticise, but a huge part of London's urban fabric has been renewed, leaving the East End as the local memories of a disappearing population and a stronger virtual reality in the form of a popular TV soap opera.

And it is upon this basis that London has been appointed as the Olympic city for the 2012 games. This will greatly promote the historic shift from a westward to an eastward orientation of urban development and, at its heart, will be Canary Wharf: now central to easy links between, on the one hand, the West End, and, on the other hand, the Stratford area that is crucial to the Olympic dream and to the government's even greater dream of a 'Thames Gateway' development that will absorb much of London's appetite for new homes.

*Above: 'The Diner' at Container City*

*Right: Richard Wilson literal 'piece' near the Millennium Dome.*

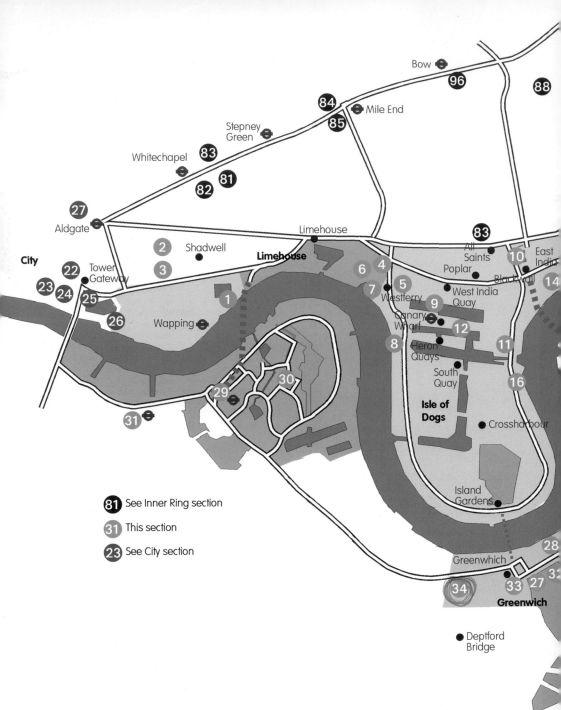

Bow

96

88

84 Mile End

85

Stepney
Green

Whitechapel

83

82 81

27
Aldgate

Limehouse

83

City

2 Shadwell

3

Limehouse

All
Saints

10 East
India

22 Tower
Gateway

6 4

Poplar

Blackwall

14

23

24

25

7

Westferry

West India
Quay

5

9

26 Wapping

Canary
Wharf

12

8 Heron
Quays

11

South
Quay

16

29

30

Isle of
Dogs

31

Crossharbour

Island
Gardens

28

81 See Inner Ring section

31 This section

23 See City section

Greenwhich

34

33 27

32

Greenwich

Deptford
Bridge

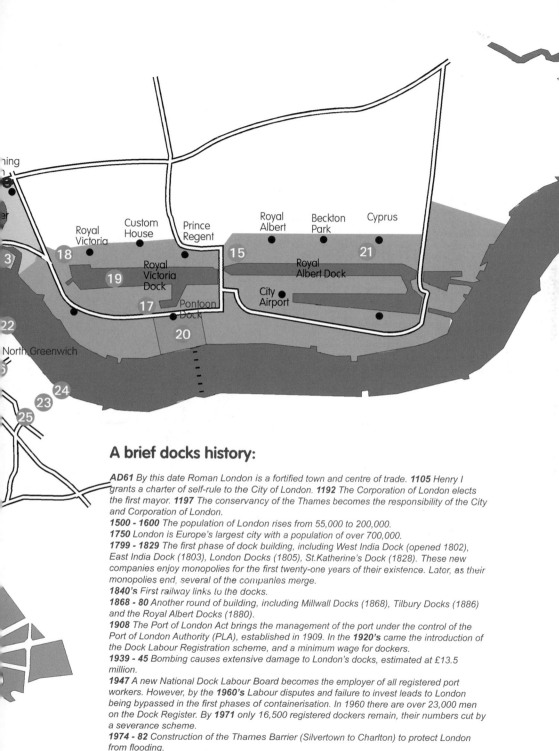

**Royal Victoria**
**Custom House**
**Prince Regent**
**Royal Albert**
**Beckton Park**
**Cyprus**

Royal Victoria Dock
Royal Albert Dock
Pontoon Dock
City Airport

North Greenwich

## A brief docks history:

*AD61* By this date Roman London is a fortified town and centre of trade. *1105* Henry I grants a charter of self-rule to the City of London. *1192* The Corporation of London elects the first mayor. *1197* The conservancy of the Thames becomes the responsibility of the City and Corporation of London.

*1500 - 1600* The population of London rises from 55,000 to 200,000.

*1750* London is Europe's largest city with a population of over 700,000.

*1799 - 1829* The first phase of dock building, including West India Dock (opened 1802), East India Dock (1803), London Docks (1805), St.Katherine's Dock (1828). These new companies enjoy monopolies for the first twenty-one years of their existence. Later, as their monopolies end, several of the companies merge.

*1840's* First railway links to the docks.

*1868 - 80* Another round of building, including Millwall Docks (1868), Tilbury Docks (1886) and the Royal Albert Docks (1880).

*1908* The Port of London Act brings the management of the port under the control of the Port of London Authority (PLA), established in 1909. In the *1920's* came the introduction of the Dock Labour Registration scheme, and a minimum wage for dockers.

*1939 - 45* Bombing causes extensive damage to London's docks, estimated at £13.5 million.

*1947* A new National Dock Labour Board becomes the employer of all registered port workers. However, by the *1960's* Labour disputes and failure to invest leads to London being bypassed in the first phases of containerisation. In 1960 there are over 23,000 men on the Dock Register. By *1971* only 16,500 registered dockers remain, their numbers cut by a severance scheme.

*1974 - 82* Construction of the Thames Barrier (Silvertown to Charlton) to protect London from flooding.

*1981* London's Docklands Development Corporation (LDDC) is set up and authorised to spend public money in buying up derelict and empty docks to build offices and housing. Closes 1998; 'de-designation' had started in 1994.

*1987* Docklands Light Railway opens at an initial cost of £77 million. *2000*, Jubilee Line extension opens. Some 35 years afer the docks closed, the regeneration effort is still going on throughout the East End.

# Docklands & Greenwich

## 1  Wapping Project

Shadwell Basin, E1
Architects Shed 54, 2000
Tube: Wapping

The Wapping Project at Shadwell Basin is the reinvention of an old hydraulic pumping station (1890), one of five that used to serve the West End, now converted into a restaurant and art gallery by Jules Wright and her architect husband, Joshua (Shed 54). It's a superb conversion — a balance of old and new, where knowing 'intervention' (why do architects use that aggressive term? policemen intervene, not designers) or its avoidance manages to produce an authenticity that is all too rare, especially where food and art are concerned. The entry space and the adjacent hall (bottom right) were given a new timber roof and diners sit on Charles Eames chairs midst the machinery. Beyond that is a large space for exhibitions and installations. These parts are linked to upper parts by an external galvanised stair and upper deck that links to large old water tanks awaiting future conversion.

Wright imbues her gallery with a 'no bullshit' undertone affecting everything about the place and it is surely one of the most worthwhile projects in London. And, since the restaurant is actually good and its profits enable the art programme to function, you should have something to eat when you go there!

*Also take a stroll around the area, around Shadwell Basin, its housing (old and new), maybe pop into the Prospect of Whitby pub opposite.*

## 2

*Nicholas Hawksmoor's baroque church, **St. George-in-the-East** (1714–29), is a haunting burned-out shell, within which there nestles a much smaller, 1960's church. It sits opposite Tobacco Dock, on The Highway, E1 with a dark, brooding quality that belongs to a church programme intended to bring moral order to the irreligious masses of early eighteenth century London. This is Hawksmoor expressing that notion of the Divine as something wonderful and sublime, but somewhat 'terrible'. Details have a chunky, robust and brooding quality.*
*St. Anne's, Limehouse, is another Hawksmoor church dating from the same period. Also compare with St. Luke's.*

## 3

*Tobacco Dock (Pennington Street, E1. Terry Farrell Partnership, 1987; Tube: Tower Hill. DLR: Shadwell) was a commercial failure but remains interesting: the original Georgian, high-tech sheds, with wonderfully thin and elegant roof members, together with impressive brick vaulting at the lower level (all 1806); and also for Farrell's restoration work and the creation of steel and cast-iron façades for the shops. The massive surrounding brick wall is original, indicative of how defensive the docks once were (pilfering was big business).*

## Limehouse Houses

Ropemaker Field, E14
Proctor Matthews Architects, 1996
DLR: Westferry

**4**

This terrace of 11 town-houses, with their 'layered' façades, stands out by being simple and self-evidently well-designed. Elements such as the entry gate, concealment of utility meters and bins, balconies to a first floor *piano nobile*, the grouping of windows and the cornice-like attic storey, indicate careful composition and detailing. The pergolas to balconies are typical of attempts to provide a sense of comfort and security, their wood detailing corresponding to that of the windows so that the various elements are unified.

*This scheme becomes more interesting when compared with the practice's later work on the Greenwich Penninsula, at* **Millennium Village** *(the area master-planned by Ralph Erskine), where the basic motifs are still employed, but now in galvanised steel and with considerably more (and questionable) gusto. And it is hugely more civilised than the practice's work at Baron's Court.*

## Westferry

Westferry Studios
Milligan Street, London E14
CZWG Architects, 1999
DLR: Westferry

**5**

This Westferry scheme sits among the better part of CZWG's work, despite its in-your-face debt to a mix of Frank Gehry and Robert Venturi. Described as a "groundbreaking scheme providing affordable living and working space for aspiring new firms in docklands, aimed at small start-up businesses", the building is notable for its upbeat graphics in brickwork on the principal frontage, and an entry court with access balconies, stair and lift at the rear. The development comprises a mix of 9 commercial units and 27 rent-controlled live-work units providing 'affordable' accommodation and, in order to reduce costs, minimum-specification shells were provided so that occupiers could tailor units to their own requirements.

**6** **Roy Square**, *in Narrow Street, E14 (Limehouse), is an Ian Ritchie design from 1987. The scheme is an exception to the neo-Victorian blocks that were also being constructed at the time. Ritchie has created an urbane 'hollow block' of 77 units formed into four pavilions accessed from a shared, central garden court that is also a podium above car parking. The formalism owes much to Georgian precedent and aims for a similar, calm regularity. It is worth looking at, but there is a security gate and visitors are not usually welcomed into this self-contained development. Compare this development with Ritchie's* **Regatta Centre** *of twelve years later (Royal Docks).*

**7** **Dundee Wharf** *(Dundee Wharf, Limehouse, E14; CZWG, 1998; DLR: Westferry) is a large, quirky block of 160 flats argued to be contextural, polite to neighbours and properly responsive to its position on a river bend. The apartments form a 'U' shape on plan, enclosing a private access and parking space conceived of as a 'new urban square'. The design is actually its 'kerb appeal', principally achieved by the likes of idiosyncratic brick coping details at roof level and a daringly disconnected 11 storey tower of balconies (said to refer to travelling dockside cranes). Other balconies, being 'V' shaped, are ostensibly a reference to ships' loading booms. (That's what they say.)*

## Docklands & Greenwich

**8**  **Cascades** *(2-4, West Ferry Road, E14; CZWG Architects, 1986–88; DLR: Westferry, Canary Wharf) is one of the most successful CZWG designs, towering high even before Canary Wharf arrived and a breakthrough against high-rise living prejudices well before towers once more became appealing to popular tastes. In the late-1980s it was a yuppie symbol but during the recession prices had plunged low enough so that the local authority was purchasing them as housing the homeless. Now we're back where we were. The long, spinal diagonal – important to the difference with conventional towers – can be explained as a fire escape but its form derives from the way apartments have been arranged and oriented to obtain good views. Much effort has gone into breaking any monolithic qualities the tower might have had. As one of the better housing developments of the earlier phases of Docklands regeneration, it is worth comparing with current parallels in apartment block living in London. (Compare with Rogers' Montevetro)*

**9**  *This is an elegant* **footbridge** *(North Quay/West India Quay, E14 ; Future Systems. Engs: Anthony Hunt, 1995 ; DLR: Canary Wharf). The floating concept lends it a metaphorical 'liveliness' to set against the ponderous formalism of Canary Wharf's first stages. However, although it looks as if it could float away (or be taken away overnight), it is necessarily anchored on sliding connections to concealed concrete piles under the water. The central portion is hydraulically operated (assisted by counter-weights) and opens to allow boats through. But there is a curiously neo-militaristic undertone — as if some romantic, war-weary 'band of brothers' was about to march over.*

**10**  **Robin Hood Gardens** *in Cotton Street and Robin Hood Lane, E14 (DLR to Blackwall; by Peter and Alison Smithson, is one of the few projects that London has seen from this team (see the Economist, in St James's). No student of the 1950's–70s would offer them less than hero worship and this polemical scheme is all about streets in the sky and attempts to make medium to high-rise housing work. It's a rather sad, bleak place and no amount of lyricism about its authors can ameliorate its failures, so typical of many '60's housing schemes. But if these architects are your heroes, you should get here and take a look.*

**11**  *Will Alsop's tiny dock gatehouse perched at the end of a steel stalk (and located at the east end of the Canary complex, on the roundabout) has somehow managed to survive the years of change all around it. It's minor, easily missed, but fun and witness to his inventiveness, even at this scale.*

# Docklands & Greenwich

## Canary Wharf

This instant Gotham City (master-planned by SOM in Chicago) started off almost accidentally during the early 1980's and grew into a speculative North American vision profoundly challenging to British architects as well as to the City of London. The first phase (around Cabot Square), up to the 1990 recession, was almost entirely North American: the initiatives, the money, the designs, the construction management. When this ended the banks took over a bankrupt development, only to have the original speculators buy it back and bounce into a booming second phase initiated in the mid '90's. What has been crucial to this success had been the DLR (Docklands Light Railway) and, later, the Jubilee Line extension. Significantly, the maturing development now incorporates some apartments, a hotel and extensive retailing (the mall is now a major East End venue) as well as additional offices. About 25,000 people worked here in 1999 and 65,000 by 2005 (in eighteen office buildings). This is set to rise to about 90,000 at full potential.

Initially denigrated by London's architects, Canary Wharf has settled down as an accepted feature of the metropolis, although still with a surprising lack of integration into the surrounding fabric (a difficulty slowly being eased as the developement grows and a deliberate policy of diversity and disinvestment by the current owners progresses, but one the highway infrastructure hardly facilitates).

The gloriously dominant building of the first phase was the stainless steel clad Canary Wharf Tower (One Canada Square), 50 stories and 114,751 sq.m. (net), floating on a raft 4m thick, in turn supported on 22 piles going another 30m into the ground, designed by Cesar Pelli, who also designed the first stages of the central shopping building and the DLR station. It was an instant London landmark, now rather unfortunately absorbed by surrounding towers. The squat, first stage lower buildings surrounding the Pelli tower were by a variety of architects: Pei, Cobb, Freed & Partners; Kohn Pedersen Fox; SOM; and Troughton McAslan (the lone British firm). All are undistinguished, although interesting

*As the Thames Gateway (the proposed residential developments for the Thames estuary area) and the 2012 Olympic facilities develop (at Stratford), Canary Wharf will find itself as a key location between these and the City and West End. Ironically (and unexpectedly), its underground shopping malls have already become a major weekend venue.*

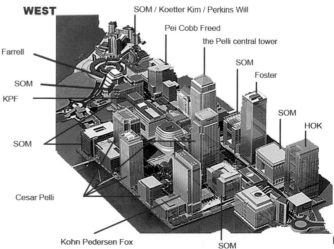

**163**

for their Po-Mo and mish-mash of Chicago-Paris values that pretend to be English: real power-dressing of the kind that frightened and offended the native architects.

During a late '90's Canary's second phase Foster built a tower for Citigroup (the relatively low, 52,284 sq.ft. 33 Canada Square) and put One Canada Square under competition with a 41 storey building of 102,191sq.ft., designed for HSBC on the north side of Canada Square (no.8). Both are rather bland. Meanwhile, SOM had dumped Post-Modernism, discovered a more European form of contemporary modernism and were designing a series of lower buildings of about 50-55,000 sq.ft. But the better designs are the neo-1950's buildings from Cesar Pelli (such as the 112,000 sq.ft 25 Canada Square building, and the 97,500 sq.ft 25 Bank Street, and from Kohn Pedersen Fox (e.g. 10 Upper Bank Street, 93,000 sq.ft). (*Note: all figures given are in sq.ft because agents addressing global corporations still insist on using those figures; just divide by 11 to get the approximate area in metres; or 10.76 if you want to be precise*)

The contrast between the first phase and second phase buildings is interesting. Step into the former and one enters a world removed from daylight, a realm of deep, cavernouse spaces and singularly uninspiring interiors locked into some pompous, post-war banker's tradition. Enter some of the later buildings — and the Barclays HQ stands out, with interiors by Pringle Brandon — and one is aware of a different agenda concerned with literal and metaphorical lightness. This ambient difference hardly shows up at the level of plans and grids.

Overall, Canary Wharf is a fine example of an instrumental, global capitalist equation: an artefactual office park pretending to be a vibrant part of the city. You either belong or you do not, and a constant filtering is always taking place. Later phases have been supplemented by peripheral hotel and residential developments and the whole has always been rendered more palatable by the palliative of an art programme aiming to create ostensible intimacy within the enormous spaces, but the place is haunted by an underlying monotime. It is interesting to note, however, that the current owners have admitted a policy of tenant diversification and are even selling off some of the buildings — a hugely significant landmark in the project's development toward long-term organicity.

Canary Wharf's character as a managed, homogenous beast largely incapable of organic change might always remain its Achilles heel. But it is nevertheless a fascinating product of our times, and worth studying. (Try 4.30pm on a Friday summer evening, when the place comes alive.)

*A typical Phase One 'club-like' interior.*

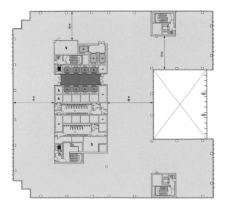

*Above and left: plan, typical atrium and entrance lobby of the Barclays Bank HQ. The building design is from HOK and the interior fit-out is Pringle Brandon. The fit-out is interesting, but security policy prevents further elucidation (!).*

*An example of Canary's first phase buildings from the late 1980's: SOM in full-blown Post-Modernist mode, designing a 'London' building while in the Chicago office. The reality is a return to an American Beaux-Arts tradition and dark interiors. Right: looking down upon a latterday example of SOM's work at Canary (in the second-phase).*

## Canary Wharf JLE station

*The **Jubilee Line Extension** project gave London eleven excellent, architect designed stations (heavily assisted by a JLE team that receives less credit than it deserves). Foster's grassed-over Canary Wharf station design owes something to its precedent at Bilbao and a bit to Stansted as well, but this one is much larger in scale and capacity (it is intended to serve up to 40,000 people per hour, served by twenty escalators — more traffic than Oxford Circus). Underground, it is a huge hall (280m long by 32 m wide and 24 m deep; about as long as the Canary tower is tall), typologically similar to that designed by Will Alsop adjacent to the Millennium Dome, but bigger. Much bigger. Above ground, it manifests as a double-curved glass canopy that belongs to a family of such forms the Foster team adapts to a variety of projects at a variety of scales (e.g. the air museum at Duxford) — like a swollen airplane cockpit bubble. Below ground is veritably Piranesian: gigantic forms, given flow, elegance and the scale of a Italian fascist train station! It's superb. The aim (characteristically) has been simplicity and clarity, avoiding a clutter of signage and producing a calm ambience enhanced by the sweeping curves of the concrete structure. Lighting has been an important feature of the design and the entry bubbles scoops enable daylight to penetrate the interiors and draw travellers out into Canary. Station servicing is via concealed gangways, entirely behind the scenes. Lighting is by Claude and Danielle Engle. The total area is about 31,500 sq.m.*

### 13 Container City

Trinity Pier, Orchard Place, E14
Nicholas Lacey and Partners, 2002
DLR: East India

The LDDC designated this part of the Docklands — Trinity Wharf, once owned by the people who trained light-house keepers on site — as a place for artists to let cheap space. Its developer (shame it's not a cooperative . . .) uses redundant containers as a relatively cheap and quick way of doing this. It's all based on the UK economy's import-export inbalance that leaves quiet parts of the country stacked with empty, old containers. Windows are cut, doors fixed open to support balconies, external staircases added, insulation sprayed on the inside, plasterboard linings put in place . . . It's all fairly straight-forward. Interestingly, the first phase has been 'architected' by Nicholas Lacey. This makes sense, but somewhat knocks the edge off a naive romance about shanty towns in London. A second phase is more knowing and strives for less overt architectural gamesmanship, although it still demonstrates a striving to provide a real sense of place within its arrival court. Local planners have

been supportive (but probably traumatised). As an aside, it is interesting to note that as Container City has established itself and become more successful as a live-work community security and the like has been put in place and it is beginning to pose as less bohemian and more corporate. Such is the gentrification of containers.
*Left: just to remind you where it came from — Habitat '67, Montreal.*

### 14

*There is something defensive and castle-like to many of Rogers' designs and this is no exception (a building for **Reuters**). It sits against the river, has multiple power connections and back-up systems, and is characterised by an air of paranoia which surrounds the place with guards, fencing and cameras. The building houses telecommunications equipment for an agency whose services are crucial to many finance houses – information worth millions. And they don't want anyone thinking it might be easy to knock the building out. It's really a big machine, with a few inhabitants, a relatively low-cost shell but expensive internals. These qualities are emphasised by the massive air conditioning plant taking up the two upper levels. The architect's ability to be more playful is restricted to perimeter escape stairs and a separate cafeteria pavilion with riverside views. (St. Lawrence Street, E14; Richard Rogers Partnership, 1990; DLR: Blackwall)*

## Regatta Centre

Royal Albert Dockside Road, E16
Ian Ritchie Architects, 1999
DLR: Royal Albert Docks

This club and adjacent boat house — described by its architects as a 'robust intervention' (whatever that means) — could have been one of the finest buildings in Docklands (sited at the end of an Olympic standard 2000m rowing course within the old dock), but adjacency to an over-bearing DLR line, the windy bleakness of the Royal Docks, and an incongruous fit-out have all fought that possibility. Nevertheless, the architecture has some fine qualities and is worth visiting, especially on a sunny day. On a grey winter day, its pavilion schema is both literally and metaphorically exposed as inadequate to the prevailing conditions (invariably more windy and colder than central London).

The Centre comprises two buildings: a Boathouse and ancillary workshop of approximately 1150 sq.m., and a Clubhouse which includes changing rooms, gym, restaurant and bar facilities (at first floor), short term residential accommodation for athletes, and a unique, powered rowing tank which utilises flowing water to simulate open water rowing.

The single-storey boathouse shed is defined by the free-standing gabion walls and a lightweight stiffened catenary stainless steel roof. The more robust clubhouse building sits back from another, north-side, gabion wall to create an access buffer zone spine running the length of the building frontage. Terraces on the second level project over the gabion providing interesting viewing from the bar and restaurant.

But then there is the damnable presence of the DLR . . .

**16**  *This **pumping station** has to be one of the more challenging and daring of London buildings: one that some people find offensive to their sensibilities and ideas of architectural propriety, but it is a building full of ideas, challenges and enjoyment — a most peculiar mix of fun, seriousness, erudition and skill. What you see on the exterior is the wrapping to a massive engineering pump installation that discharges surface water into the Thames. But what fun Outram has had. He explains the design almost mythologically: the pediment is like a mountain; the columns are trees on the mountain; water runs from a cave (the fan) and down to the plain where the water runs over the area around the buildings*

*as different coloured blocks; and the sides of the building are layered as if ground strata. The front gate includes a middle-eastern 'evil eye' (we are not sure what it is warding off) and the decorative scheme is pure beaux arts (in the manner of recreated, painted, classical temples) with a slight Chinese influence. There are even references to the work of Alvar Aalto in the way the side pilasters have been clad in half-tiles. Nevertheless, whatever Outram's rationale, the fan and pediment have the formal playfulness of a 1950's child's drawing of a propeller-driven aeroplane and the colouring is like a cross between Classicism and a Chinese pagoda. On top of all that, Outram is sincerely concerned with honest, explicit construction of an entirely Modernist manner. He desires everything to be functional and he wants you to know how it's all put together. For example, he uses the columns with pre-cast capitals ('blitzreig' concrete made from redundant broken bricks) as duct risers, the fan is entirely functional, exhausting any build-up of methane gas, and the outer walls are bomb-blast proof. All in all, it's a rich architecture, not only erudite in its search for meaning, but significant at the more immediate level of an experience of the thing itself, in all its directness. Few architects — anywhere in Europe — have dared to employ such an agenda and play such a game. To call the work Post-Modernist does Outram a disservice. (Stewart Street, E14; John Outram, 1988; Tube/DLR: Canary Wharf)*

# Docklands & Greenwich

**Peabody trust housing**
Evelyn Road / Boxley Street, E16
DLR: Custom House (north side) or new station
at Thames Barrier Park

The area around the Royal Victoria Docks is witness to some 35 years of Docklands regeneration — an undertaking that has only slowly crept eastward (and will possibly do so more quickly now that we have the Thames Gateway concept and the 2012 Olympics). It is here — on the south side of the docks and near to the Thames Barrier Park — that we find a group of three housing projects that tell us much about London's contemporary architecture.

All three projects have the Peabody Housing Trust as their client. That's where the similarity ends. The oldest of the three is, as it were, the real thing: what Peabody normally does (five storey, pitched roof block with lower terraces in between). Except as a contextural background of academic interest, you could ignore this work. In front of this relatively large, multi-storey development is two 'experimental' schemes promoted by Peabody. Both have similar briefs, serving small households at the lower end of the social spectrum (typically being aimed at 'key' workers). Both are by 'young' practices with strong reputations. And both are worthy of your attention. But that is where all similarity ends.

The first of these 'experimental' schemes is by Ash Sakula and seeks to continue and terminate a long existing terrace of rather mean dockland worker homes, keeping to their height and (rather bizarrely) continuing the strip of garden in their fronts. It comprises four apartments (see plan overleaf). The aesthetic keynote of this scheme — faced in yellow corrugated plastic — is one of deliberately irreverence and being 'in your face' in the sense of directness, lack of conventional fussiness and an implicit denial of formal values. The second experimental project is by Niall McLaughlin. As befits this man's poised erudition and declared 'Miesian' training, his design strives to strike a note of considered detailing and aesthetic cool that is entirely different from the more funky ambitions of Ash Sakula. This is an architect who delights in formal games and he offers us two in particular.

*The magically irridescent quality of McLaughlin's facade shows up even on the most grey day.*

*The modern Peabody: the 'experimental' housing is in the foreground; the real thing that Peabody normally builds is in the background. The Ash Sakula housing is immediately opposite (out of camera shot, to the right).*

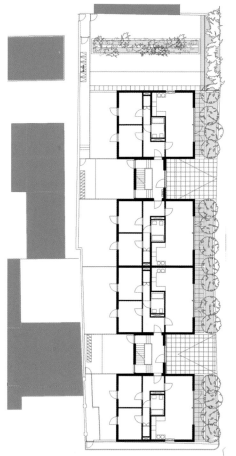

The first is one of scale: one looks at the three blocks of 12 apartments and sees four storeys — and then looks more carefully and notes there are, actually, only three levels. This obfuscation is encouraged by the blocks' most diversionary architectural feature: their glimmering south façades. You might at first think this is solar panelling, but this is England 2005 and such devices are still rare. No, it is entirely an aesthetic conceit — a very successful one, but (disappointingly to most people) without any impact whatsoever on the interior.

Two further things are interesting about these projects. The first is the planning. Whereas McLaughlin provides a well-considered but orthodox plan which never betrays an allegiance to a kind of neo-Miesian order, Ash Sakula dare to aspire toward something more spirited and ambitious: for example, minimising the conventional room sizes and enlarging the circulation so that the hall becomes a living space. The second is that, although the AS housing nudges around the edges of a frontier aesthetic not a million miles from timber packing crates, the Mclaughlin housing strives to provide a narrative overlay akin to those provided by Libeskind, revealing historical traces which might literally inform the aesthetic of the blocks i.e. the wooden packing crates once common in docklands. These — with their irridescent steel straps — are given as the inspirational source of the architecture's motifs. Like all such architectural conceits — no matter how clever — they serve to flatter clients and planners, but are of questionable pertinance to the lives of a generation who probably have little or no memory of the docks and enjoy no particular sentiment that lingers over its sometimes unsavoury history. On the other hand, it is clever. One hesitates to declare which scheme is more appropriately and considerately addresses the philosophical question of 'ought' and everyday issues of dwelling. You literally pay your money and take your choice. (Incidentally, the officer within Peabody who promoted these — and Bedzed in south London — received little thanks for his diversionary experimentation).

---

**18** This **pumping station** at the Royal Docks (west end, Tidal Basin Road, E16; Richard Rogers Partnership, 1987) looks utterly different to Outram's, but they are both equally expressive as well as sharing the common denominator of brightly coloured paint. Outside, it is all pipework, industrial railings and ducts like ship's ventilators. Inside, it is basically the same, although the engineer's plans do look more elegant. The aesthetic is reminiscent of an architect's idea of either ship or an oil rig (take your pick) and, in that sense, is profoundly romantic as well as functional and instrumental. From that perspective, the design is not so far away from that of Outram as at first seems.

**19** **Royal Docks Bridge:** This competition-winning bridge has been offered in two stages. The first provides a purely pedestrian link across the dock and the second will add an enclosed, travelling car slung beneath the bridge. At the moment, it's a gesture awaiting potential users among those who will live along the Royal Victoria Dock. The southern termination is at a small, semi-circular apartment block leading through to the first of the housing developments. It is quite a structure and comparatively large, but shrinks against the massive scale of the Dock.

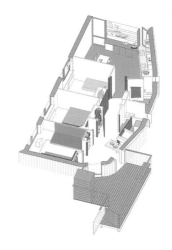

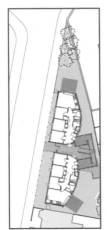

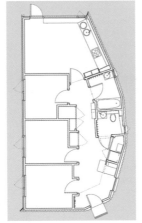

*The internal planning of the (symmetrically arranged) Ash Sakular apartments is well-considered. The exterior treatment raises eyebrows — this part of Docklands hardly carries the refinements of Knightsbridge, but the 'stockade fence' front gate is tonally idosyncratic (timber posts plus corrugated plastic with coloured wire inserts plus Astroturf corner edging) and quite out of tune with the McLaughlin references.*

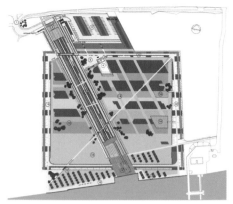

# Thames Barrier Park

North Woolwich Road, E16
Groupes Signes, Patel & Taylor, and Arup Engineers, 2000
DLR: Prince Regent, Custom House

We are familiar with the park in its manifestations as Renaissance garden, the apparent informalities of the English landscape tradition, and the dense, formal cuteness of the Victorian municipal garden. Within the Renaissance tradition, mannered artifice was everywhere self-evident, mostly as geometry coloured by symbolism and myth. In the English tradition, artifice is at once concealed as an 'improved' nature and made explicit as artefactual contrivances such as the resident hermit, grotto, folly, and ornamental cottage — aesthetics devices less concerned with ratiocination and its manifestation as something erudite and clever. Against such a background that we have the Thames barrier Park: a post-modern municipal park returning to the explicit formalities of the Renaissance, now in the guise of public art, Anglo-French style. After a long absence, geometry has returned as the tool of artifice and contrivance. The folly is there as public loo and café (an elegant neo-Miesian exercise in timber from Patel & Taylor), with the equivalent of the band-stand, now as floating canopy propped with irregular columns vaguely evocative of a farmed pine forest. The tradition of the walled villa garden is now a huge slot (appropriately reminiscent of a dock) that wilfully slices through the landscape and manifests a taming and repression of the underlying industrial pollution, dominated by playful geometric delights and fragrances that thrive in its microclimate, and oriented toward the Piranesian engineering act that keeps modern central London from drowning: the Thames Barrier. Even the edge of terraced housing (by Goddard Manton) is reminiscent of the grand terraces of Regents Park (now with, of course, nautical overtones). This is the culture of the West End coloured by Francophile influences and introduced into the formerly industrial docklands of the East End as a civilising act of vision and reform serving a programme of urban reinvention within the new Town tradition. However, the place is simultaneously a local park — somewhere to walk the dog and play with the kids — and deeply embedded within a London tradition of open spaces that have always served the needs of a growing, changing city: a successful ornament to London. So what is the problem? Lack of proper maintenance, which the local municipality has only more recently sought to attend to.

## The Design

*The designer's challenge was to create a park from a heavily polluted wasteland adjacent to the City Airport, linking it into a larger urban design framework of urban renewal and regeneration that includes an extension of the Docklands Light Railway (DLR) along the park's northern boundary. The key elements of the park include a 'green dock' (instead of a 'dry dock'), a permeable eastern edge of housing (originally intended to be a series of pavilions rather than the solid terrace implemented and fenced off by Barrall), a water feature, a street entrance, a plateau of greenery and trees with subtle changes of level, a network of paths that cross the park and leap the dock as steel bridges, and a riverside walk and performance area (now a memorial pavilion).*

*The 'dock' is a topographical slice between the direction of the bridge over the Royal Dock and the Thames Barrier, emphasising a potential linear movement from the Barrier to the DLR and Excel Centre on the northern side of the Royal Victoria Dock. This formally planted device is 6m deep at one end and 4m at the river end, creating a microclimate a few degrees warmer than the surroundings. A 100m rebuilding of the river wall and adjacent walk area (separated from the plateau by a ha-ha), where a dock was once located, includes a tall canopy (The Pavilion of Remembrance) propped by a random set of steel columns simulating a grove of trees (in a distinctly neo-Barcelona style). Another pavilion (more in the tradition of 'the primitive hut' as revisited by Mies) serves as toilets and a cafe, and has a concrete service part married to a green oak frame with glazing in between — it's a fine building.*

*The park's axes link to surrounding developments prompted by the 24 acre park, potentially giving a local population of about 30,000 people who could, one day, be using the park.*

*The area to the north of the Park (which includes the so-called 'Silo D' building) is to be called the Sivertown Quays / Pontoon Dock development. This 24 hectare scheme will include an aquarium as well as housing.*

# Docklands & Greenwich

**20** The **Thames Barrier** — one of London's best loved engineering structures — is the capital's flood defence: the end of central London and its true river gateway with a very serious defensive role to play. If necessary, water flow can be stopped by six huge steel gates (1500 and 750 tonnes) which rotate up from the river bed. The gear for all this is within the zinc-clad, sculptured housings that straddle the river. It's an impressive sight, underscored by the massive dangers to life and property if the system doesn't work when the occasional mix of conditions arises that places central London at risk of flooding. The engineers were Rendel, Palmer & Tritton (1984). A visitor's centre is on the south side (Unity Way, off the Woolwich Road), but you'd be better off just seeing the engineering itself, probably from the Thames Barrier Park side.

**21** Ted Cullinan's **University of East London** Docklands campus design for 3000 students is strung out along the northern edge of the Royal Albert Dock (DLR to Cyprus). At its core is a building described as a 'pedestrian hub' — meaning a stubby east-west 'street' that feeds into the various facilities on either side. Along the (windy) dock edge itself, a series of brightly coloured, isolated residential towers lend an identifying theme to the campus. One suspects that a design strategy predicated on the idea of pavilions keenly rationalised in terms of net:gross and available funds — rather than a network of outdoor spaces and people places — is at odds with the exposed conditions of the Victoria Docks. (Bring back the cloister?)

One of the more pleasant parts of the park is this simple pavilion from Patel and Taylor: Tado Ando meets Mies meets the Abbe Laugier's dreams of 'the primitive hut' — all of it complete with capuccino and public lavatories. The cafe part is a post and beam construction in green oak — immediately grey, cracked and redolent with not inappropriate rustic ovetones. Patel & Taylor, as executive architects, did all the detailing within the park and also designed the memorial pavilion adjacenet to the Barrier (a rather Barcelona-inspired structure emulating a grove of trees, with 'random' columns and a flat, sheltering canopy overhead.

# Millennium Dome

The Dome — an attempt to recreate the success of the Great Exhibition of 1851 in 2000 — was a brilliant way of doing something inherently stupid. The project's fundamental problem was that it became a symbolic act founded upon an abstraction (the number 2000), and a set of arbitrary forms madly searching for an appropriate, celebratory content (required to be at once meaningful, significant and entertaining). In reality, the project became its own content (the only authenticity about the whole thing). The Rogers' part (the driving partner was Mike Davies) included the tent, the peripheral plant housings, the interior comfort pavilions, and the central arena, together with overhead gantries, lighting rigs, etc. It was and remains gutsy stuff that any architect would be proud of. The basic figures include coverage of more than 8 ha, over 12,000 piles, 12 bright yellow masts, each 90 m long and stacked on 10 m high steel 'quadrapods', holding the 400m diameter cable-net structure which is about 50m high at its apex. Because the site was formerly a gas works, the engineering included the careful isolation and capping of more chemical nasties than one likes to think about – resulting in a profoundly symbolic equation combining a balance of dream and nightmare. So, the real heroes of the phenomenon were surely Buro Happold, the engineers on the project. The Dome has always had an 'about to happen' future that never materialises, but the 2012 Olympics could change that — for a while.

*Since the Dome is currently surrounded by a security fence denying access, I suggest you view it from the perimeter walk around the Peninsular, or from the north side of the river e.g. at Trinity Buoy Wharf (Container City). The building is currently being converted for events and - they hope - a casino.*

**22**

Gate 1, Drawdock Road, SE10
Richard Rogers Partnership, 1999
Tube: North Greenwich

*Take a walk around the tip of the Greenwich Peninsular (e.g. walk westward from the Yacht Club near to the Millennium housing) and you'll see sculpture of a scale to suit the river. 'Quantum Cloud' (left) is by Antony Gormley; the 8m ship part is called 'A Slice of Reality' by Richard Wilson.*

## 23 Millennium Housing

Greenwich Millennium Village, John Harrison Way SE10
Ralph Erskine (with Proctor Matthews), 2201
Tube: North Greenwich

Ambitious plans for inhabiting the Greenwich Peninsula have been master-planned by Rogers and then by Farrell, and taken to a detailed level by Erskine Tovatt Architects, with EPR and Proctor Matthews (who designed the second phase of housing within the Erskine framework) as executive architects. Like BedZed, it's a very green scheme with 'low energy impact' ambitions and much talk about 'self-sustainability' [sic].

Essentially, the scheme is a series of taller apartment blocks surrounding low-rise terraces with mixed accommodation types. The former are in concrete and the latter are timber and steel framed. Efforts have been made to keep the car at bay whenever possible, but this surely runs against the grain in such an environment. Even though the Jubilee Line is ten minute walk away across the Peninsula's pleasant but wind-swept park designed by Robert Rummey, this remains as implicitly car-based as any suburbia.

The timber-framed and light steel framed terrace designs are certainly upbeat and well considered (apart from some notorious noise transfer difficulties), but (as with BedZed) one has the feeling that the fiercesome, extrovert cheerfulness of it all and the symbolic proclamation of values might overwhelm the less extrovert personality. Will it last? Can it be easily maintained? Will the upbeat tenor of it all pale? (Will the potential scheme even be fully constructed?) At the time of writing the answers appear to be positive, as another concrete-framed block by the late Erskine is erected. Certainly, the location — within minutes walk of the Jubilee Station and easy access to the road network — suggests long-term success for the peninsula. Nevertheless, the Proctor Matthews designs prompt issues about English housing design and comparisons with what is deemed to be both preferable and acceptable in other European countries (most foreign architects I have taken there are not impressed by the mix of materials and features).
*Also see Baron's Court, p.244.*

*The Erskine apartments.*

## 24 Yacht Club

Old Greenwich Yacht Club, 1 Peartree Wharf, SE 10
Frankl & Luty, 2000
Tube: North Greenwich

Designed to exploit panoramic views, this yacht club building (unusual in London, but the club was founded in 1908) is possibly an example of suburbia creeping in and linking up with the Docklands redevelopment (and welcoming visiting sailors): the river here is wide and useable in a manner hardly feasible further upstream. Whilst the building itself — the social focus of the Club — sits 45m offshore on an existing jetty, the boatyard and parking area is on the land side (on the other side of the riverside walkway recently constructed). And Clare Frankl, one of the designers, is even a member of the club!

## School / Health Centre

**25**

50 John Harrison Way, SE10
Edward Cullinan Architects, 2001
Tube: North Greenwich

Cullinan's school and community building extends this architectural practice's impressive portfolio of social work and has many of the old Cullinan features, updated by a younger generation in the office. Designed to provide education, health centre and act as a community centre (with crêche, one-stop advice centre, sports facilities, etc), the more private sides of this low-energy building face south to landscaped garden areas; the more public faces are faced in 'rippling' vertical larch boarding and introduce a timber fortress keynote that is at once playful, endearing and somewhat peculiar.

**26** *North Greenwich Jubilee Station*
*has two parts: a massive underground concrete box, 400 m long, 30 m wide and 25 m deep, by Alsop Lyall & Stormer and, above ground, a bus station beneath a curved, flowing, metal roof designed by Foster & Partners. Alsop's gutsy, Piranesian design employs huge diagonal struts covered in blue mosaic. These carry the roof structure and the suspended concourses, whilst blue glass panels screen ducts help and lend the interiors an especially lively spirit. The Foster station is designed as a large, bird-like, curved roof that draws vehicles beneath sheltering arms, low on one side and opening up on the other, the curved, 'shell' roof appearing to be 'draped over' (not propped by) a forest of structural 'trees' is not entirely convincing and it is not until one is in an aeroplane taking off from the City Airport, when the 'big roof' idea become readable and convincing, taking on the form of some beautiful giant moth hugging the ground.*

## 27 Maritime Museum

Romney Road, Greenwich, SE10
Rick Mather / BDP, 1999
DLR: Cutty Sark

The National Maritime Museum is a part of the Greenwich Palace and Naval Hospital complex designed by Sir Christopher Wren and adjacent to the Queen's House designed by Inigo Jones, with access from both the north front of the building and the west colonnade of the Queen's House. In addition, it sits on the edge of one of London's finest parks and an old village area now accommodating the Cutty Sark and offering a very busy weekend market. Access can be via the DLR at Greenwich or via the old Victorian pedestrian tunnel under the Thames between Greenwich and Island Gardens (another DLR station).

    The key to the design is Mather's enclosure of the central courtyard and the insertion of a single-storey building with an upper podium (where a cafe is located). Together, these elements hold the complex together and, from all points, give a central reference. The design is simple and robust and Mather even provides an uncharacteristic, seamless extension of the existing classical detailing.

    Visitors enter through the triumphal arch of the existing building, into a lobby area and then out into the lofty enclosed courtyard where there is a central block and cafe mezzanine (the roof – at 2500 sq.m. – is claimed to be the largest free-span glass roof in Europe; see his similar but smaller exercise at the Wallace Collection). From here, there is direct access into two floors of galleries, where Mather's hand is always evident, sometimes in spite of the tacky entertainment quality that typifies some of the gallery exhibits. Other accommodation includes a restaurant, library, shop, etc. (as you would expect).

**28** *Trinity College of Music (a distinguished music school) occupies the east wing of King Charles Court (in what became the Greenwich Naval Hospital, now Greenwich University), designed by John Webb, 1662-69. The interiors were always utilitarian and McAslan continues in this mode with a low-budget conversion. There are plans to roof over the central courtyard. (Univ. of Greenwich, King William Walk, SE10; John McAslan + Partners, 2001; DLR: Cutty Sark Gardens)*

**29** *Like North Greenwich, this Jubilee Line station in Surrey Docks designed by Eva Jiricna is in two parts: the **Canada Water JLE** (1999) underground platforms and a bus interchange above ground. The main part of the scheme is a large, cantilevering bus shelter and ancillary accommodation. Below ground works are by the Jubilee Line Extension Architects, who engineered and detailed a concept design by the late Ron Herron (a typical procurement route for most of the Jubilee Line stations). Also see Ian Ritchie's Bermondsey Jubilee Line station in nearbt Jamaica Road.*

**30** *Surrey Docks is now a maturing development within the context of the Docklands regeneration exercise and is worth a visit for that very reason. Take a walk, for example, from the Design Museum to Rotherhithe and walk along the water feature at the heart the former docks (now mostly infilled, apart from Greenland Dock).*

*Richard Reid (responsible for some notable housing designs and Epping Town Hall, 1990) designed **Finland Quay** (at Onega Quay, off Redriff Road, SE16, Surrey Docks east) as a 'necklace' of 7 pavilions designed at a time when Po-Mo architects felt they were rediscovering a warm and comfortable vernacular tradition. (The housing market didn't discover Modernism until the mid '90's.)*

*The Lakes housing scheme (also here in the east of the Quays), designed by Shepheard Epstein and Hunter, 1990, Norway Dock, Redriff Road, SE16. An unusual scheme: many of its detached, suburban villas are romantically surrounded by an area of shallow water which lends the development a special character.*

*Wolfe Crescent (CZWG, 1989; at the heart of the area) includes some pleasant 4-storey apartment brick towers that sit adjacent to the small, central canal. Their nearby terraces are also interesting.*

*Whilst in this area it is worth walking between Rotherhithe (on the western side of the docks) and Bermondsey, where a mix of old and new has produced a convivial ambience. One can say something similar about the Bermondsey / Cherry Garden Pier area further west again. Look out for* **St. Mary Rotherhithe**, *a church by John James of 1716 (in St. Marychurch Street). And see Hawkins Brown's* **Hope (Sufferance) Wharf** *(Rotherhithe Street, SE16) — four storey terraces completed in 1999, leading onto the river. Alternatively, get there by walking from City Hall (see diagram).*

*Overall, Surrey Quays provides a good case study in London housing during the 1980's — an intermediary phase between the social housing provision of the 1950's and '60's (best seen in areas such as Camden) and the 'modernist' taste suddenly discovered in the mid 1990's. It is some somewhat incongrous: suburban values in the heart if the capital. But this no doubt is a strong value for those who live there and, during a period, when many more apartments are constructed than houses, possibly enhancing the area's value in the long-term.*

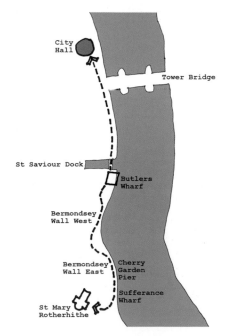

**31** *Ian Ritchie has designed* **Bermondsey JLE Station** *(in Jamaica Road) and three nearby vents: one in Ben Smith Way, of wavy concrete forms; one in Durands Wharf, looking like an up-market pill-box (both these designs close the vent with cable-net) and one in Culling Road, adjacent to Southwark Park. The latter is perhaps the most interesting, being an exercise in playfully cladding the large vent with bands of pre-patinated copper cladding — apparently, to keep the nearby funeral director happy. The station itself is most interesting inside.*

## Docklands & Greenwich

**32** Immediately adjacent to the Maritime Museum is Inigo Jones's **Queen's House** (1616–35; enlarged by John Webb, 1662). This is England's first Palladian villa, described by Pevsner as being shockingly chaste and bare when constructed and designed by a significant architect given the attribute of Vitruvius Brittanicus. For some peculiar reason concerning convenience, Jones's design straddles the former road to Dover, making it novel as well as architecturally pretentious (the road was diverted north in 1693). Internally, as one might expect for a neo-Palladian villa of this date, the underlying keynote is a profound concern with number, proportion and geometric harmonies. The colonnades linking the building to the NMM are by Daniel Alexander, 1807-16. Inside, there are some impressive (if sparse) spaces (esp. the central cubic hall). The current entry arrangements (and misc. disabled access issues) were dealt with by Allies and Morrison.

Go here and perhaps make a comparative visit to **Kenwood House** in Hampstead in order to see what a later generation — the Adam brothers — was making of the suburban London villa.

The **Royal Observatory** Greenwich (Wren & Hooke, 1675-6) is just up the hill, in Blackheath Park (from which you'll get splendid views). This is currently undergoing refurbishment etc. under the guidance of Allies & Morrison. (A new 120 seat planetarium is planned for completion in 'Spring 2007'.)

Apart from the remaining City churches, the two most important Wren buildings in London are **St Paul's Cathedral** (p. 51) and the **Royal Chelsea Hospital**. The latter was intended to house some 412 veterans and was mostly completed by 1692 (two additional courts being started in 1686). It comprises a three-sided court, with accommodation on two opposite sides and a chapel and hall in the main part. Parts of the comples are open daily. (Royal Hospital Road, SW3)

**33** Across the road to the Maritime Museum (on the east side of Greenwich village) is the former **Greenwich Naval College** and Hospital, a palatial, scheme now partly taken over by the University of Greenwich. Much of it was planned by Sir Christopher Wren (1696–1702); other parts are by Nicholas Hawksmoor, James Stuart, Yenn, and John Webb (son-in-law of Inigo Jones). As well as being listed Grade 1, the building is a World Heritage Site (see the Painted Hall and the Chapel). It is well worth a visit, particularly since such grand, baroque formalities and axial gamesmanship are comparatively rare in this country (especially within the London area).

Another significant building in this area is Nicholas Hawksmoor's church of **St. Alfrege** (left), built 1712–18 (Greenwich High Road, SE10). It was bombed during WWII and the interior is a reconstruction, but the exterior still bears Hawksmoor's trademark. The pedimented portico onto the street is especially impressive. Greenwich itself is an interesting London 'village', with a central weekend market and — as its central feature — the Cutty Sark, which sits in a dry dock.

## Laban Centre

Laban Centre, Creekside, SE8
Herzog & de Meuron, 2003
DLR: Greenwich

The Laban is the kind of brief and project content most architects would die for: some 8000 sq.m. of facilities for the country's premier dance school. A tight budget, yes, but Herzog and de Meuron have injected the project with the kinds of decision-making that carefully allocate available funds. It's cheap 'n' cheerful, but with elegance and wit — a refreshing place to visit that provides a level of architectural gamesmanship that is rarely experienced in London (or anywhere).

Intended as the catalyst of regeneration in the area (the borough is one of the most deprived in the country), the new building sits astride Deptford Creek and reinvents a former refuse depot, populating it with a 'pavilion in a landscape'. It is, as the architects claim, respectful, sensitive, and engaged — although the area offered little enough to engage or respect. Strategically, the architects have attempted to create a dialogue with this weak context — principally in the form of a façade curve (distinct, but hardly generous) that orients this and the entrance toward Thomas Archer's St.... Paul's Church, Deptford (1713-30; a superb baroque work and the only building of merit within quite a distance). They then develop the concept of interior arrangements as an urbane village, with streets, courts, views (for example, to the church

again) and the presence of nature — once again adopting weak contextural references (e.g. street lines), but using them strongly and consistently. A basic conceptual narrative is thus provided and the design is given 'coat-hangers'; it's all rather arbitrary, but it works.

Herzog also refers to the design as 'figuratively' oriented rather than 'systems' oriented — a building that is 'a vibrant, inspiring focal point for the community, accessible and welcoming all', one that implicitly negotiates an instrumental agenda. On the other hand, there were clearly budgetary and programmatic pressures that suggest the design as a dual personality, with one architectural narrative on the outside and another on the inside. Externally, the reality is that the Laban is actually a simple, compact, low-energy, low maintenance shed which comes close to communicating itself as a proverbial black-box fortress with constant CCTV surveillance, set well behind a tight perimeter security fence and defensive landscaping — all of which is disguised and glamourised by softly tinted polycarbonate cladding and the long curve to the principal façade. And, internally, one notices that the entrance arrangements have obviously been impacted by late-design instructions for coping with security. The power of a simple equation of Director's office / reception desk / cafe / and ramp up to the auditorium entrance is intruded upon by barriers and restricted access arrangements at odds with the fundamental design.

Perhaps one carps. But there are some curious design decisions that have been made. One of them appears to be to have a 'tight skin', without openings. This means that the black-tinted glazing of the cafe — located on a south-east corner, adjacent to the Creek, does not open up onto a nearby terrace — even though the camera-scanned no-go zone between entrance gate

*View down entry ramp towards the entrance. The projecting element at ceiling level is one of the two central courts.*

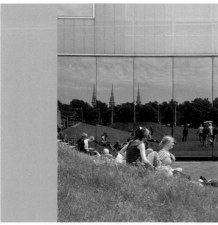

*The exterior areas are very pleasant but strangely cut off from an internal life, as if they have been reluctantly accepted into the general scheme and seek to disguise their other reality as a security zone.*

and entrance door is strongly landscaped and argued to be intended for recreation and performances. It's all somewhat at odds with the PR-speak.

From the outside, it is not until the light fades that the vibrant richness of the interior is revealed: a place of colourful streets and courts and internal transparency, with 13 dance studios, offices, a 300 seat auditorium (with public programmes), a dance health suite, long ramps and all kinds of internal delights tempered by the consultancy of artist Michael Craig-Martin. It is here that the architects have been able (despite the budget restrictions) to exercise ambition and real skill that 'dances' (one has to say) between the strictly programmatic and the poetic. In other words its a terrific building to be in and use.

The roof of the (apparently two-storey, but actually three-storey) concrete structure is pitched (and also the place of deliberately cultivated inhabitation by rare Redstart birds!), so that the upper interior studios all enjoy different configurations and personalities. These (as well as offices and other rooms that subtly background themselves) are accessed from wedge-shaped 'streets: carefully considered, front-to-back corridors dealt with as sensuous, lively spaces that feed one's ears as well as one's eyes, their geometries informed by alignment with the Creek and the main street, thus generating the wedge geometry.

It may be flawed, but the Laban is a rare kind of architectural gamesmanship that offers genuine satisfaction and commands admiration: an inner, as well as an outer, landscape rooted in the idea that the interior is as much an urbane village as the outside community is — the former described by Harry Gugger, the building's design partner at Herzog & de Meuron, as "an urban life within the envelope".

But one wonders about the fundamental strategy, even before the architects drew a line. The Goldsmith's campus, where the Laban was located (and which retains a building used by them), would have been hugely and more plausibly improved by a new building like this in its midst. Instead, we were given a Will Alsop's arts building providing kind of injection. If the Laban had stayed on that site, the Goldsmith's campus (a fascinating urban mix) would have been extremely strong; almost anything would have helped Deptford Creek.

*View from the entry gate toward the pavilion.*

*The two black concrete spiral stairs penetrating the black flooring are expressionistically strong features.*

*The Laban's internal corridors are especially characterful and almost always provide some link to externalities. Even the cross-corridors relate to the two internal light-wells.*

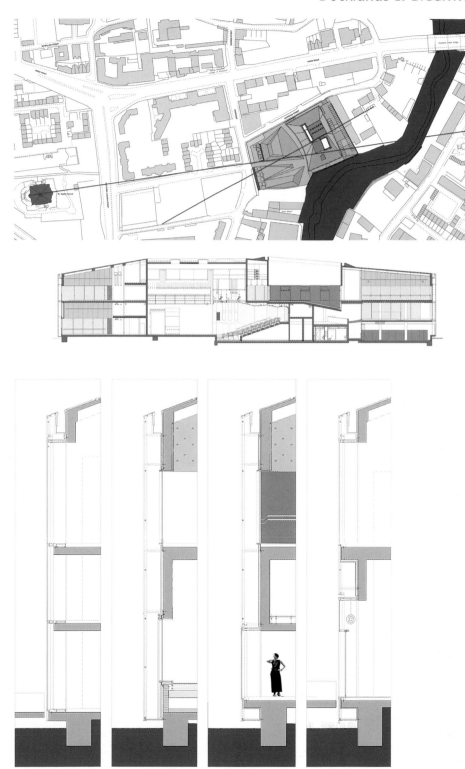

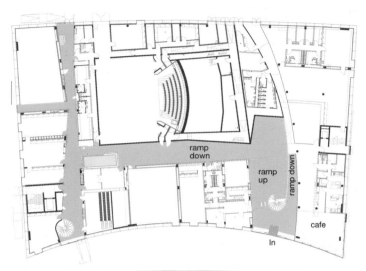

The Laban has an internal architecture that is at once simple and complex. Tightly bound within the confines of the external geometry which arbitrarily accords with geometric abstractions, the internal arrangements struggle for coherence and actually win through. What reads, on the outside, as two levels is revealed, on the interior, to be more complex than that.

The ground level introduces the user to what is, in essence, a simple circulation routing — which immediately splits into ramps leading up and down, and even up in order to then go down! Note the lecture theatre on the ground level.

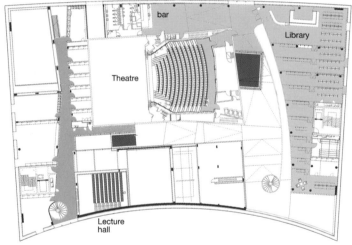

The so-called mezzanine level has two principal parts: the lobby and access to the theatre auditorium as well as the school library; and — at the opposite end of the building — an access corridor to offices and dance studios.

The latter are dotted around the place and all appear to be different. Most are to be found at on the upper level (below).

Two other (orienting) features should be noted: the two light-wells; and the two large spiral stairs.

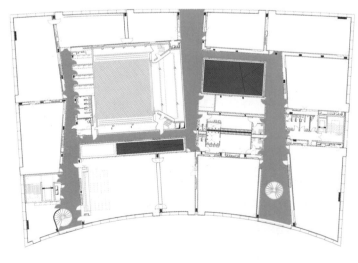

Staff are given facilities that would make Scandinavians blush in horror, but this is England. Academic staff have windowless box rooms where tutorials can be given. But it all appears to work quite well — above all in the dance studios.

Each corridor is given a diverse geometry that widens out to an external view. That above the main entry door is on an axis to St. Paul's church — the only, as well as a worthy — baroque work of architecture to the west.

## Features of a personal top list (no order) :

*Each of the recent buildings I have chosen is flawed. But then name me an architecture anywhere that isn't. To note this is not to carp or be excessively negative, but to acknowledge both a truth and the fact that it is exactly such flaws that metaphorically let us in — that enable us to penetrate the architecture, accommodate it to us and vice versa. To quote Harry Gugger, the partner in charge of the Laban design, "There is no solution. There is always only an idea. And it works in some parts, and works not so good in others. Nothing is perfect. In architecture this is certainly true". One could easily be philosophical on this point, quoting the likes of Hegel and Zizeck. One could also quote cultural traditions which invite the 'deliberate flaw'. But any ruminative architect considering the wonder that anything of merit is ever realised would be forgiven a neglect of deliberate and artful flaws. Contingent impediment is sufficient!*

*Another point of note is that these current favourites only make sense when set against the background of all the other buildings of note in London — and when I say 'buildings', I am conscious that one is often referring to parts and isolated features (as well as those characterful places made up of groupings of buildings): London is a city of the 'almost all right' and is best enjoyed on this basis i.e. as a rich mix inviting discovery. In the words of the late Theo Crosby, "Much of the pleasure of cities comes from small scale, invention and complexity: a doorway, a bay window, a spire, an element suddenly seen and exploited in the context of the street. These are fragments, the result of intelligent intervention or forethought, that provides the markers by which one remembers and creates a mental structure of a city. [...] It is those fragments [...] that remain memorable. [...] To recognise the [architectural] language and the players, to be able to see the jokes, is the richest pleasure of living in cities; to play the game is in itself a mode of establishing identity". (from The Necessary Monument, 1970).*

*The contemporary buildings listed on the right are merely a tiny part of such a scenario.*

• **The Laban Centre**
Why? Although I query its location and cannot get excited about the site strategy, the Laban is possibly the most masterful piece of contemporary architectural gamesmanship in London, lifting that bar and asking for a native equivalent. But a visit is almost deceptive; one has to study the plans and sections in order to understand what is going on and what moves have been made to realise a design making the most of a constrained budget. Certainly, no other London educational facility comes anywhere near the quality of this building.

• **Fawood Nursery**
Why? I believe that Fawood marries intelligence with considerateness and artfulness — qualities that are surprisingly rare in architecture. It's on-target and — incidentally — a complement to the Swaninarayan Mandir temple just down the road and Wembley Stadium on the other side of the North Circular. No other nursery in London comes near it. few other buildings mix such intelligent considerateness and outrageous playfulness.

• **Idea Store nr 2**
Why? The very notion of an 'idea store' is nauseating and this place is still far from what one expects of a good metropolitan library, but Adjaye here demonstrates some of the promise that media hype has already attributed to him. It's cheap 'n' cheerful and the client has screwed up some principal intentions; however, the Idea Store — like Alsop's Peckham Library before it — delivers an architecture of substance.

• **Institute of Cell & Molecular Science**
Why? One wonders if plans for the exterior will ever come to meaningful fruition and, on the inside, the 'pods' simply don't work as well as they should and nor are they well detailed. However, this is a great place for the post-graduates who use the place and will be (when they complete it) terrific for visiting children. In having such ambitions, the brief is unexpected, generous and (again) intelligent. And the design takes it head on.

• **One Centaur Street**
Why? It's simple. It's unpretentious. It's refreshing and poses as if site constraints and a ludicrous adjacency didn't exist. London needs much more like this.

• **Chelsea College of Art**
Why? (Possibly in spite of themselves) Allies & Morrison have here pulled off an artful mix that has the new dancing around in between the old bits, enlivening them, changing them, releasing potential: it's fine gamesmanship again. If they gave up doing worthy office buildings we might get more of this quality of work from them.

• **Hampton Gurney School**
Why? BDP's efforts on this tight corner site hardly constitute a poetic wonder, but this is damned powerful stuff that delivers an architecture whose benefits are literally and metaphorically multi-layered. The kids, teachers and parents clearly love it.

• **The Wood Street *assemble*, in the City**
Why? Because there is no equivalent in London of such a mix of new buildings in an aged part of the metropolis by — I admit — equally aged, establishment architects. Terrific fun to read, juxtapose and deconstruct.

• **Silvertown**
Why? Niall McLaughlin and Ash Sackular at odds with one another against a background of dreary residential orthodoxy is a rare mix illustrating aspects of the mixed architectural values enjoyed in London.

• **The Great Court, British Museum**
Why? Despite implausible aspirations regarding routes across town, the Great Court — like the work Spencer de Grey also realised at the Royal Academy — is a marvellous architectural work almost justifying that horrible term 'intervention': truly a worthy architecture and beneficial collaboration with possibly the UK's best engineers, Buro Happold.

The Inner Ring referred to by this section actually goes quite a way out from the centre, embracing most of C19th developments and taking us into those areas developed to serve the motor car in the period prior to WWII.

184

# Inner Ring

*Right: Cumberland Terrace, on the Outer Ring Road of Regent's Park.*

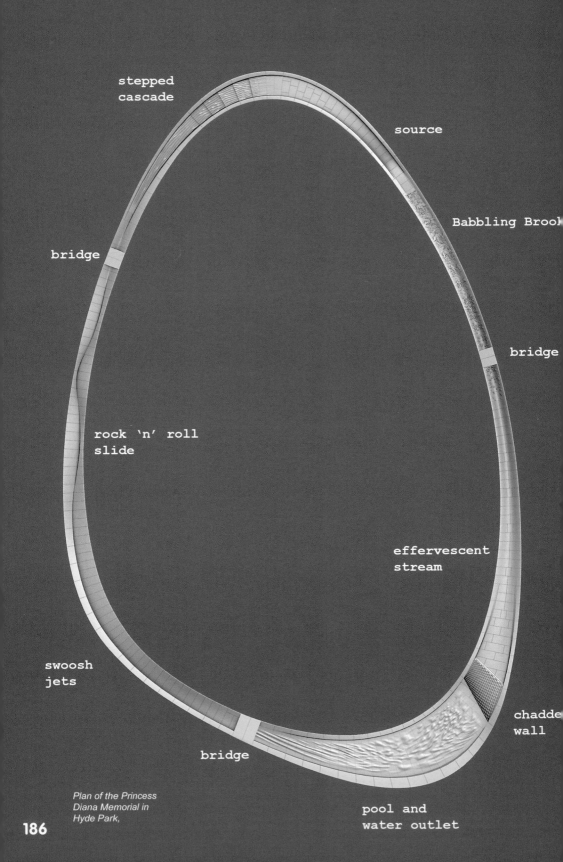

stepped
cascade

source

Babbling Brook

bridge

bridge

rock 'n' roll
slide

effervescent
stream

swoosh
jets

chadde
wall

bridge

*Plan of the Princess
Diana Memorial in
Hyde Park,*

pool and
water outlet

There is a degree of truth in the generalisation that the 80:20 rule applies to London's architectural geography: most of it is central, approximately within the Circle Line. But one of the things emerging in recent years is a novel spread of architectural commissions across the capital — in part, because much of this work is residential. But there is still a bias toward distinct pockets of development and toward the East End and Docklands. Some of the reasons are obvious; others are to do with arcane issues of location value and development potential. However, it is true that it is worth getting away from the centre and exploring London's outer areas.

In this section we indicate where the better architecture is outside the City and West End. As always, boundaries are arbitrary and merit does not respect them, so it is worth cross referencing the maps along their edges, looking for adjacencies and accessible groupings.

The map divides between the north (numbers in deep red) and the south (rather fewer numbers in orange) — a schema I justify on the basis of convenience rather than any geographical prejudice. In fact, south London has become a vibrant area of general development, rich in character and nowadays much more accessible because of an improved bus system.

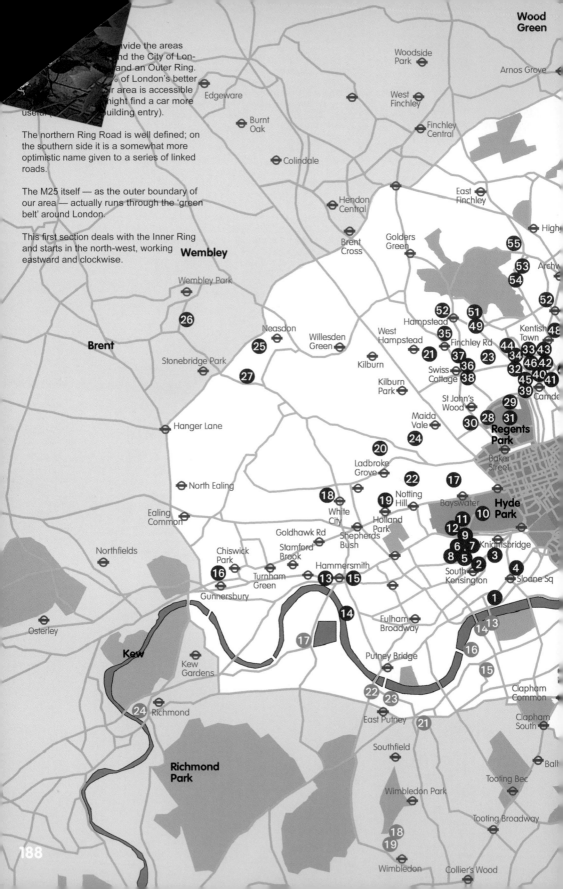

...vide the areas
...d the City of Lon-
...and an Outer Ring.
...% of London's better
...r area is accessible
...ight find a car more
...uilding entry).

The northern Ring Road is well defined; on the southern side it is a somewhat more optimistic name given to a series of linked roads.

The M25 itself — as the outer boundary of our area — actually runs through the 'green belt' around London.

This first section deals with the Inner Ring and starts in the north-west, working eastward and clockwise.

## Inner Ring

Tite Street, SW3
Tony Fretton Architects, 2002
Tube: Sloane Square

### 1 Red House

Not your average house, but a design for an art collector within the more than average affluence of Chelsea. The design is mindful of the street history and plays contextural games that politely front an interior arrangement that is distinctly pre-WWII: an entrance to the left for staff, a car bay in the centre and the owner's entrance on the right (compare with Goldfinger's house). The double height piano nobile ('salon') echoes the traditions of the Georgian London terrace house, but is clearly for entertainment, with a 'small living room' to one side and a concealed mezzanine library above. An attic storey is set behind a parapet — a retreat for hedonistic pleasures, with guest bedrooms and an outdoor 'tropical hot-tub' with planted courtyard. All this is faced in a sensuous red limestone.

    *Also see the **Camden Arts Centre** (p.206) and the **Lisson Gallery** (p.105).*

**2** *The mosaic wrapped **Ismaili Centre** near South Kensington Station (Cromwell Gardens, SW7; Casson Condor, 1983) is an unusual piece of Modernism in the Islamic tradition — sounds awful, but it's actually very good and in no way is a pastiche of anything. It sits as an island, scaled to nearby houses, chamfered to give them daylight, with a top floor garden, with escape stairs at each corner and the content of the design strives for an Islamic spirit without obvious quotation. On the first floor is a large prayer hall and the roof has a delightful garden. (Often open for Open House.)*

**3** *This building at **60 Sloane Street** SW3 was Stanton Williams's first major job (assisted by YRM; 1994). The challenge was to convert and extend an existing 1911 building of some character. The outcome is an elegant marriage of old and new, the latter betraying distinctly Catalonian architectural traits as it marries itself to the older five-storey block and integrates itself behind and above the two-storey wing, as if the old façade had been 'peeled back'. Retail content on the ground floor is about 3350 sq.m. and the offices above comprise about 7150 sq.m.*

**4** *The **Royal Court Theatre** (Sloane Sq.; Haworth Tompkins, 2000), is a familiar exercise (like Hackney Empire) in updating a much-loved theatre without destroying the ambience of its distress. The theatre was rebuilt, new dressing rooms etc added, and — at basement level — the theatre punches through under the road and square to form a bar and restaurant. Worth a visit. Also compare with Allies & Morrison's exercise at Chelsea Art School.*

Science Museum, Exhibition Road, SW7
MacCormac Jamieson Prichard, 2000
Tube: South Kensington

## Wellcome Wing

**5**

*The entrance to the Wellcome Wing: a darkened space characterised by blue lighting.*

Deep within the Science Museum, strapped onto its rear end, sits a huge, galleried hall loaded with technology and bathed in blue light. The lighting serves to add drama to the content whilst simultaneously disguising a monumental architectural equation that harks back to 1960's notions of infrastructure and changeable parts floating within it. The former comprises a massive, acrobatic structure and a differentiation of parts, together with exposed services; the latter is a dazzling whizz-bang-press-button set of displays designed to entertain and inform. In principle, the design is quite simple. One has to imagine a gigantic, inverted 'U' shape — this is the side-wall structure and roof. Hung within the inner space is a set of galleries ('trays') that carry the displays and the underbelly of an Imax Theatre with escalators that ride people up into it like something out of a 1930's futuristic movie.

The far end is fully glazed, but obscured to give a hint of the outside but deny daylight any entry. Visitors enter at the opposite open end from the older Science Museum gallery spaces. The wrapping structure is clearly derived from Foster's Sainsbury building in East Anglia: a form of infrastructure that keeps out the weather and whose side wings bear within them toilets, ducts, escape stairs and the like. The infrastructure concept also facilitates the series of galleries (or 'trays') that are slung across the inner space on 'gerberette' column and beams conceptually derived from Rogers' Lloyd's building; these carry the ducted service and cable trays, and have a grille ceiling exposing everything to view (a celebration of the architectural technology). The tall, fully glazed end-wall is a virtuoso exercise of layering that gives a dim view out and awareness of external life whilst admitting a mere 4% daylight.

The exhibits include a series of aluminium pods and all kinds of sophisticated 'interactive' displays that, unlike those at many venues, actually work. A cafe designed by Wilkinson Eyre is on the ground level.

## Exhibition Road area

*This street is about to have a make-over that addresses the realities of the number of visitors to the museums and the number of students at Imperial: it's going to become a tree-planted, re-lit, 'pedestrian-friendly' new paving together with the ubiquitous public art. Meanwhile, Imperial has been giving itself a make-over in recent years, adding some significant architecture.*

## Museum Land

*Alfred Waterhouse's **Natural History Museum** (Cromwell Road, 1873–81) includes two contemporary designs worth searching out: Ian Ritchie's **Ecology Gallery** (1991) and the late Ron Herron's dramatic, stainless steel, structural insertions into the **Dinosaur Gallery** (1992). Ritchie offers an intriguing mall lined in glowing glass and crossed by zoomorphic bridges. Herron's work is especially clever, installing a spinal armature that weaves between the existing columns and is immediately in tune with the subject. 2002 saw the opening of the **Darwin Centre** — a zoology research and storage centre with a collection of some 14m soft-bodied sea creatures housed in ethanol, designed by HOK. The Science Museum has two pieces of contemporary design to see: Ben Kelly's basement **Children's Gallery** (brash, cheerful, direct – a successful design); and an 'interactive' **bridge** designed by Chris Wilkinson with Whitby & Bird, meant to demonstrate stresses with sounds and lights (it is a nice bridge design but less successful as something meaningfully interactive).*

Exhibition Road, SW7
Foster & Partners, 2004
Tube: South Kensington

## 6 Faculty Building

The Foster studio has three buildings here: the Alexander Fleming Building (1998), used for medical and biological studies); the Flowers Building (2001), with research labs and support offices; and the Faculty Building of 2004. The former are rather inaccessible, although notable as features of the current work at this campus which is radically modifying its character as well as its facilities. However, the Faculty building is worth attention. It appears as a rather Alsop exercise plonked into the heart of the campus until one realises its adaptation to strategic campus issues in the manner that a dramatic diagonal route cuts through its heart. The colour, too — bright blue — is part of current attempts to enliven the campus scene. From another perspective, this is a deliberately neutral-looking office building for faculty staff (somewhat in the tradition of an enigmatic quality that also pervades, for example, the Gherkin). And perhaps that is where one has to carp: this is the usual strong Foster strategy, but one longs for his teams to demonstrate that love of

the material, ritualistic and symbolic stuff of the building in the sense that Herzog & de Meuron do. One worris that, at the end of the day, all we are offered is a satisfying equipmentality and not much more (especially not as a practice aspiration).

Exhibition Road, SW7
Foster & Partners, 2004
Tube: South Kensington

## 7 Tanaka Business School

The Tanaka building serves as a gateway into the Imperial campus, as well as being home to a business school. One enters through a 24m high glazed (of course) façade into a very large space topped by equally big translucent ETFE pillows and dominated by a huge drum that houses lecture rooms. It commands respect, but is a somewhat soulless place which hardly welcomes incidental student

activities. The external steel frame appears to be one of those neo-Venturi et al 'ghostly' references to the massing of the early C19th blocks opposite (which Grimshaw possibly did more cleverly at Camden some years ago).

*Above: the street elevation of the tanaka is 'sketched out' in steel framing that ghosts an alternative massing.*
*Left: the entrance lobby is a large hall which includes a circular drum of stacked lecture rooms.*

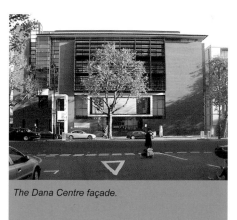

*The Dana Centre façade.*

## Dana Centre

165 Queen's Gate, SW7
MacCormac Jamieson & Prichard, 2004
Tube: South Kensington

**8**

We are told that the Dana Centre is a collaboration between the BA (British Association for the Advancement of Science) and The European Dana Alliance for the Brain (EDAB) making it unrivalled in its expertise and depth of knowledge of scientific and technological fields. As a place, it offers the public all kinds of information access, debates and the like — all, as they say, in "a stylish, purpose-built venue, complete with a cafébar, appealing to adults" and events such as 'punk science'. Architecturally, it would be pushing it to call MacCormac's Wrightian-inclined flair 'punk', but it sings out an artfulness that is comparatively rare (and an interesting contrast to the Foster buildings next door at Imperial).

*Also see this same practice's work at Paternoster, in the City, and for the BBC in Portland Place, in the West End. Friendship House (p.242) is a good example of their residential work.*

## Royal Geographic Society

Exhibition Road
Studio Downie Architects, 2004
Tube: South Kensington

**9**

This rather fine pavilion building is the visible outcrop of an fine and extensive programme of work focusing upon the need for an education centre and a 750 Ondaatje Theatre as parts of a listed Norman Shaw building. The pavilion houses the Society's archives and provides a lecture / meeting / gallery space as well as an undergound reading room. The entry sequence and consideration of views to notable adjacent buildings (including the Albert Hall) are well handled. Overall, the clarity and directness of the strategy and the gamesmanship command respect even though one might carp at one or two of the secondary level detailing.

(The pavilion, for example, has a daring concrete structure, but its relations to services and its external resolution don't quite get there.) The relations between internal spaces and the new garden work particularly well. The currently obligatory conceit of artistic presence adopts the form of glazed façade panels from Eleanor Long set along the paving wall (why the architects could not have done the same thing remains obscure).

# Inner Ring

## 10 Princess Di memorial

Make no mistake: Gustafson Porter know how to design landscape. And this is a very good example of their work — a very pleasant surprise in the heart of Hyde Park. But here is what Gustafson has to say: "Princess Diana was a contemporary princess and we wanted to design a contemporary fountain to remember her. The concept is based upon the qualities of the Princess that were the most loved and cherished. These were inclusiveness and accessibility. It is an environment that you can walk into, be part of. It is a large oval, the size of a football pitch, that is a novel use of water, that is brilliant in the sunlight, that cascades down, that you can touch and you can be interactive with and that you can become part of. We wanted to create an environment in which people can remember Diana, not an icon that they can only look at. The fountain also reflects parts of the Princess's life: on one side the water bubbles and effervesces down a gentle slope, whereas on the other side it tumbles down, cascades, then 'rocks and rolls' from side to side in a joyous way, before turning over on itself, perhaps representing the turmoil in her life. Both sides finally flow into a tranquil, peaceful, calm pool."

Well, whatever . . . despite such implausible allegorical sentiment the design reality works, simply as a pleasant place to be, whoever it commemorates, on whatever absurdist terms. Really. It will surprise you as a demonstration of self-evident, inventive architectural skill that is effective both as a unity within the gardens landscape and as a linear promenade that offers a series of events along its length — there's a sensuous, eventful and skilled architecture to this thing. And also ignore the media fuss about accidents — it's also nonsense.

*(See the plan on page 186, at the begining of this section.)*

*See a larger plan on page 186.*

**11** *John Miller's work at the **Serpentine Gallery**, a 1934 building in Kensington Gardens, Hyde Park, leaves the building looking outwardly the same, but inwardly totally changed (1997). Ad hoc arrangements have been replaced and reorganised, together with air conditioning, louvres to roof-lights, etc., including a shop and education room as well as the galleries themselves. It is an artful piece of work that stays in the background – both its strength and weakness. You can compare it with Miller's work at the Whitechapel Gallery, at Aldgate. Recent summers have seen a series of excellent 'garden pavilions' designed to front the gallery (by Hadid, Libeskind, Toyo Ito, etc.) and its opening has now become of the celebrated social events of the year. (Tube: South Kensington / Bayswater)*

**12** *The **Albert Hall** (Kensington Gore; Francis Fowke, 1871) and the **Albert Memorial** (Kensington Gardens; Sir George Gilbert Scott, 1872) are twin curiosities. The former is not that interesting; the latter was considered by Scott to be his 'most prominent work': an exuberant shrine protecting a statue of Victoria's deceased husband, Prince Albert, surrounded by symbols of Britain's then elevated global status. Ever since, we've all been astounded but not quite sure what to make of it all.*

## Doctors' Surgery **13**

Hammersmith Bridge Road / Worlidge St.,
Guy Greenfield Architects, 2001
Tube: Hammersmith

The planners wanted this doctors' surgery in Hammersmith, tucked under the principal road out to Heathrow, to be a 'landmark' building and were delivered this frontage of tall white, insulating screens to internal corridors serving the accommodation in a two-storey building. The result is an unexpectedly calm interior with top-lighting and slotted views out to the mundane drama of traffic jams. The corridors give access to the medical and other rooms overlooking a courtyard well screened from the noise and business outside.

**14** *The **Richard Rogers' studio** is a part of a small complex of buildings. There are three things to see (and do) here:*

*• See the barrel-vaulted Rogers' studio, converted from an existing 1950's brick and concrete warehouse. Other accommodation nearby is rented out to creative trades. • See the adjacent brick buildings of apartments with huge, slung balconies facing onto the river. They include the 'Deckhouse' designed by John Young, Rogers' partner as the ultimate in bachelor pads; look for a glass block bathroom tower on the roof. The riverside is the most dramatic façade. • Enjoy the River Cafe (run by Rogers' wife Ruth, together with Rose Gray), located in an adjacent building facing toward the river.*

**15** *The **Ark** (Ralph Erskine, 1992; Talgarth Road; Tube: Hammersmith) is an idiosyncratic, dark, brooding lump that serves as a gateway to London as visitors arrive from Heathrow. The exterior might have been even more interesting if the colouring had been different (brown glass of a complex geometry and copper spandrel panels that resist going green), so one has to wait for the breath-taking effects inside: white, airy, light, soaring and exhilarating spaces topped by a huge Douglas Fir ceiling. The heart is an atrium filled with meeting structures inspired by Italian hill villages (corny, but very effective). Around this are stepped, open office galleries. Scenic lifts glide up and down and disappear into the roof, where they pop out to an upper level viewing gallery which offers amazing views over London.*

*In terms of the stock of office buildings in London, the Ark is hugely significant, breaking conventions and demonstrating alternative possibilities. That was the theory and is the reality, but its curved floor plates were not the rectangles your average agent or facility manager was used to and the building took a long time to find its tenant (a difficulty that has been latterly entirely overcome).*

## 16 Chiswick Business Park

566 Chiswick High Rd, W4
Richard Rogers Partnership, 2000
Tube: Gunnersbury

CBP is a new generation Stockley Park (see p.252): more dense and urban (4 stories instead of 2 or 3), characterised by a lean budget that makes the achievements of the Rogers' team all the more remarkable. To get there (keenly encouraged by the demands of Stanhope's, the client), they honed the design equation to a simple set of architectural parts that, nevertheless, look expensive. The 1.5m gridded geometry is as compact as it comes, the frame is concrete, with post-tensioned floors and plenum access floors; the cladding is mostly glass, screened by high level louvres, access walkways and fire escapes. Net to gross is 87%. Parking is below. Go there and keep telling yourself this was low-cost, shed construction. It's difficult to believe. Here is the contradiction of Pevsner's famous claim that aesthetic intent differentiates Lincoln Cathedral from a bicycle shed. These buildings not only demonstrate that it is sheds most of us work in these days, but that these workplaces of the *volk* certainly enjoy considerable aesthetic intent.

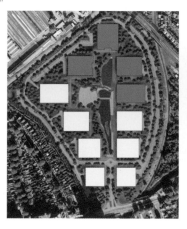

*Photo: Richard Rogers Partnership*

**17**  *The **Hallfield School** (Denys Lasdun, 1954; W2) on the south side of the Hallfield Estate (Tecton / Lasdun & Drake, 1954), is a fine modernist icon that now enjoys two new additional pavilions by Caruso St. John (2005). The latter are in the manner of the 'cool & understated' school of post-Smithsons architecture and if you want to see the place it's best to make access arrangements. Sometimes open for Open House, in September.*

*Lasdun's other exemplary London buildings include the **National Theatre** (p.138) and the **Royal College of Physicians** (p.88).*

## BBC White City

The first stage of this large complex provides some 50,000 sq.m. of offices and production space set out as 18m deep floor-plates divided by lively atria and set above a ground level of shops, cafes and restaurants that seek to offer a (one-sided) mall within the heart of the complex. In order to mediate the scale of it all with the surrounding urban fabric (public housing blocks on the west), perimeter blocks of a different scale have been introduced. These considerably present their fronts to the street, enlivening these whilst lending them a comparatively deferential relationship to existing residential buildings — which means they are scaled down to the form of rather elegant terraces whose character engenders questions with regard to the more orhtodox, corporate character of the main building. Overall, there has been an aim to obviate instrumental regularity by providing penetrative pedestrian access into the central (mall) heart, where pleasant landscaping has

**18**

Wood Lane, W12
Allies and Morrison, 2003
Tube: White City

*Does it work? It is a fine master-plan, but one has to admit to reservations regarding the ground floor retail content and a distinct timidity regarding its expressive character. Similarly, the idea that the BBC has provided a publicly accessible realm is (appropriately) media spin. Yes, one can enter, but through massive gates that signify you can be readily locked out and under the gaze of security guards who come rushing out to prevent any photography. This is a reality that tells it's own story.*

been designed by Christopher Bradley-Hole. Then comes the art: the facades facing onto these places are enlivened by a colour programme for shutters designed by Yuko Shiraishi; in addition, Tim Head has created a light projection 'piece' said to be visible from the adjacent major highway (the A40). The cladding is, as usual, immaculate (*compare with 123 Bankside, p.146*).

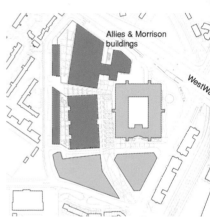

Allies & Morrison buildings

**19** *John Pawson has established a reputation for a kind of superior minimalism with pseudo-religious pretensions posing as rather apart from the tasteless customary fray. He's good, and this block at **18 Lansdowne Road**, W11, is a rare example of his work. The north (entry) façade lacks something. This is what he says about the project: "The idea here was to create not another conventional block of flats, but a series of lateral houses, each 'house' occupying a single floor, with an upper duplex apartment. The equivalent of a London terraced house in terms of floor space – considerably more in the case of the duplex — these apartments enjoy the privacy and individual character of a conventional house, with the security, open interiors and aspect associated with apartment living. A key architectural challenge was the project's corner site, meaning that the design had to deal simultaneously with two strikingly different contexts — the dignified villas of Lansdowne Crescent and the larger scale structures of Ladbroke Grove". Ironically, the scheme had a difficult planning history against the objections of neighbours and was, upon being awarded permission, sold on and another architect (Paul Davis & Partners) reworked the interiors so as to create the 'lateral apartments' claimed by Pawson. (completed 2004; Tube: Holland Park.)*

# Inner Ring

**20** *Trellick Tower*, by Erno Goldfinger (1973; now listed) sits in Golbourne Road, W10 (near the top end of the Portobello market and adjacent to the Regents Canal) overseeing west London in the form of what was once the tallest block of flats in England (31 storeys). It was an experiment in access (one external corridor serving three maisonettes) and 'Brutalist' architectural form. Now it is a gritty Brutalist icon. Architects like to love it, partly because it has a content of professional expertise, in part because of its peculiar beauty, and partly because it's such a radical design statement. Whether that makes it good housing is another issue. However, since it was constructed, people have grown to enthuse about the city and density once again and the Trellick has become an admired model for metropolitan living. The media tell us the tower is a very desirable piece of real estate (currently being refurbished by John McAslan), but a visit makes this hard to believe except with major qualifications — the white middle class families who have been deserting central London in droves are not about to rush back to Trellick Tower.

**21** The massive social housing development of **Alexandra Road**, NW8 – the last of a series of 'infrastructural' housing schemes promoted by Camden Council and designed by Neave Brown) had a brief for 1660 people in 520 units, developed into the form of two curving, raked concrete terraces, facing one another. The resulting canyon is both incredible and frightening – testament to how architecture can go badly wrong. It is worth comparing such developments with Lubetkin's Hallfield Estate in Bishop's Bridge Road, W2 (1951–59).

**22** Perhaps this triangular building (a lavatory and flower shop in **Westbourne Grove**, W11; 1993), built on the foundations of a Victorian lavatory, is one of the best things CZWG have designed – at once utilitarian, cheerful and frivolous. It is a poised, single-storey design that is simple and makes you glad it is there – not the easiest thing to achieve and something that encouraged a lot of community support against a local authority alternative (including a large donation from a local resident). As with most CZWG buildings, don't expect any internal surprises but (after relief in the lavatory) enjoy the flowers, the polycarbonate projecting canopy, the turquoise glazed bricks and the big clock.

**23** *Sarum Hall School* (Allies & Morrison, 1995, 15 Eton Ave., NW3) is typical of their work: considered, well mannered; fussed over but not fussy; unrhetorical, carefully composed and detailed. And not coping with a speculator's instrumental brief. It's a contextural design, conscious of Arts & Crafts, leafy, domestic surroundings that bring together a variety of features in one building: the entry porch, canopy and gateposts take ideas from neighbours (but keep the language contemporary) and the architects have arranged the accommodation so that repetitive elements are on the rear and varied ones are on the street.

**24** This housing in **St. Mark's Road**, W10 (Tube: Ladbroke Grove), is by Jeremy Dixon and was completed in 1980 — it makes an interesting comparison with what is now going on. The scheme comprises 44 family units and attempts to be contemporary whilst contextually offering a traditional London arrangement, e.g. half-basements, walk-up steps to a piano nobile, etc., in a terraced format with a stepped gable overhead. Another scheme by Jeremy and Fenella Dixon is at 171–201 Lanark Road, W9 (1979–82) – a scheme that is also in radical contrast to those being designed only ten years earlier.

**25** *If Future Systems redream 1960's technological optimism, this Hindu community centre, **Shri Swaminarayan Mandir,** redreams community and spiritual harmonies, having thoroughly researched their subject in order to recreate this Hindu jewel in Neasden. The focus is upon the incredible craftsmanship of stone-carving that was imported from India, but the heart of this place is a community/prayer centre that includes a column-free space for 2500 worshippers. (Run by Bochasanwasi Shri Akshar Purushottam Swaminarayan Sanstha (BAPS). What you experience here is not some Disney recreation, but investment in the power of architecture to be a sign and a symbol, to represent a whole gamut of values. To experience this architecture is also to experience a community spirit – which is what most good architectural experiences are about; visitors are very welcome (although security necessarily gets tighter each year). The address is 105-119 Brentfield Road, NW10; the architect was C D Sompura (1995); the nearest tube is Neasden.*

*Also see the **Gurdwara Karamsor** Sikh temple on p236.)*

## Wembley Stadium

Anyone venturing into north London will find it difficult to miss a new landmark as prominent as the City's 'Gherkin': the 315m span and 133m high arch of the new Wembley Stadium. Not complete at the time of writing, the rebuilt stadium will be open by mid-2006, catering to some 90,000 fans of soccer, rugby, music events and even athletics. Apart from serving as metropolitan landmark, the arch lends critical support to a roof that includes a sliding section (some 25% of the total roof area), thus obviating the need for supporting columns and, importantly, allowing natural daylight onto the grass pitch (as well as sheltering spectators during events). The latter sit in one single bowl as opposed to the old stadium's four sectors, but they will be able to enjoy some traditional Wembley rituals — such as trophy presentations from a Royal Box. At the time of writing everyone is rather upset that the building has not only cost a considerable sum, but that it is too late for crucial annual soccer matches. No doubt all this will be soon forgotten.

**26**

World Stadium team (Foster & Partners, with HOK), 2006
Tube: Wembley

*Image: courtesy of Wembley National Stadium Ltd.*

## 27 Fawood Nursery

Stonebridge Estate, Harlesden, NW10
Alsop Design Ltd, 2005
Tube: Harlesden

It is not difficult to dismiss Alsop's work as arbitrary and wilful, gestural and gimmicky — especially when seen in magazines (and it has become increasingly fashionable to criticise his work from such a perspective). However, experience the reality and one is (surely?) immediately struck by an intuition of design intelligence as well as wit and a striving not to be bound to conventions. (Yes, I am aware that I am now in controversial territory.) Of course, the ostensible wackiness of his work courts the danger of fashionability and unfashionability, and it will be interesting to see how Alsop survives and offers relevance to a younger generation.

Here, at Fawood — in a derelict area undergoing demolition and reinvention — the local authority has provided the community with a symbol of caring and hope which, bizarre as it might appear, certainly does the job.

The building — which provides a nursery for three-to-five-year-olds, nursery facilities for autistic and special needs children, and a base for community education workers and consultation services — looks like a simple shed: a lid and a steel mesh wrap, within which Alsop has located a series of architectonic units: mostly three storeys of old containers, but including a yurt. The result is arguably a kid's paradise of spaces and places blurring the boundary between indoors and outdoors, admits lots of light and keeps the children safe from that nasty world outside.

In one sense the ground plan is within the tradition of the grand living or library room, as perhaps found in a stately home or ministerial office i.e. one space with lots of sub-scenarios: reception zone, climbing platform, yurt, outdoor eating area (piazza), sandpit, water garden, stage, cycle track, play house, four trees, etc., all bounded by what is sometimes (unkindly) called the cage of steel mesh.

"With a tiny budget, we had to stretch our imaginations," says Alsop. "We decided to buy the biggest, cheapest and most robust structure we could find, which is effectively a standard portal-frame mass-produced for farm buildings. This has allowed us to cover as much space as possible — in fact, the entire site — for little money, leaving the rest to create spaces that, hopefully, will shape the children's imagination. They already think of themselves as being at sea when they're inside the sea containers, and they like to hear stories told inside the yurt, which is a far cosier and more magical space than a conventional classroom can ever be."

I would argue this is intelligent architectural design. It's also artful. But it sports gestures — such as the woven mesh 'flowers' on the exterior — guaranteed to upset many architects. However, if a fraction of the architects in London had this man's daring and inventive wit, its architecture would be a distinctly livelier scene.

(I can already hear the chorus of disagreement!)

*The 'piazza' corner (bottom left of the plan, opposite).*

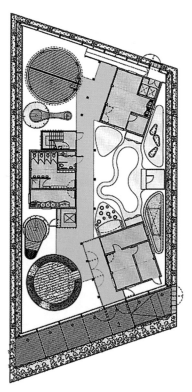

*Exterior view, entrance side.*

The Fawood Nursery plan is basically a shed populated with internal pavilions that bears a passing resemblance to many an interior office arrangement or, perhaps more appropriately, a native village conglomeration. As a nursery, it is hugely successful and serves as a model of what can be achieved. As an architecture, it works at every level, from the urban down to the details of its places and spaces (which, of course, could always be improved by a little more money being thrown at them). Clad in glass and used by an ad agency it would be hailed as a revolutionary novelty in work-place design

*A decorative 'flower' on the exterior steel mesh.*

*Roof view from an upper gallery. The construction is rudely industrial.*

*The internal pavilions are simply stacked steel pavilions accessed by spatious galleries. The spaces provided are there to serve an 'inclusive' grouping of children of all abilities.*

# Inner Ring

**28** *A set of Po-Mo private Villas self-consciously recreating the era of John Nash, who conceived of a Regent's Park populated by expensive villas. Three of them – the Veneto, the Gothik and the Doric – were built in 1992 and have since been added to by four more (another was going up in late 2005). Located in the north-west corner of Regent's Park, on the Outer Circle (opposite the American Ambassador's residence), they are designed by Quinlan and Francis Terry and in a tradition of English eccentricity married to latter-day Establishment values, Post-Modernism's reactionary undertones, and a good dose of hi-tech carefully hidden away. They supplement the five villas realised by John Nash in the 1820s and straddle the edge of the Regent's Canal adjacent to Hanover Lodge, providing a conspicuous display of architectural taste that attunes the lifestyles of affluent owners with that of the Ancients who gave us a symbolic classicism.*

*Perhaps to merely show these villas and suggest they are worth a look is to court ire — these are very fashionably unfashionable buildings. However, whilst they may nostalgically refer back to a bygone era when a decorous architecture might more plausibly pose as bearing pretences to eternal truths, universal harmonies and the like, they nevertheless exhibit real architectural gamesmanship. Despite claims that Terry's architecture is pompous and not nearly as erudite as he pretends, one suspects that the real debate is about political correctness and the wrath that is poured upon someone who dares to go against the grain of the zeitgeist as majority opinion conceives it — which is surely all the more reason to go to Regent's Park, open one's eyes, see these residences for the rich, and make up one's own mind. Who knows, you might enjoy them. (There is a more accessible example of Terry's work at Richmond.)*

**29** *The London Zoo (Outer Circle, Regent's Park, NW1), includes **The Aviary** in London Zoo — attributed to the late Cedric Price, to Lord Snowdon and the also late engineer Frank Newby — is a by-product of enthusiasms for Buckminster Fuller's geometries and tense gritty structures designed during that era, and is one of the first pieces of acrobatic modern architecture in London. You can see it from the pathway along the Regent's Canal, north side of the Park (a very pleasant walk from Camden Town to Lords). Given Price's predilection for saying a lot but turning away from formal issues and building very little, one suspects Newby is the real author here.*

*The Verity Stand is oldest on the site and remains the most prestigious because of its historical associations and continued use as the principal club house.*

*Grimshaw's contribution at Lords is characteristically acrobatic and well executed.*

# Lord's Cricket Ground
## summer in the city

**30**

It is difficult to reconcile oneself to the idea of the gentlemen of the Marylebone Cricket Club (the MCC, formed in 1787) becoming patrons of contemporary architecture. However, encouraged by an architect-member called Peter Bell, they have given us a number of modern buildings that, in turn, have helped to revitalise the game at Lord's, home of English cricket. Behind this is the realities of a spectator sport, that is a million miles away from soccer: a summer ball game lasting all day leaving the pitch and stands at Lord's unused for much of the year, only coming alive as a venue on only 10–12 days a year when international matches are played – also when corporations indulgently entertain valued clients and customers from within their own boxes and less favoured enthusiasts bring luncheon boxes from which to picnic. And, perhaps most importantly, cricket at Lord's has — like other sports — become fodder to an international media machine hungry for content.

When completed in 1987, the Mound Stand designed by Michael Hopkins' office was notable because it offered us an architect pigeon-holed as Hi-tech betraying both contextual sensitivities and an enthusiasm for dealing with a range of low-tech constructions. Observers were surprised by Hopkins' acceptance of the existing stand, together with his embrace of its brick arches (and their extension from six in number to a row of 21, all properly built as load-bearing), as well as by the acrobatics of the new overhead structure. They were also suspicious that an inspiration for the scheme was not only technical and instrumental, but the notion that an expansive, white, tensed fabric roof had a symbolic appropriateness to the ambience and traditional sartorial garb of summer cricket.

Just after the Mound Stand, Hopkins also completed the Compton and Edrich Stands that stretch around the east side, beneath the Media Centre. These are simple concrete raked decks that sit upon a more complex arrangement of tubular steel arms.

**31** *David Morley's '**Hub**' sports facility (changing rooms) set within the northern part of Regent's Park (2005) is described by the architects as a design set within the framework of Nash's notion of park buildings being ornaments. (One could hardly say less in such a setting.) The building comprises a mound housing changing rooms, above which is a simple, circular cafe with an elegantly structured central roof-light.*

St. John's Wood Road, NW8

Mound Stand, Sir Michael Hopkins & Partners, 1987. Grand Stand, Nicholas Grimshaw & Partners, 1998

Cricket Shop, English Cricket Board offices, and Indoor School, David Morley, all 1996–8. Media Centre,

Future Systems, 1999. Tube: St. John's Wood

# Inner Ring

Cricket has no need of summer at David Morley's Indoor Cricket School (1994), an exhilarating interior of green plastic carpet, white finishes, masses of daylight filtered from above, huge powered doors that open in summer, and lots of eager kids properly kitted out for their practice sessions. The entry side incorporates its own viewing terrace and seating, looking over the Nursery Ground.

Morley also designed the 275 sq.m. single-storey Lord's Cricket Shop next door (1996), with inflated roofing panels made of continuously pressurised, translucent ETFE foil cushions. Beside this sits a third Morley design: a simple, but elegant, 1200 sq.m.. two-storey office building for the Test and County Cricket Board (1996) with an exterior dominated by large 'light-shelves' which push daylight into the interiors.

Opposite the Mound Stand sits the Grand Stand by Nicholas Grimshaw (1998). His team offers the same basic arrangement as Hopkins, but eschews the tensed fabric motif and provides the structural acrobatics we have come to expect from this firm in the form of a two-storey spine truss and two 50m span roof trusses supported on three columns. It has many structural similarities to the Mound Stand and, like it, was constructed in two winter phases so as not to disrupt the summer games. It is a splendid design, a sophisticated and elegant structure that is well detailed and built (better, in these terms, than the Mound Stand), but misses the emotional connection Hopkins touched upon and Grimshaw would probably dismiss as sentimental design motivation – what John Pringle, the job architect on the Mound Stand, describes as 'a five-day boat cruise', complete with upper promenade and steerage class passengers.

The most interesting building at Lord's is the newest: the NatWest Media Centre (1999) designed by Future Systems – architects with a name reeking of 1960's technological optimism who are into designing 'things' (complete with obligatory rounded corners) and who marry retro and progressive postures into a single and skilled post-modern stance. Propped upon two concrete access towers, the structure accommodates special desks plus alcoholic support from a bar at the rear and characteristically an inhabited architectural blob with the exotic, sensuous, other-world quality of Hi-tech engineering (racing cars and yachts, combat aircraft, etc.), from which it borrows its forms and techniques. Taking the form of a 'semi-monocoque' aluminium yacht construction poised high above ground at the east end of the luscious green field, the Centre reads as a UFO dropping in for the splendid sights offered through its massive 40m front window. This is carefully raked so as to avoid reflections back onto the field and so that the media people can easily see out and be fed 'ambient sound'; however, the BBC considered an air-conditioned box as an affront to their commentating history and insisted on a small openable window for themselves so that they could actually hear the crack of leather on willow (a distinctly Heath-Robinson affair; see photo on right).

In fact, most journalists appear to dislike the place. The Independent's columnist comments, 'You cannot feel the match: the mikes don't work properly and you don't get a proper sense of what's happening. And it's so very bright that you can't see your laptop. We just need windows that open and better tellies (for the replays). And The Times' man says, "There's a bank of televisons above our heads and for the second half of the day you're looking into the sun and can't see them" Being high up in a glass-faced, westward-oriented pod is clearly not their idea of fun.

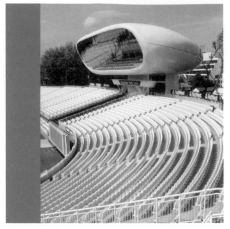

*The Media Centre* is constructed from 26, prefabricated aluminium sections of 3-4mm thick plate, shipped to site and welded together. CAD and numerically controlled machines were crucial to analysis and the fabrication carried out by yacht builders. The structure – acting as a semi-monocoque of ribs and skin – is supported on two concrete stair / lift towers clad in GRP panels (the architects originally wanted one, but members said this would spoil their view of existing trees). The top half rests on these towers, with the bottom half bracketed off concrete ring beams. Internally, the accommodation is principally a raked bank of journalists' benches and an upper, mezzanine level of small rooms (one being for the BBC, with its openable window that is, apparently, rarely used). The rear part accommodates the all too necessary bar. The internal mezzanine floor is hung from the roof and the 9m high raking glass front (made of 12mm laminated glass plus  an annealed glass layer and designed so as to be both safe and not dazzle players) rests into the floor but is supported by the mezzanine, requiring carefully designed movement joints. The powder blue interior is argued to result from the need to avoid any distractions to players; to say it is impractical would be an understatement. In a gesture of '60's mannerism, doors are formed as hatches, complete with curved corners. The engineers were Ove Arup.

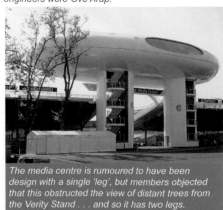

*The media centre is rumoured to have been design with a single 'leg', but members objected that this obstructed the view of distant trees from the Verity Stand . . . and so it has two legs.*

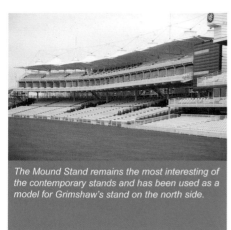

*The Mound Stand remains the most interesting of the contemporary stands and has been used as a model for Grimshaw's stand on the north side.*

Overall, Lord's has become capitalised and globalised, part of a telecommunicating cultural stream of commercialised contemporary sport whose only parallel is possibly the manner in which the City of London manages to marry history, tradition and modernity. If the Media Centre, for example, were simply an instance of advanced engineering techniques transferred to the sexy form of a building it would be less interesting. However, as an unconscious embodiment of so many contemporary cultural streams, this object comes alive and, for a while, will speak to us and echo dreams which increasingly seem to end up focused upon the playing field.

*The Mound Stand sits above an existing stand of 1899. This has been retained, but its load-bearing brick piers have been extended (using reclaimed bricks from a demolition site). The additional seating at the upper level is held up on six columns at 18m centres, giving minimal disturbance to the existing structure as well as views of the game. Below the open upper deck sits a structural box incorporating some storage and service facilities. below that is a mezzanine housing private boxes. The translucent fabric roof is a PVC coated glass-fibre weave with an additional PVDF flouropolymer topcoat. The Stand is a simple construction and, by 2005, it was looking rather tired and in need of renewal (happening over the '05 winter) but it's still an excellent building to visit.*

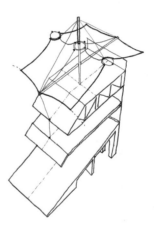

**32** *Ron Arad has to be one of London's best designers: an architect who prefers customers (for his chairs and other products) rather than clients (who end up having to be nursed) and a man whose work is inherently rhetorical yet (ostensibly) devoid of any intent to impress for the sake of it – a rare characteristic that applies to his studio as well as his product designs and craftsmanship. The studio is the conversion of an old warehouse tucked in a mews and has a positively Dickensian approach guaranteed to put off the casual visitor to the Fagan-like character hiding away up there behind the peeling paint. But it is worth the effort of climbing the decrepit access stair to see the way the studio has been formed in a marvellously whimsical yet wilful manner, the wavy wood floor and the superb furniture in the showroom. (One Off Studio, 62 Chalk farm Road, NW1; Tube: Chalk Farm)*

# Inner Ring

## 33 Newbury Mews

Newbury Mews, NW5
Brooks Murray Architects, 2005
Tube: Chalk Farm

A site that was garages and workshops, now redeveloped as mews houses only having frontal aspect, at a density of 140 units/ha — which is quite high. A major planning issue concerned neighbours and overlooking — hence the blank rears and a section profile, together with a 'sedum' planted roof, so as to offer existing inhabitants in adjacent houses a nominally 'green' outlook (as opposed to derelict shed roofs). Overlooking issues were also crucial to the face-to-face confrontation between units and it has all been well handled.

## 34 Haverstock school

Crogsland Road NW1
2005
Tube: Chalk Farm

New school buildings for an existing institution of 1250 students — while they were on the site. The intentions — which include longer opening hours and access for the community — and the process have been ambitious. In part this is reflected in the bold street facade design. (It's interesting how the lettering used by Gehry and Venturi some years ago in a more distinctly Po-Mo period is only now being aggressively used in London's architecture — probably by the generation who were then still studying). Otherwise the building is illustrative of the current govenment's programme all capital provision onto a public-private partnership basis which, needless to say, has queues of critics bemoaning this wholesale shift to instrumentalism and commerciality as the basis on which the nation provides for its educational needs.

## 35 Camden Art Centre

Arkwright Road, NW3
Tony Fretton Architects, 2004
Tube: Finchley Road

Tony Fretton has rightly established himself in recent years and this modernisation work is a good demonstration of his sensitive ability to knit old and new together into a fresh whole which now provides enhanced gallery spaces and studio facilities for classes and talks, and a new cafe and bookshop. The architects write that: "An entirely new feature is the relocation of the entrance to the ground floor in a new accessible public hall which gives a wide line of sight through the building from back to front and makes visible the bookshop in its new position, the ceramic studio, and a new cafe and garden behind."

## Hampstead Theatre

HT — London's first new theatre since the National opened in 1976 — is a classic 'egg-in-box' (like the Royal Festival Hall) scaled down for more local audiences, the outsides animated by lots of glass, wood shutters and lighting design by artist Martin Richman. But, in truth, one should forget the polite and timid exterior (compare with Hackney Empire, for example) and go straight inside. The auditorium with adaptable seating for up to 325p is slung above the foyer areas and their gallery, and an underground level provides additional facilities — all of which comes across as a lively and very pleasant atrium space that connects levels, disparate activities and public / private realms. Now, about that dreary exterior, which surely could have been so much more self-celebratory . . .

**36**

Hampstead Theatre, Eton Avenue, NW3
Bennetts Associates, 2003
Tube: Swiss Cottage

## Central School of Speech & Drama

The architects for this educational building offer much unnecessary hype about contexturalism — none of which is evident on the pavement. What does come across is a strong ambition to make an urban contribution to what is currently going on at this busy road intersection and to participate in a grouping that includes Spence's library (opposite) and Bennett's theatre (above). The planning is all about linkages and project staging as well as facilities.

**37**

Eton Avenue
Jestico Whiles, 2005
Tube: Swiss Cottage

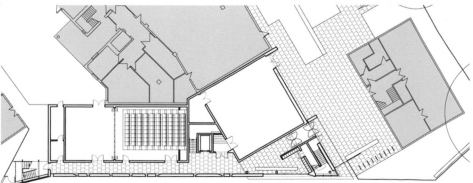

*The Swiss Cottage area has been undergoing significant changes. Apart from the Central School, John McAslan completed a refurbishment of Spence's Library (p.208) and Terry Farrell is completing a leisure centre in 2006. There is also the Hampstead Theatre (above) and, up the hill, the Camden Art Centre (opposite).*

## Inner Ring

**38** *Swiss Cottage Library was designed by Sir Basil Spence in 1962-4 and beautifully refurbished by John McAslan in 2003 (Tube: Swiss Cottage). At a time when libraries have to be disguised with bizarre names like 'ideas store' it is refreshing that such a place has been refurbished as a central feature of redevelopment work at Swiss Cottage (all to a fraught Terry Farrell master-plan). It is useful to compare this older library with Peckham and the two idea Stores — none of them have the traditional leisurely quality achieved at Swiss Cottage. And, by the time you read this, a large new Camden sports facility will also have been completed next door (by Terry Farrell).*

## 39 Latitude House

Oval Road / Parkway, NW1
AHMM, 2005
Tube: Camden

This small block of 12 apartments is a really fresh and worthwhile addition to Camden, replacing a filling station that was on the site. Having said that, its outstanding interest to the urban observer is one of architectonics and formalism. For example, its general character returns to a mix of 1950's offset window grids, now combined with an apparent tectonic of prefabricated perimeter units set as those ground to eaves slabs that were fashionable with Stirling and Gowan et al in the 1960's — all updated via Arups at Plantation Place, Parry's neo-Terragni exercises in the City, etc. It is well done, but strangely lacks substance and plausibility (it's actually a conventional concrete frame). In other words, it's tectonic theatre that doesn't quite convince the observer to suspend disbelief. One can hardly condemn it for that, but one does demand more artfulness in playing the game: either play with offset planes that hang or float, or persuade us these are load-bearing panels. Playing the architecture game means playing it seriously — and well — or courting the danger of falling into a paroditic exercise without the irony. Still, this is a lot better than most new housing in London.

**40** *Of these two houses, at 44 & 42 Rochester Place, NW1, designed by **David Wild** from 1984 on – Wild's own (no. 44) was built first and a neighbour loved it, asking him to do one for them. This is architecture on a budget, without grandiose gestures, and indebted to the London Georgian house (piano nobile with bedrooms above), le Corbusier (the city villa type, with ground level undercroft parking and a roof terrace) and Adolf Loos (who advocated non-rhetorical aesthetics). Private London has many small, local works like this (e.g. in nearby Camden Mews — which, for a few years, was crammed with architects — such as Ted Cullinan — building small houses for themselves in one of the few locations where they could get planning permission).*

## Sainsbury's battleship supermarket

**41**

Camden Road, NW1
Nicholas Grimshaw and Partners, 1988
Tube: Camden

The architect's brief for this supermarket was to design an inner-city supermarket that really wanted to be out-of-town. What the client got was a cranky and now ageing development with an aggressive note to it. In fact, its all rather admirable, although the battleship grey (latterly softened in some areas to greyish baby blue — a mistake, apparently) and grey aluminium cladding betray the technocratic concerns and military roots of Hi-tech — whicch, mixed with Sainsbury's low maintenance standards and the love of Camden youth for graffiti, hasn't engendered a lovable image. But it's a clever design.

Grimshaw provided an entirely column-free shopping area, together with loading areas, administration facilities, underground car parking and housing along the canal, on the north side of the development. Two features stand out. First, the main façade makes an attempt to build up the massing of the supermarket shed and to provide a bay rhythm corresponding to the Georgian terrace of late eighteenth century houses opposite – a sound move, realised with the aid of characteristic Grimshaw structural acrobatics. Second, the terrace of maisonettes along the canal have only northern light (their southern side being directly onto the service yard), yet Grimshaw manages to cope well, providing a double height space with garage doors giving onto canal balconies (which frequently offer that key signal of domesticated contentment: flowers).

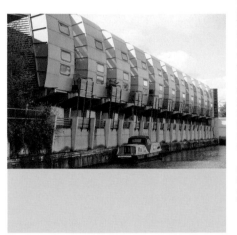

Located in the suburbs, one suspects the building would have been of higher quality and better maintained — which is a shame, because this scheme is still capable of being a real boon to Camden Town.

42 *The façade of **MTV** (Formerly TVAM – now MTV; Hawley Crescent, NW1; Terry Farrell Partnership; Tube: Camden) was arguably once one of the most exhilarating in London – straight into an architectural tradition going back to Googie coffee shops of '50s L.A. and even the spirit of the 1950's British Pop movement reinvented in latter-day terms: the converted garage reinvented as a metaphor of the rising sun, complete with a dark horizon (the base) and layers of diminishing textures rising into the sky. At the centre is a rising sun/arched entry, its 'keystone' scrawled in neon. The egg cups on the canal-side are fun but less successful. Inside, the original scheme was well-planned, but eclectic and thematically over-the-top and emphatically global locations from where the news was coming.*

*Just like those 1950's Googie coffee shops in California, TVAM was here today and a memory tomorrow.*

*TVAM lost their licence and in came MTV who toned the whole thing down, stuck roundels over the TVAM logo at each end of the sweeping façade, and generally ruined the whole thing in homage to good-designer taste. For a while Camden had the only pure Pop building in the UK. And it is still there, just beneath a surface of denial, out of fashion but nevertheless addressing the issue of the building façade read as a sign. Meanwhile, its spirit is carried on throughout Camden High Street in the form of huge fibre-glass boots and similar features that increasingly adorn the run-down façades of the institutionalised flea-market. Who knows, the old TVAM façade might one day be resurrected as an act of retro.*

*As an aside, Grimshaw and Farrell's careers have strangely paralleled one another since they broke up, both receiving knighthoods and, here in Camden, building next to one another. (See the Sainsbury supermarket.)*

**43** The **Talacre Sports Centre** is a sports / community centre within Kentish Town from the practice that did the Indoor Cricket School at Lord's. (Prince of Wales Road, NW5; David Morley Architects. 2002; Tube: Camden / Chalk Farm). It's a good example of a local community building of this type.

**44** The **Isokon flats** have an iconic status within London's architectural tradition: one of the few impressive examples of inter-war Modernism (Wells Coates, 1934; Lawn Road, NW3). The 22 apartment block is simply a walk-up, deck-access scheme of relatively small flats, financed by an arts patron, the furniture maker Jack Pritchard, and initially tenanted by (now) famous names, with the Pritchrad's in a penthouse apartment. But its living attraction is clearly its formal, abstract qualities which are simultaneously a welcoming habitat. It seems like a complete gesture — especially now that it has been renovated — and architects love this image of wholeness and unity. We're told that the current white paintwork dates from 1983 and the building was originally 'pale greyish pink' (sounds rather Po-Mo). Incidentally, both Denys Lasdun and Patrick Gwynne (see p.253) briefly worked for Coates.

**45** **Camden Gardens** (Jestico Whiles, 1994), is a difficult site opposite the Grimshaw housing on the Sainsbury site, with five villa-like apartment blocks (18 units) tightly squeezed onto it. Three villas face the street, and further accommodation provided in a terrace that faces onto the canal. Europeans might wonder what the big deal is, but (until recently) London has all too little of this kind of considerate housing.

**46** CZWG's **Green Building** in Camden (2001; Jamestown Road, Camden Lock) comprises apartments above a ground floor of retail units. Unusually for such a location and building type, huge amounts of glass have been used — which certainly helps to lift an area that can sometimes be less than salubrious. Having said that, it is worth nosing around the area, especially on the market weekend days.

**47** *David Chipperfield's* studio (Cobham Mews, NW1) is in a similar location to Arad's – tucked away in a mews – but meaningful correspondence stops there. Chipperfield goes for a more cool, architectonic aesthetic, for a simple play on materials and abstract surfaces also evident in his designs for shops like Equipment (now closed) or the Wagamama restaurant in Soho. The Maison de Verre influence is again evident in the way the façade cladding has been handled.

**48** The **Burton house** (1989), 1b Lady Margaret Road, NW5, Kentish Town tube), is a two-person, timber-framed house by and for Richard Burton, of ABK. It is pushed against its northern site boundary, facing south in order to benefit from solar gain. But this is more than another timber-framed / highly insulated eco-exercise: Burton manages to give his home extremely livable qualities that are totally integrated with the technical strategies. Access from the 'moon-gate' is through a glazed access corridor (semi-open, as it were), off which are three rooms (study, living and kitchen-diner). From here, a stair goes to the bedroom upstairs. All this is supplemented by a garden studio pavilion and by an additional apartment for a member of the family — a splendid small grouping hidden behind Burton's brick wall.

**49** This fine, two-storey **Hopkins House**, at 49a Downshire Hill, NW3, was completed in 1975 and stood as an understated model of Hi-tech and eccentric living for many years (somewhat in the manner of the California houses built after WWII by Entenza, Eames et al, from which it drew inspiration). The former came from its simple, 3.6 m span, steel and glass structure; the latter came from a home / work equation that optimistically placed a lot of reliance on louvres for spatial divisions, foreshadowing the latter-day enthusiasm for loft spaces and similar non-prescriptively defined spaces that are easily changed and adapted. The overall character is emotively 'hot' as well as shed-like in comparison with the calm elegance of the John Winter house.

**50** **St. Paul's Church,** Wightman Road, N8. (Inskip & Jenkins, 1993). The diagrammatic qualities of this church's massing bear comparison with John Nash's All Soul's at Langham Place and, like the Nash church, it works. The key (as always) is context – in this instance, a hilly, Victorian domestic suburb, with pointed gables and dormers. The geometry gives the church a real presence and the simple interior is well handled. It's not only the church's name that draws a comparison with St. Paul's in Covent Garden, but also its 'barn-like' qualities. There aren't many contemporary churches in London, so it is worth a visit if you are in this area.

## Inner Ring

**51** These terraced houses built by Erno Goldfinger at 1–3 **Willow Road,** NW3 in 1938 (4C 44) are a fascinating and intricate design that marries 1930's Parisian avant garde values with design traditions informing the London terrace house that stretch back to the late 1600's. In Goldfinger's design, Modernism as an ostensibly radical lifestyle found a place to root and nest within cosy Hampstead. Elegant living and salon conversations enthusing about Surrealism and socialist politics found resonance in spaces profoundly indebted to the good manners, tastes and support from the invisible servants of London's 17th.c Georgian terraces. The fundamentals of their architectural form – especially the 'vertical living' between party walls (as opposed to a 'horizontality' between floors characterising Continental apartments) was enthusiastically taken up by this talented architect and his wife who saw no difficulties in attempting a synthesis of tradition with Modernism. No. 2 Willow Road epitomises a distinct period between quite different eras in England's architectural history: between architectural traditionalists sceptical of the new ideas coming from the Continent and architectural values that were to be at the heart of a large post-war programme of urban regeneration; and also between pre-war and post-war social values. Here, in this small, pre-war family house in Hampstead, overlooking Hampstead Heath, the Goldfingers literally and demonstrably brought the issues home, set stylistic themes and standards that were to be copied by many post-war architects and lived a life that manifested the kinds of social changes that saw their servant's quarters modified into a family apartment. Goldfinger's own unit is now owned by the National Trust and is open to visitors. (Tel 020 7985 6166 for daily opening times and tours.)

**52** Camden's rich legacy of social housing from the 1960's through to the mid - 1970's is epitomised by this development of a hillside in Hampstead Village, tucked away in **Branch Hill,** NW3. Designed by a local authority whose programme gave young designers marvellous opportunities, this scheme (designed by Gordon Benson and Alan Forsyth, 1970–77) bears reference to Corbusier's beloved Mediterranean hillside villages as reinterpreted in Switzerland by Atelier Five. Tucked away, this scheme is frequently forgotten. But if you are interested in housing, Camden probably offers the best localised example of late 1950's to early '70's public housing, designed in a time when its team was rather prestigious and acclaimed for its work — the ways in which people live don't change that much!

## Lawn House

**53**

South Grove, Highgate Village, N6
Eldridge Smerin, 2001
Tube: Highgate

The Lawns is the conversion and extension of a house originally designed by Leonard Manasseh in the '50's. The new work — mostly in glass — entirely wraps and engulfs the old house and doubles its size with expansive, double-height spaces, so that the new is played off against the old. And a complete new floor is added, replacing the former pitched roof. For historical and planning reasons the house is set well back from the street — generating a large forecourt and underscoring a space syntax that elevates the house's status as the visitor parades to it or swings into the car area. Inside, the interior is well-organised, playing off old and new with real panache. And there is even a third generation here: the Manasseh house was built upon a retained Victorian basement, now used as an apartment for the children of the household. The house was short-listed for the Stirling Prize in 2002.

**54** *John Winter's* own home at 81 Swains Lane, N6, sits opposite the gates to Highgate Cemetery *(where Marx is buried). It's a marvellous three-storey design (completed in 1969), with piano nobile at the top, bedrooms in the middle, and kitchen / family / dining on the garden level. Its rusting Corten steel cladding and large panes of clear glass peek above crusty brick walls, looking at once aged and modern. The influences are entirely North American again, this time the California Case Study houses of the late 1940's and early 1950's, and the work of SOM, for whom Winter worked in the 1950's (plus a bit of Saarinen on the Corten). (You can see what Winter built for himself in 1959-61 and extended until moving to Highgate, near Regents Park, in Regal Lane.)*

**55** *The **Highpoint** flats in North Road, N6 (Highgate Village) have an almost suburban location, high above London, with terrific views. Berthold Lubetkin and the Tecton group designed them in 1936–38 as exemplars of modern rational thinking. The first, Highpoint 1 offers us all of le Corbusier's 5 Points (car port, piano nobile on piloti, roof garden, free plan with minimum columns, and horizontal windows), together with a splendid common hall and a plan that makes architects swoon. (And then there are those characteristic balconies.) Highpoint 2 further echoes the example of le Corbusier, with double-height studio spaces. Its entry porte coche is daringly held up by neo-classical caryatids copied from the Erectheum in Athens – a gesture that some people consider to be facetious and incomprohonsiblo, but it certainly lifts the spirit. (Also see Bevin Court, near Kings Cross, and the Finsbury Health Centre a little further south of that.)*

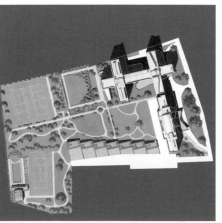

**56** These two houses — **'Venus'** and **'Cargo Fleet'** — are around the corner from one another and make fine examples of how London architects (Chance de Silva) strive to make something out of difficult sites. Both serve as end-of-terrace designs and make quite a contrast with the neighbours. (Venus, left; Cargo Fleet, right.)
• **Cargo Fleet:** 14 Whistler Street, N5 (2004)
• **Venus**: 1A Elfort Road N5, (1998)
Tube: Arsenal

**57** The studio of **Jo van Heyningen and Birkin Haward** (1998) at Burghley Yard, Burghley Road, Tufnell Park, NW5, is the conversion of a former warehouse into one of those equations that pays the studio bills. The front half has been converted into apartments and studios are provided at the rear. Intermediate structural bays have been removed to provide a courtyard in between and the rear wall has been demolished and rebuilt one bay in, in order to provide the studio with a patio. It's necessarily an economic design, but sensitive and carefully considered. The pruning manages, for example, to retain the roof trusses and boarding, complete with the patina of age and wear, thus lending instant warmth to the simply arranged, main studio space at the upper level.

. . . And this Orion (see the Graduate Centre, opposite), Libeskind's "spatial emblem of the Northern sky" and his "guiding light". It's form is traditionally taken a human figure, as if a warrior with sword and shield (and, incidentlally, prompts all kinds of neo-Wittgenstein debate on language and signage, as if it were a diagram taken straight out of his 'Philosphical Investigations'). Alternatively, you could draw a variety of lines between the stars and invent another, alternative, symbolism. Thankfully, Libeskind neither went that far or insinuated the mythology into the Graduate Centre design. But it is fascinating to experience the power of this arbitrary narrative on the client and users — they love it (a point on which it might be too easy and unnecessary to be cynical).

## Graduate Centre

London Metropolitan University
Daniel Libeskind Studio, 2003
166-220 Holloway Road, N7
Tube: Holloway Road

**58**

This 700 sq.m. exercise in trophy architect branding is actually a simple and well worked out architecture with fairly minimal accommodation (two seminar rooms, a lecture room, and space to hang about and enjoy celebratory views). It is all well handled on a low budget. In principle, this accommodation is added onto a 1960's building, meeting it at a common circulation corridor that runs in between. The lecture room is in the upper part and comes complete with a 'constellation of Orion' ceiling pattern to its light fittings. The building certainly brightens up this part of the Holloway Road and for those attending the University. Libeskind's own words on the graduate centre project are both illuminating and obfuscatory; "ORION — the spatial emblem of the Northern sky — is the guiding light for developing a unique icon for the London Metropolitan University on Holloway Road. The Orion project provides a landmark attracting visitors to the cultural program within by its articulated forms. The Orion project has an enlivening impact on the wider urban context and particularly on the image and accessibility of the University. The three intersecting elements that form the building strategically emphasise certain relationships: one creates a connection between the public, the new building and the university behind, one form gestures from the university toward the tube connection to the city and one more regular form stitches the new building into the context of Holloway Road. A small plaza at the entrance provides an accent and an engaging gateway."

*The plan of the Graduate centre (top) indicates how it has to be read as an addition to the existing complex, one that deliberately seeks to integrate itself into the University's circulation routing whilst maintaining a discrete identity and pstrong, idiosyncratic presence on the street. The Orion link apparently comes from Libeskind standing on the site and casually looking up at the night sky - and he accidentlay noticed Orion and thought 'Well, I am in North London — perhaps this Orion thing is significant'. Whether you read this in terms of marketing hype or a neo-mythical sentiment in the guise of something far more rational hardly detracts from the reality that the affective charge at issue stirs just beneath the symbolic surface of architecture. It is fascinating to see how everyone grasps at the narrative on offer.*

## 59 Straw Bale politics

9–10 Stock Orchard Street, N7
Sarah Wigglesworth & Jeremy Till, 2001
Tube: Caledonian Road

Once upon a time two architects found an industrial site adjacent to one of London's main rail lines. Later, they found the money to demolish and start work on a dream house and studio — calling in the builders to work from a small model and the TV crews to record it all. That anything was realised at all — and that it has distinctive merits — is remarkable. The house / studio was apparently always intended to be as much political as 'green': a feminist statement of protest against 'patriarchal' values ostensibly driving a high-tech agenda and prompting a programme of 'as-found' materials that are easily handled. Such possibly naive, pseudo-hippy, urban-farmer ambitions are, of course, a rich psychological field and easily criticised, but this might be to miss the daring and bravery of what has been done. In essence, the scheme is a T-shaped plan, with the office part along the rail lines, defending itself against the rattling express trains by cement-filled bags. However, it is raised up on concrete stilts, so that the criterion of protecting the inner garden area is distinctly undermined.

*The street approach offers a bizarre mix.*

And in this latter area is a self-sufficiency garden programmed for the holocaust coming, complete with vegetable patch and garden shed. But the attractive part is the adjacent house architecture: a mix of Rudolf Schindler (again raised up) and romantic turrets (described as a reading and lookout tower, and as a 'thermal flue' and natural vent, as well as 'a book stack') from which a lady might gaze out over north London's urbanity (which now includes some

massive, real-life apartment blocks immediately sitting opposite, which set a contrast in values). At the very end of the garden is a bedroom tower (which, the TV programme informed us, came about because of slow site progress and the need to provide some basic shelter on the site while the complex was completed). Here, the straw bales used in much of the construction, are exposed behind corrugated plastic. The structure is a mix of steel and concrete and timber, and the gabions propping up the upper parts actually surround a concrete inner reality. These are topped by sprung cushioning devices intended to absorb the vibrations from the trains. Overall, the whole thing — an on-going project always awaiting extra funds to bring it to completion — is a mad, eccentric and very English delight. But it is one which (despite its pretensions) hardly posits a plausible agenda of change in urban living (arguably, the apartment blocks across the lines — quite an alteration to the Londoner's tradition of terrace housing — do that). A French architect described it all as baroque. It is also eclectic, erudite in its way and (especially with the neo-Schindler parts) betraying real architectural enthusiasms. These authors have not only stuck their necks out, but have enjoyed the commitment.

*The studio block has cement-filled bags to the railway side and is faced with plastic fabric on its other sides. Till jokes that his builder suggested this was a nappy keeping the 'architectural shit' in!*

## Platform One

**60**

2 Donegal Street, N1
Gollifer Langston Architects, 2002
Tube: Kings Cross

Not so imposing from the outside, but this is a very good example of the architect working with a strong social brief, with the client, to design (in this case) an extension to an existing school in the form of a busy and well equipped adult learning centre for a large and diverse ethnic community. On the interior, this is a more exciting place, both architecturally and socially.

## Victoria Miro Gallery

**61**

16 Wharf Road, N1 7RW
Trevor Horne Architects, 2000
Tube: Old Street / Angel

This is a marvellous conversion hitting all the right notes. Much of this is down to a sensitivity toward the characteristics of the existing, former mattress-making warehouse and knowing just where to intervene and where to hold back. The retained roof is terrific. (Also see Allies & Morrison's work at Chelsea Art College for a comparison, of sorts.) Oh, and you might enjoy the art they show. The architects say: "The conversion [...] was undertaken in two stages — initially, we stripped out the building for the inaugural exhibition Raw. During this period, working with a group of the gallery's artists and through the use of a model and drawings, we developed the final scheme. The brief was formed to make two separate galleries. The ground floor gallery would be the 'white box' fully serviced with power and data to accommodate painting, photography, video and film works and a smaller space where more intimate works can be shown. Also on the ground floor is the project room and storage space with the office discreetly at the rear with access to the canal waterside. On the upper floor we left the structure and roof structure of the building exposed giving the space a less finished feel not as formal as the lower gallery allowing for large sculptures and installations". *Also see the Gagosian, p.98.*

**62** *This house sits at the end of a Georgian terrace (40 Douglas Road, N1 by **Future Systems**; Tube: Highbury Corner), its four storeys straddling the two flank walls and wrapped in a 'skin' that rises as a front wall of glass block on one side, over the roof, and down the southern garden side as a splendid, falling wall of glass. The front, with its glass blocks (vaguely Maison de Verre), stepped stainless steel approach to the threshold across a 'void of stones' (vague undertones of aeroplane access stairs providing access to a parked industrial object) and groovy 1960's, round-corner entry door (hatch) is probably the most interesting because it gives much away about the values and enthusiasms of these designers.*

*Incidentally, it is worth noting that architects currently have a problematic relation with art and artists. Any self-respecting work of any scale can hardly do without an artist on board the project. This often has self-evident benefits. However, placed in the context of an historical fragmentation of the architect's role and a divestment of all numerical-based skills which leaves their core-skill and project role somewhat ambiguous, architects might be playing a dangerous game. Having an artist on board may be flattering to them and the client, ostensibly underscoring urbane good taste and judgement, but it simultaneously suggests the architect is without sufficient capacity to exercise aesthetic judgement and is in danger of effecting an impression contrary to that intended. Since architecture as an aesthetically-oriented vocation is sometimes the principal 'added value' an architect brings to a project, there is an argument that the prudent practitioner must surely be wary in posing as 'artist' rather than elevating and articulating the unique values of being 'an architect'.*

## 63    Dalston Cultural House

Gillett Street, N16
Hawkins Brown, 2005
Tube: Highbury
Rail: Dalston Kingsland

Go to the Gherkin or to the Royal Festival Hall and one experiences a cultural dimension to the architecture that is easily taken for granted. Go to Peckham Library and that aspect becomes pertinent and unavoidable. Similarly, at the Dalston Culture House, architecture gets mixed with an ethnic vibrancy that is very London and not at all the City or the South Bank. You can go and mix architecture and jazz any evening, but also try a Saturday afternoon to see how the DCH swims within a sea of local entrepreneurial culture — except that some of this is about to be swept away in a tidy-up to the car park in order to create a new Gillett Square (part of Mayor Livingstone's 100 squares programme for London).

The principal architectural event — where the Vortex is — is simple enough, but strives to impact upon the whole square in the way its façade lights up at night. And then, all along its adjacent facade is a series of rented sales booths selling everything imaginable. The whole thing tests and perhaps defines the fluid cultural boundaries of what architecture is and does, what it strives for and is forced to do. Whether, for example, the entirely worthy make-over of the car park into a sanitised realm of design decency (the image shows us the white middle - classes sipping cappuccino outdoors and sitting by fountains) is at once relevant and irrelevant to the community, how it is served and how it signals identity and self-esteem to itself. Compare it with Trafalgar Square's make-over by Foster, Stanton Williams' scheme at the Tower and (when it is completed) the latter's efforts at Sloane Square. (Other public spaces in this scheme include Kensington High Street, Exhibition Road, the Victoria Embankment, Highbury Corner, Barking Town Centre, etc. — most of which are in the process of being realised.)

## City & Islington Lifelong Learning Centre

**64**

28–42 Blackstock Road, N4 2DG3
Wilkinson Eyre Architects, 2004
Tube: Finsbury Park

An adult education centre with a public library, incorporating a remodelled 1880's school. The new parts wrap the old and the incorporation of the library is to encourage a cross-over of usage. What you see on the street frontage is only a part of what is going on (see diagram below).

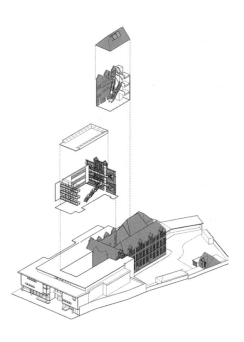

## Raines Dairy

**65**

Northworld Road, Stoke Newington, N16
Alford Hall Monaghan Morris, 2004
Rail: Stoke Newington

Another Peabody Trust experimental housing development, this time one of the better examples of what to do with 'volumetric' housing. This time, 11.6m x 3.8m units are stacked from 3-6 storeys in an overall T-shaped plan. There are 41 two-bed units and 11 three-bed units, plus one one-bed and eight one-bed live-work units (127 in all). The constructional logic takes advantage of the fact that cost goes down per sq. metre with size and a reduction of the number of units per household. Access is by conventional access decks at the rear. (Compare with Container City.) About 55% of the project was constructed off-site. All windows, doors, internal walls and fittings were factory-fitted, but balconies, etc. were on-site. The project was built in about 50 weeks (estimated to be a 40% saving over conventional build methods). As an example of so-called volumetrics, this is one of the better schemes.
*Also see Baron's Place (p.244) and Murray Grove (p.222).*

## 66 Mossbourne Academy

Mossbourne Community Academy
Downs Park Road E5 (opp. Hackney Downs)
Richard Rogers Partnership, 2004
Rail: Hackney Central

This school (described by the architects as 'log cabin meets Lloyds) for 900 11-16 year olds is part of a government programme to bring private money and leadership into inner-city schools. The scheme occupies a triangular site, up against rail lines and so the architects have developed a linear design that sits along two sides of the site, and faces away from the trains toward Hackney Downs. These façades show the laminated timber construction. Internally, the scheme seeks to mix facilities and break down conventional barriers; externally, there was a similar intention to erode boundaries that was compromised by landscape budget cuts and a security fence. (The site diagram speaks of 'open arms to Hackney Downs' and indicates the V-plan opening out in that direction.) Nevertheless, this is a fine design. All teaching spaces face out to the court and the landscaping of the Downs.

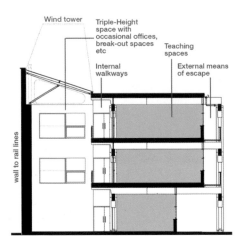

Wind tower
Triple-Height space with occasional offices, break-out spaces etc
Internal walkways
Teaching spaces
External means of escape
wall to rail lines

## 67 Hackney College

Falkirk Street, N1
Hampshire County Architects/Perkins Ogden
Hawkins Brown, 1997
Tube: Old Street

This large 'community college' in Hoxton, just beyond the northern edge of the City and adjacent to Hoxton Market, serves about 14,000 students. It mixes brick, timber, metal louvres and stretched fabric sails as key features of buildings that race around the perimeter of a large, 2.8 ha site, defining a landscaped and colonnaded inner courtyard at the heart of the complex whilst ensuring the outer edges maintain a definition of surrounding streets. The aesthetic is crisp and fresh, although the understandably heavy security presence contradicts the open arms, community message. Hampshire County Architects, experts in this field, are responsible for the scheme; Hawkins Brown refurbished two Edwardian schools included on the site. Artists were brought in to design gates and screens, courtyard benches, water features, etc.

## Hackney Empire

Matcham completed this innovative 'variety palace' in 1901 (within 5 months!) and Ronalds did this superb refurbishment incorporating an 'eat-your-heart-out-Venturi' sign on the exterior. The original's lobby area is described as 'flamboyant Rococo Baroque style'. After serving as a live TV studio in the '50's and a bingo hall in the '60's the Empire returned to theatrical events in the mid-'80's. The Ronalds team have entirely refurbished and restored the interiors, added to the fly-tower and provided new back-stage areas.. . . and they gave us that wonderful signage (currently a recurring theme in London's new architecture, but never so full and neo-Venturi on as this).

**68**

291 Mare Street E8
Frank Matcham / Tim Ronalds, 2004
Tube: Bethnal Green. Rail: Hackney central

Photo: Siobain Macgrath

Photo: Siobain Macgrath

**69** *This is one of the better warehouse conversions in London, although the most interesting parts – zinc-clad roof pavilions and the central court – are not readily accessible. The building, located in* 10-22 **Shepardess Walk,** *N1, fills a whole block and is centred around an open court fitted with new access balconies, a glazed lift, and minimal landscaping with Scottish beach stones and three silver birch trees (parking is underneath). The ground floor is commercial space and the upper levels are 50 apartments. It is all very direct, no gimmicks, with robust, consistent detailing and very satisfying. The designers are Buschow Henley (1999; see their TalkBack building in an earlier section).*

**70** *The* **Rushton Street Surgery,** *on the south side of Shoreditch Park, N1 (Penoyre & Prasad, 1999) divides doctors over two floors around a central, top-lit mall running through the centre of the plan and the street façade offers itself as the presentable face of the building, embracing on-site parking, whilst the rear (south) side is quite plain – architecturally, a layering of accommodation along the central axis. It is the kind of design that is deeply considerate of users' needs, operating costs, etc., although some details have suffered from a procurement process that, at the final stages of the job, distanced the architects.*

**221**

# Inner Ring

## 71 Gainsborough Studios

New North Road / Poole Street, N1
Munkenbeck & Marshall, 2003
Tube: Highbury / Old Street

A good example of what the younger English middle class is into today: a block of apartments that sits adjacent to the Regent's Canal and wraps itself around an inner court with a rather nice art installation (possibly because it is intrinsically architectonic). The building was originally a power station (its chimney was demolished in World War II as a potential target for Nazi bombers); it also housed the famous British film studios where Alfred Hitchcock made many films. The scheme comprises 280 new build apartments, office and studio space and a restaurant. A quarter of the residential area is affordable housing. The new blocks are built around a square and canal side walk beside the Canal. The tallest of these is 14 storeys. Its successes are mixed with curious lapses, as if five different people were doing the design, but it has its moments — particularly the steel sculpture that dominates the central court.

## 72 White Cube 2

White Cube
48 Hoxton Square N1
Mike Rundell, 2002
Tube: Old Street

2002 brought us a two-storey addition to the top of White Cube's building in Hoxton Square, designed by Mike Rundell and providing additional office, conference and related spaces for this trendy gallery in a trendy part of town. It's an incongruous addition, but strangely elegant and entirely appropriate both to the gallery and in this area, epitomising the nature of optimistic regeneration. The interior of the gallery is, as you might imagine, a squeeky clean white box. (Rundell also designed the well received but ill-fated Pharmacy restaurant for Damien Hirst et al.)

*This part of Hoxton, just to the east of Old Street Underground station, has enjoyed high fashionability in the last ten years (in parallel with the City's expansion outside its traditional boundaries), although the high prices and status are belied by a crummy reality. It all rather underscores the fact that so-called 'hygiene' factors possibly have merely coincidental relation to well-being. In this instance forms definitely follow function in the sense that the latter are social factors at work, engendering architectural change in their wake. But progress to date suggests real change in Hoxton has a long way to go before condition of the urban fabric catches up with the caché the area enjoys.*

**73** *So-called 'volumetric' housing has become a new enthusiasm among architects in recent years, despite confusing economics. This — commissioned by the Peabody Trust — was one of the first examples of container-sized units assembled Safdie, 1960's style and given some architectural lipstick (**Murray Grove**, N1; Cartwright Pickard Architects). The Japanese, one suspects — for whom pre-fabrication has historically been taken for granted — would be bemused by this focus upon technology rather than any enhanced consumer service it provides (and I argue that point that from consultancy experience). Sound transmission problems have apparently been obviated in later developments such as Raines Dairy (p.219) and Baron's Place (244).*

# Amnesty International HQ

This conversion and addition to a former furniture factory building (1911 and 1954) is definitely a cut above the ordinary — and from a young practice. The facilities serve 20 staff and 50 volunteers in what is a half private / half public building where all staff are located, meetings and training sessions held, etc. The old buildings have been entirely refurbished and a new entrance building added on the street side (what is called the Human Rights Action Centre), providing lecture hall, exhibition space, etc.

**74**

17-25 New Inn Yard, EC2
Witherford Watson Mann Architects, 2005
Tube: Old Street

# Lux Building

This was designed as a small cinema and art gallery for the Film Makers Co-operative and London Electronic Arts in a trendy location within then 'up and coming' Hoxton. Contrived to look as if the accommodation is in two separate buildings, the blue, composite brick/concrete structure (which is a composite of both precast and in-situ concrete) has an intentional heavy, industrial quality whilst the large windows promote a continuous 'dialogue' between interior and exterior. It is worth a visit if, as a contrast to the manifestations of global capitalism at the heart of the City, you are prowling peripheral areas in search of authenticity. However, the cinema went bust in 2002 and the place now has other uses.

**75**

2-4 Hoxton Square, N1
Maccreanor Lavington Architects, 1998
Tube: Old Street

*Purely coincidentally, compare the Lux building with this late C18th Georgian house in Nelson Square, SE1 (near the Palestra building) — it has more glass than brickwork, but without the concrete behind.*

**76** *Nicholas Hawksmoor's **Christ Church**, Spitalfields, E1, sits on the eastern edge of the City monumentally towering above the domestic properties that sit beneath it's magnificent tower and steeple. Commissioned as part of the Fifty Churches Act of 1711 that attempted to bring religion to London's masses, it was designed in 1720 and has been recently restored, so is well worth a visit. And, if Hawksmoor interests you, you might want to read Peter Ackroyd's book of that name. It has our master-builder as a character of arcane interests and magical inclinations burying people in the foundations of his churches! Fictional, fun, and definitely an enlivening notion of architectural endeavour. Go one block further east and you are definitely out of the City and in Brick Lane.*

*Another new project in this area — just being completed at the time of writing — is **Fairmule House**, by Quay2c architects (Waterson Street, E2; Tube: Old Street). It introduces London to a form of large, solid timber structural panels that have long been common in Germany. But this is pre-fab from Po-Mo architects of the Venturi mold crossed with latter-day predelictions for narrative, picking up on facts such as an adjacent spilll-over graveyard where Thomas Fairchild is buried. (He who crossed a Sweet William with a Carnation to produce an artefactual hybrid called the 'Fairchild Mule'.) The architects handle all this with some wit, insinuating 'Mule' motifs and even managing to stretch the gardening references to the rationale given for selecting the timber structure. A mix of double and single-bed, double-aspect apartments are provided, together with seven business units. The artist involved Julia Manheim.*

## 77 Geffrye Museum

Kingsland Road, E2
Branson Coates Architecture, 1998
Tube: Liverpool Street, then 149/242 bus

The Geffrye Museum is a pleasant London oddity. Formed from almshouses (1715) and devoted to the history of our domestic interiors. It sits on the edge of the East End, on a busy arterial road, but offers a village-like setting: tall trees define the boundary; beyond them is a green forecourt, and arrayed around three of its sides are the cottage-like former almshouses, calmly dominated by what was once a chapel at the architectural focal point of the grouping. The visitor approaches the Museum off busy Kingsland Road and enters in one corner. From here they progress along the frontage of the almshouses, following an architectural promenade on a temporal theme, through what was once an individual series of homes, now transformed into room sets displaying domestic interiors from different historical periods, beginning in the C17 and ending at the new C20 gallery by Branson Coates. The promenade terminates at a place where a new focal space has been created between three brick gables. This space – formed beneath a roof that spans between the gables and conceived as if it were an exterior place — houses a restaurant and shop, and it is also a foyer space that leads on to the C20th. gallery itself. One of the three gables is a termination of the almshouses, where they turn the corner; two of the gables are actually the ends of the same, horse-shoe planned building. One leads into the shop the other forms an entrance to the restaurant kitchen. Entering between them into the new gallery, the visitor has the C20 sets arranged in an arc, all around. The backwall is solid masonry and the roof structure is a heavy, open timber truss. At the centre of this top-lit space is a grand, curving concrete and glass staircase that leads down to a lower set of rooms mostly used for educational purposes. From the outside, the new addition is a blank, two-storey, brick-clad building, with a sheltered ramp wrapping around the outside. Try and go here — you'll enjoy it.

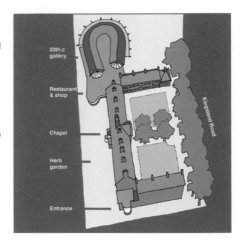

**78** There was a time when London was proud of its welfare housing programme, begun with schemes like the Arts & Crafts **Boundary Estate** (1897–1900), at Arnold Circus, E2, just north of Broadgate, an estate of 5500 people at a density of 200 per acre, designed by LCC Architects. The programme ran right through to the 1970's and, even though the Boundary estate is now a sadly neglected and decrepit example, it still speaks of values to be proud of. Laid out as a series of apartment blocks radiating from a central, landscaped roundabout, it is comparable with the better preserved Millbank estate of the same date, behind the Tate Britain. (And it is pleasing to see that the estate is at last undergoing renovation.)

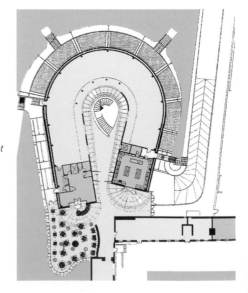

David Adjaye's Dirty House (for artists Tim Noble and Sue Webster) has to be seen in the flesh rather than as a photograph. The latter is all pose. The real thing is richly attuned: an experience that is contextural and tonal as well as direct and simple. Since it's private, there is nothing to see of the interior life behind the external brick wall plastered with anti-graffiti paint to give a textured effect that unifies the whole even as it lets its rough, uneven character show through — well, nothing except the floating flat roof that hovers above the defensive screen with its flush opaque glass windows at ground floor level. It's at night, of course, that this floating lid delivers its poetic effect.

*While here, have a look at the nearby Boundary estate. Note that this location is just north of Brick Lane and the Sunday morning markets that transform this area.*

## Tin House

This house off Brick Lane (more or less directly east of Christ's Church) is an indicator of how the area has recently changed: cheek by jowl with Bangledeshi restaurants sits this galvanised steel and glass beast that manages to blend in surprisingly well. The lower floors are bedrooms and the top, double-height space is the living area. It's very elegant and comes across as a rather polite English version of the houses Frank Gehry used to put up in Venice (LA).

**81** *David Adjaye also has a domestic insert near here in Ashfield Street, E1, near the Alsop building (overleaf): the* **Elektra House** *(2000). Its blank (but mildly articulated) facade betrays zero hint of domesticity and perhaps indicates that, merely a few years ago, the Planners were desperate for gentrification in this area. Having said that, it's not at all a bad strategy, merely rather defensive and introverted, as well as simultaneously 'in your face'. (The architectural equivalent of flashing your bum to the neighbours?) Only the hint of glass at the roof eaves gives anything away about a life beyond the facade. . . And yet, it stays in the memory and an architecture with that minimal degree of the 'tingle factor' that draws one's attention.*

## 82 Medical School

Institute of Cell & Molecular Science
Stepney Way, E1
Alsop Architects / Amec, 2005
Tube: Whitechapel

This is basically a Queen Mary University medical research building for PhD students, attached to the adjacent hospital. The intelligence of the design derives from the aspects of the brief linked to the building's funding: a call for a single lab space (cutting across the usual departmental boundaries); facilities for 'write-ups'; and an ability to put everything on display to parties of school children — thus encouraging them into science. Since the single lab space was so large, it was decided that the best place to locate it was underground, filling the entire site area. The above ground parts then divided themselves into three 'slices': a thin building handling reception, a cafe, and a lecture theatre; a parallel slice of public open space; and a third slice which is a galleried atrium — the gallery accommodating write-up benches, with the heart of the atrium as an opportunity to float meeting 'pods'. And it works splendidly.

The real delight is the interior: a veritably vibrant scene straight out of a Hieronymous Bosch painting — all the madness of the *Garden of Earthly Delights* and all that. (The 'mushroom pod' off the entrance is actually a platform rather than a 'pod' like the meeting three spaces. And one of these — the one for children — was without the funding that will furnish it as of early 2006.)

If there is a problem with this building, it is the comparatively cool blandness of the external appearance and the Bruce Mclean art works that adorn the surface like well-designed but nevertheless gratuitous advertising bill-boards. In fairness, the central piazza space awaits (in early 2006) some public furniture. But the space cries out for trees and it is sad that the budget did not extend to structurally accommodating these above the labs. As for that underground space, it is surprisingly pleasant. And, above, the hundreds of galleried PhD students also appear to be content with the facilities provided. However, all experimental ventures always have problems — this one includes such things as the neoprene skin to one of the pods that acts as a perfect sound transmitter.

*The exterior of the building is simple but stylish, and enlivened by decorative Bruce McLean glass-works on a microbiological theme. The area between the long building which is mainly for plant and the building with the galleried atrium is an open pizza that stil awaits whatever will turn it into a desirable place to linger or play (although it is unlikely the latter would be allowed).*

Photo: Hanne Lund

*Below left: one of the pods (with a spikey one behind). Centre: view along the gallery with a stainless steel clad service tower on the left. Below right: view down from the gallery to the basement lab space and its benches.*

*Left: the non-territorial lab spaces are simply organised according to a hierarchy of functionalist specialism and danger, with the simplest functions set out as an array of long benches.*

Idea Store 2004 , Chrisp Street. DLR: All Saints, E14
Idea Store 2005, Mile End / Brady Street, E1
ub@: Whitechapel
Architect: Adjaye Associates

## ...ng

## two sharp ideas

It is a strange reality that libraries can't be denominated as such any more. In Tower Hamlets, they have become a new invention called an 'idea store' . In contrast to the absurdity of the term, these two 'stores; by David Adjaye confirm his status as a rising talent on the London scene. The first 'store', just north of the Isle of Dogs, was relatively small, but has all the ingredients one sees amplified and refined at Mile End. Both are sharp designs and the second store — set midst a strong Bangledeshi community — has real architectural substance. *Note the two locations with the same number on the map.*

## Idea Store One (Chrisp Street):

Compared with the second (two storey) Store this one is a more tentative project — the idea is being tried out at a local, 1960's market, above a row of shops (just north of the Isle of Dogs). The architect's challenge was therefore to accommodate the new Store to the old structure. The outcome is a rather Post-Modern mix of grids — steel structure, timber beams, timber cladding primary structure, glazing bars, light fittings, etc. — that deliberately bear no relation to one another. The overall concept is an arrival hall with lots of computers and an escalator up to the first floor. The latter has seminar and meeting rooms down one side and the books stacked in mid-height plywood shelving that sinuously curve around to create interesting nooks and crannies. Everything is fairly simple, cheap 'n' cheerful, well considered and well detailed.

## Idea Store Two (Mile End):

The second Idea Store — now much larger and five storeys — is a leap forward: its feels distinctly similar to the first in all respects, but there is an added confidence and refinement to the scheme and the detailing. It is full of references: Alsop at Peckham; Herzog & de Meron at the Tate and at the Laban, and all the more interesting because of that. The basic concept is that of the retail department store with particular — and considered — ways of relating to the street and its activities and flows. Inside, visitors move straight to any floor (a cafe is on the top) and can withdraw books at a variety of points around the building (there is no conventional desk, although a diminutive version is located on the ground floor).

*Above: the Idea Store in Chrisp Street (just north of the Isle of Dogs).*
*Below left: the Idea Store in Mile End.*

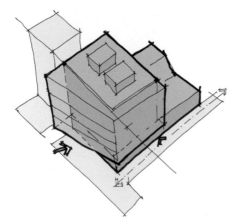

*The second Idea Store's principal architectural moves include a street projection well beyond the building line (see diagram left). This wraps two sides of the building and serves as a shelter and canopy which houses the escalator drawing visitors up to the first and second floors — a simple and clever move that announces the library to those walking along the street, where one of London's largest street markets is located on a daily basis. From the 2nd floor, visitors can continue up into the building so that every floor is well used; the cafe, for example is housed on the fourth floor. Originally, the escalator was to have gone all the way to the top by wrapping itself around the building — but the Council made budget savings! Nevertheless, the resulting void on the east side provides a dramatic three storey height relief to the sandwiched floors of the upper parts (top right. opposite).*

The Idea Store at Chrisp Street (above) sits as part of the Lansbury Market and is actually on East India Dock Road (the DLR is across the road). Above: the entrance area, with escalator up to the main library (sorry, ideas) floor.

    The later Store (below and right) is simply a much enlarged version, but feels to be a more refined work, despite the greater complexity (and just as much cost cutting by the local authority). If it has a problem it's that the main roof sports incongruous exposed steel beams (shades of Mies) and plant rooms that appear to be distinct after-thoughts. In fact the rear massing is altogether untidy (a not unimportant consideration given that this façade is almost as important as the street façade).

    The colouring of the cladding is argued to be prompted by the canvas covers to street stalls at both these locations. Whether this is a subtle point or an effete narrative prop effecting itself purely at an abstracted conceptual level distinct from the experiential reality is something you can only decide for yourself by visiting the building. Both the mannerism (of off-set grids and coloured glass) and the conceit (of narrative) are currently rather fashionable, but they certainly seem appropriate to this project.

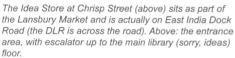

## 84 Queen Mary College

Queen Mary College, Mile End E3
various architects
Tube: Mile End

Queen Mary College has a number of interesting buildings on its campus, including the **Westfield student accommodation** by Feilden Clegg Bradley (2004); a **student Union building** 1999) by Hawkins Brown; a science building by Sheppard Robson; and a **Library** by Colin St. John Wilson (1989; Wilson also did the British Library); **student housing** to the south of Westfield by MacCormac Jamieson Prichard (1991); and a small **graduate building** (rather po-faced and sub-Libeskind, but not bad) from Surface Architects (2005; situated as one enters, adjacent to the canal).

The **Westfield** buildings are by far the most architecturally ambitious: 5 buildings and accommodation for 1000 students. Formerly a gravel yard, the site sits hard up against the main line railway to Liverpool Street and overlooks Regent's Canal and Mile End Park. The buildings are set around simple garden courts 3 of which are four storey brick buildings, to the north is the 7 storey slab of larger flats (clad in oxidized) copper that attempts

to dispel the noise from the railway. The Eastern block which contains apartments for visiting academics, a ground floor cafe, shop, common room and laundry, is clad in pre-patinated copper. The internal layout tries to offer as much internal layout variety as possible with 17 possible types.

The obvious comparison to make with the library is the same architect's design for the British Library at St. Pancras. The 'bagged' brickwork on the exterior is more timid than Lewerentz's precedent of St. Mark's in Stockholm, but it is the only example you will find in London and always takes courage to execute. The interior is comparatively cheap-and-cheerful, as one might expect for a contemporary university library.

(*Of course the most lively building is Alsop's cell & Microbiological research building, fuurhter west of this campus.*)

## 85 Mile End Park

Mile End Park, E3
CZWG / Jonathan Freegard, 2000-02
Tube: Mile End

This East End park is a fascinating example of regreening: an area bombed in WWII, grassed over, left to dereliction, and reinvented with the assistance of lottery money and the energies of a local charity (Environment Trust) together with the local authority, etc.

The Park sits alongside the Grand Union Canal, its linear development is zoned for ply, ecology, art, sport, etc. Since a main road crosses the park, it was decided to build a 'green bridge' (CZWG) so as to lend the park continuity (an appropriate and well executed idea that isn't half as novel as it's authors pretend) and which includes retail accommodation in glazed green bricks.

The Ecology Park includes two half-buried buildings whose open side fronts the canal by Jonathan Freegard Architects. One is an education centre and the other is an arts gallery, both trumpeted as having 'been designed to be as energy efficient as possible using a 'Passive annual heat storage system' (PAHS). Another two are planned.

## Stratford Circus

**86**

Theatre Square, Salway Road, E15
Levitt Bernstein, 2002
Tube: Stratford

A successful project conjoins many things together. To isolate any one would be unjust. And yet the design of this building is clearly a major part of what makes the Circus such a lively and valuable community resource (much like Peckham Library). The Circus' programme is focused upon the performing arts, on schools and out-reach projects. At the heart of the building is a central hall with a cafe and a suspended gallery level, off which there are studios, dance and theatre spaces (Circus 1, 2 and 3). It's tight (clearly too small) and buzzing. Every community should have one of these. *(Compare with The Broadway, in Barking centre.)*

> *When there, also look at the adjacent **Picture House** by Burrell Foley Fisher, 1998, a place with a restaurant and bar as well as cinemas. Like the station, it's a welcome, fresh design for the area. There is also the **Stratford Bus Depot** (by London Transport).*

## Stratford Station

**87**

Stratford Station, E15
Chris Wilkinson Architects (concourse)/
Troughton McAslan, 1999

This is quite a statement and just what Stratford needs (the place is virtually a large, inhabited and isolated roundabout designed by highway engineers). The main building – serving as an interchange and terminus for the underground and DLR – is a soaring, curved roof structure and a simple solution to a complex design problem with design criteria for crashing trains and collapsing roof beams, and the accommodation of underground trains and a river. In addition, the big volume acts as a simple solar ventilator, drawing air from the shed and the lower passages. But it's the way Wilkinson plays off the big statement against considered detail and a thoughtful use of materials that makes this building sing. The ceiling, for example, is almost invisibly lit and appears as a gigantic ribbed and shimmering surface. The JLE platforms are by Troughton McAslan (now split; and Chris Wilkinson is now Wilkinson Eyre).

> *Stratford, you should be aware, is the centre of some of the ambitious eastern gateway plans coping with London's housing needs and the Olympics. Arup and Fletcher Priest are master-planning the vast former railway areas to the north of Stratford centre and the general planning intent stretches down the Lea Valley to the Thames. All kinds of issues are at stake: from wild life to the need any metropolis has for derelict, low-rent areas (we can't gentrify everything) to conflicts between commercial, Olympic, and political interests. And many people are afraid the Olympics will engender one-minute wonders that leave Londoners with a burden of media-oriented architectures. It's a very confused and confusing scene whose story will, no doubt, be one day written (after the Olympics, one presumes).*

## 88 Pumping Station 'F'

Abbey Lane, E15
Allies and Morrison, 1997
Tube: West Ham

The Lee Valley is not the most attractive part of London, but it does possess a curious, post-industrial authenticity. Here sits a gleaming aluminium beast: the enclosure to hi-tech pumping machinery that deals with some of London's prodigious waste: a large industrial barn, some 57m long, 29m wide and 23m. high — a gleaming enclosure to sophisticated pumping machinery, the fifth of a series of sewage pumping stations built here since 1869. Four sewers are brought together into one large concrete culvert that forms the base of the entire building. Using 16 submersible pumps, the sewage is pumped up 13m and discharged into the upper level culvert, and from there into the 1869 main outfall sewer and the treatment plant at Barking (in the same manner it has been done since that time). Four diesel generators — sitting in the middle of the building — power the whole affair whilst a central gantry and two side-aisle travelling cranes are

for lifting the submersible pumps and other machinery for maintenance. The enclosing superstructure comprises lightweight steel 'A' frames, bearing internally upon a rectilinear frame that carries travelling cranes necessary for maintaining the interior machinery. It is this structure that is at the heart of the design and becomes the key to the expression of the gable ends.

*Inevitably, one can't but enjoy comparisons with London's original 'barn': St. Paul's in Covent Garden (right; Inigo Jones, 1633), John Outram's pumping station on the Isle of Dogs (another shed elevated into architecture; Stewart Street; 1988) and the Richard Rogers pumping station at the Royal Victoria Dock (bottom right; 1987).*

## 89

*This timber-framed and clad SureStart school and community centre (**Abbey Children's Centre**; North Street, Barking IG11, designed by Cazenove Architects, 2005; rail — Barking) offers a welcome architectural relief in an otherwise bland suburban area. The building form wraps itself around the perimeter of the site, thus providing enclosure to an inner playground. However, things go awry when the architects tell us that, "Its identity is underscored by timber framing that strives to make references to a tradition of fishing boats for which Barking was once famous"!*

# Plashet link

Plashet School, Plashet Grove, E6
Birds Portchmouth Russum, 2000
Tube: East Ham

Technically, there's not a lot to say about this pedestrian bridge for Plashet School in Newnham: an artfully propped, prefabricated, 67m, blue painted steel construction, covered with tensed fabric, linking two halves of a girls' school across a busy road, (one from the 1930's, the other an eight storey 1960's building).

But it's where utilitarianism ends and the enjoyment of designing a contrived artifice begins that this simple link bridge elevates itself into the alchemy that transforms the mundane into the valuable. It's a joy to see, to pass under, to walk through, giving the anonymous school buildings a new identity. The sinuous curve (argued as necessary to preserve an existing tree, but they would say that wouldn't they?) is interrupted by an intermediate hang-out with steel benches.

It's cheerful, inventive and — in the details that incorporate lighting and get rid of rainwater — distinctly quirky. You'll either rank this, together with Alsop's Peckham Library, as two of the best pieces of London's contemporary architecture — or dismiss it as over-wrought mannerism posing as instrumentalism. We hope you'll join with us in seeing this as the celebratory act that is good design: entirely rooted in its substance, in contingent factors and it is and does. This is architecture at its simplest and most sophisticated: on target; both appropriate and authentic (two words that are difficult to employ these days).

Doesn't it have problems? Well, of course: in particular, the magazines never show you the most difficult and unresolvable part of the equation: the ends where the new bridge hits the two schools. And it's smaller than you think. And the fabric gets dirty. However, few designs can induce the feeling that such criticism is carping.

**91** Another project at central Barking, adjacent to the Town Hall, is Tim Foster's refurbishment of a 1936 theatre, which provides a new multi-purpose auditorium as well as a foyer extension, rehearsal and teaching spaces for the Performing Arts Department of Barking College (**The Broadway**; 2004). The architects tell us that 'the glazed façade reveals the activity within and welcomes the community inside'. Certainly, the refurbishment is a welcome change. (Compare with Stratford Centre.)

**92** At the time of writing AHMM has two large, twin blocks being constructed in front of the old inter-war years **Town Hall at Barking** (Clockhouse Avenue, Barking IG11; Rail: Barking. This strident, 'U'-shaped plan will accommodate a library (now a 'life long learning centre') and 206 one and two bedroom flats. The building — about as strident as designs get in such a context — should be complete by mid-2006 and will include a 'new civic square'. The adjacent Town Hall is a 1936 design (built 1954 - 8).

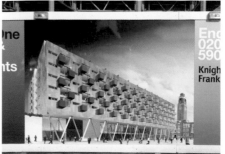

## Inner Ring

### Two from Barber

Peter Barber's work has begun to make an impact, particularly in these prize-winning designs for East End areas where everyone is seeking to concentrate housing activity. Contexturalism — certainly in formal terms — is given two fingers and a breath of Mediterranean bloom (prompted, in part, by the UK's current building Regulations) has been dropped into the midst of areas that, historically, are better known for distress and that peculiar London quality of semi-suburban meanness. But to address these schemes only in terms of their novel aesthetic would be unfair: these are well considered design schemes striving to cope with issues of urbanity, density and cost. A language of perimeter geometries, terraces and courts are mixed with features such as oriel windows, Romeo & Juliet balconies and the like.

*Images (top to bottom): Donnybrook; axo of Donnybrook scheme and two images of Tanner Street nearing completion. Note the inter-war mock 'tudorbethan' housing on the left.*

### 93 Donnybrook Quarter

Architects text: "The project is conceived as a celebration of the public social life of the street. Every aspect of the design is configured to promote buzzing, thriving public space made with a hard edge of buildings. Streets overlooked by balconies, bay windows and roof terraces. Streets where people might enjoy to sit out, kids to play, people going to and from their homes or just passing through. Dwellings are laid out as a unique double stack hybrid, terrace/courtyard typology. Every unit having its own front door on the street and its own good sized outside space."

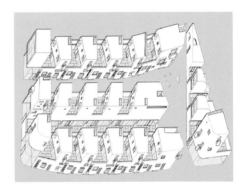

### 94 Tanner Street

Architects text: "Tanner Street Gateway is a dense street based urban quarter in the Thames Gateway laid out as a network of intimately scaled streets defined by a hard edge of buildings. At the heart of the scheme is a delightful, new tree lined public square, where a spectacular, 10 storey landmark building marks the junction of a number of important public routes. The new neighbourhood has around 200 dwellings in a mixture of town houses and unusual double stack apartments. Every unit has its own front door and its own good sized outside space."

A ten-storey block of 40 apartments adjacent to the Barber scheme (bottom left) is by Jestico & Whiles. The intention is that this acts as a landmark building on an approach from the town centre.

Donnybrook Quarter, Parnall Road, E3 (at Old Ford, nr Victoria Park) Peter Barbour, 2005 Tube: Bow Road. DLR: Pudding Mill Lane

Tanner Street housing, Barking 1C Peter Barbour, 2005 Tube: Barking

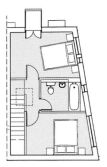

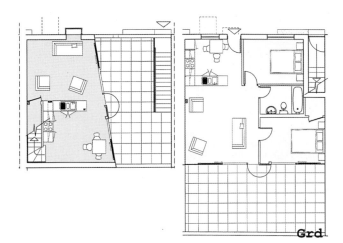

*Typical plans indicating what is meant by the 'hybrid' schema. (right to left; ground, first, second.)*

## Doris' Place

**95**

14 Broadway Market, E8
Peter Barbour, 2002
Train: London Fields

Another Barber design — a precursor of success with the larger schemes shown overleaf (designed with marion Lewis). The architect tells us that: "Doris' Place is an ultra-dense mixed use urban regeneration project on a 4.5m wide slot site in Hackney. The project wraps a retail unit, two maisonettes and a live/work unit around a central courtyard which is located at first floor levels. [...] The roof section of the scheme is topped by a dramatic tilted parabolic vaulted roof which has become a popular local landmark."

## BowZED

**96**

56 Tomlins Grove, E3
Bill Dunster Architects, 2005
Tube: Bow Road

With a more ecologically committed stance than most housing schemes, Bill Dunster demonstrates an apparent monopoly on ecological residential design (see Bedzed). Familiar features (apart from a daft name) are displayed e.g. solar panels and a wind cowl as at Bedzed, as well as ample balconies. Four apartments are fed by a single 15kW wood stove and solar panels and the planning is arranged around a central core that feeds up to the familiar wind cowl. It all fits in rather well to the Victorian terraces, but is it dreary to long for such an agenda to be handled by architects as equally enthused by living now as much as saving the planet's future?

## 97 Not Blue and Not Wood

Blue House, Garner Street, E2
FAT (Sean Griffiths), 2002
Train: Cambridge Heath

FAT's designs exhibit their '80's training and the 'Blue House' (actually pale turquoise; and it's not wood either, but fake wood boarding) betrays its author's PoMo enthusiasms (Venturi plus a touch of Arts & Crafts). The authors tell us: "We are more interested in the effect the thing has, than how you might produce it". Contexturalism here is a purely cerebral, transatlantic game that refuses parochialism: the house is two small apartments pretending to be a villa in Maine, deriving every possible benefit from its tight site and given odd features such as an end elevation capped by what is supposed to be an Amsterdam skyline. Like Venturi's work, the house deliberately obfuscates the boundary between fun and high architecture: 'the window seat [on the stair rising to the first floor] may be Loos on the inside, but on the outside it refers to the Amsterdam red light window, with its game of seeing and being seen'. But its well done and worthy of attention.

**98** *The **Gurdwara Karamsor** Sikh temple (400 High Road, Ilford ; Rail: Ilford / Seven Kings), is designed by Marindar Assi of Agenda 21. There was originally a Labour Party hall on the site, converted to a temple and then demolished and rebuilt as now, in 2005. They say about themselves: 'Aesthetically the building gracefully combines traditional sikh and mughlai designs with modern western architecture. Its façade and distinctive domes are perhaps its most striking features. Carved entirely from pink sandstone in Rajasthan-India, it was shipped to the UK and reassembled in-situ. The foyer is a grand and simple space with a skylight bringing in natural light all the way from the third floor. It has prayer halls on the first and second floors with the Langar hall on the ground floor. The interior is all white and uncomplicated. The ambiance of the place naturally lends itself to the main purpose of a Gurdwara which is to worship and realise the Lord'. Like all such places, they make excellent hosts and visitors are welcomed. The surprise is a contemporary interior behind the traditional façade. Also see the **Swaminarayan Mandir** Hindu temple on p199.*

**99** *It's quite a way out and you'll need a car, but if you're tackling it easy and exploring way out east try this building: **The Millennium Centre**; Penoyre & Prasad, 1997; the Chase, Dagenham Road, Rush Green, Romford, RM7; Tube: Dagenham East. It's an educational / community eco centre — in truth, looking for a role in life — but quite a pleasant architectural exercise for those into bird watching. The building has a steel frame, lots of recycled timber stuffed with paper and all that.*

**100** *The **Whitechapel Art Gallery** was designed by Charles Harrison Townsend in 1901 (Whitechapel High Street, adjacent to Whitechapel Underground station) and given a make-over in 1988 by Colquhoun Miller Partners. It is well worth a visit if you are in that area e.g. visiting the Adjaye or Alsop buildings.*

*Note: this is not on the map — simply locate Whitechapel station, on the east side of the City.*

## Goldsmith's College

Goldsmith's College, Lewisham Way, SE14
Alsop Architects, 2005
Train: New Cross

1

Goldsmith's is a campus with a potential to envy: most of it appears to be just another mixed bag of London architecture, but even the apparently residential terraces turn out to be occupied by the College. The Laban used to be here and it is highly questionable whether they should have moved or improved the campus with new facilities here rather than at Deptford Creek. But whether the College will realise this potential remains in doubt.

The most slaient building here is a recent work by Alsop — one of those 'generic' buildings beloved of universities, accommodating a mix of studios and offices (what they have in common remains an open question), one that is simultaneously asked to fulfil a branding exercise by standing as a 'trophy' work of excellence. In fact, it is a rather early Frank Gehry exercise topped off by a wild, swirling Alsop sculpture (quite a feat for an architect to intrude upon an art college's territory). In planning terms, the key to this castle-keep of a building is the links it engenders to the rear parts of adjacent terraces, thus fostering better inter-communications between these buildings. Overall, the building is an interesting exercise in branding and 'instant character', although its entrance canopy is a formal oddity and one wonders just how genuinely considerate the whole exercise is.

The **Goldsmith's Library** (by Allies & Morrison, 1997) is a simple, direct building of 1500 sq.m. of accommodation. Internally, it is designed with economy and offers exposed concrete surfaces and natural ventilation to the users. Externally, it has a long, robust façade coping with the orientation and

a busy road outside. The large fins are solar protection and stiffening for the glazing, but also lend image-quality to the building. As always, the design is elegant and well composed – the work of a firm who will probably be around long after more strident and fashionable firms have come and gone.

*The Library building by Allies & Morrison.*

## 2  Peckham Library

Peckham Hill Street, SE15
Alsop & Störmer, 2000
Train: Peckham Rye

Peckham Library has been a social as well as architectural success, but the building is simply one part of a larger story: the third part of a plaza that terminates a new urban park (Burgess Park) as it meets the local Peckham High Street, aiming to give a regenerative civic dignity to the locale. Apart from the park itself, the first part of the equation was the arching shelter designed by Troughton McAslan — a gateway to the park, a place to linger, to protect market stalls, and an art-work in coloured lighting; the second built part was the Peckham Pulse, the local fitness centre.

The library rises up to stand tall above its surroundings and locates its raison d'être — the lending library — on the 5th, upper, floor, requiring lift access. This engenders a large open space at ground level that integrates itself to the adjacent plaza and also offers a massively protected area akin to standing within the giant orders of some neo-classical, pedimented portico (where people can meet, gather, trade, etc.). Alsop underscores this experience by wrapping a (not quite dense enough) woven stainless steel mesh up the inner façade and across the underbelly of the library above. He explained: "We elevated the library above the ground so that it would be a little bit apart from the normal humdrum life of Peckham [...] People would come out of the lift and into another world. We wanted to reveal views of the city that people wouldn't have seen before. And we wanted the library to be like an attic, where people can concentrate without distractions". The exterior sports a large white 'Library' sign and the dark red prow of the roof-light roof (described by one critic as 'like a beret') — adding sculptural effect to the copper-clad L-shape of the main block. The rear of the block — facing north, over a large builder's yard and toward the not-so-distant towers of the City — is glazed, using a pattern of differently coloured glass sheets.

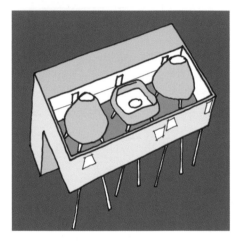

The pods — apparently inspired by the work of the sculptor Richard Deacon — are constructed from pre-shaped timber ribs, assembled on site, clad in OSB (oriented strand board) and clad in stained 1.5mm

plywood sheets cleverly sized and arranged so as to overlap in a simple geometry that also accommodates the curves and takes up construction tolerances (the original intention was to use leather). Inside, the construction is lined with white painted board. There is an office / interview room pod on the ground floor, study pods on one of the intermediate floors and three large 'pod rooms' within the main library hall, propped on concrete legs, each of them accessible from the upper gallery. Two of the library pods are fully enclosed and top-lit by roof-lights with internal 'butterfly' hinged louvres: shaped plywood panels that are operated by pulleys and small electric motors, so that a degree of black-out can be achieved — crude but effective. Fun has been had with some of the 'sculptural' light fittings that look as if they are giant 'Brillo' pads.

*But 5+ years is a long time in the current life of a London Library (Idea Store? Life Long Learning Centre?) and there are now plans to move on and make changes. Compare with* **Swiss Cottage Library** *and the* **Idea Stores.**

3  *Quay House by Ken Taylor's practice Quay2c (Kings Grove, SE15; 2002) is a former dairy building and yard converted into the architect's home, a studio for him and another for his artist partner together with street-frontage flats that are a fine example of how inventive architects can be in imaginatively transforming derelict sites. It's all very upbeat and cheerful, complete with bedrooms designed as first floor 'beach huts' and two mini-galleries on the street (M2 and 2M2, reflecting their sizes at one and two metre cubes). It's a good example of putting such things together.*

*The artist involved is Julia Manheim.*

# Horniman Museum

The Horniman was originally designed by Charles Harrison Townsend in 1901 (he also did the **Whitechapel Gallery** and the **Bishopsgate Institute**) and the A&M work was part of a long overdue delapidations and extensions programme that called for an exhibition space, education facilities, a shop and cafe. It also called for clearing away unsatisfactory extensions and attempting to make a connection between the interiors and the surrounding parkland. The result is a delight, both in terms of what A&M have done and what the Horniman now is.

Townsend's building is now a small complex of inter-linked pavilions in a park. From the street it reads as four: two belonging to the Townsend design, the gable end of the A&M extension, and a 1994 Centre for Understanding the Environment, from Archetype (actually quite a nice 'green' pavilion in itself, complete with the obligatory grass on roof). To the rear is another (a glass-house). Inside, the Museum is a mix of old and new and the collection is, on the whole, a superb and idiosyncratic mix of ethnographic pieces. The parts handled by A&M are excellent (especially the new music room) and one only wishes the funding could have extended to a revamp of all spaces. (Perhaps that it didn't remains a part of the pleasure of the place.) This is possibly A&M at their best: picking up contextural themes from the existing parts of the Horniman — particularly the barrel vaulting — and reinventing them. The detailing and proportioning is,

*The Archetype building overtly displaying its ecologically worthy values sits rather incongruously adjacent to the later and more elegant A&M work. Otherwise, it is an interesting enough work whose neo-Venetian wind chimneys lend a distinctly jaunty air.*

as always, superb (vaguely Scarpa inspired) and the scale is (again as always) well handled. It's a lively mix, often thronged with children and the place offers the especial pleasures of expert but non-monumental architecture somewhere out there in suburban London. If there is a sour note it's that frequent English disparity between cultural and design intent, and management actions (manifest here, for example, in the stink of frying chips that fills the otherwise fine cafe).

## 5 Dulwich Picture Gallery

Gallery Road, Dulwich Village, SE21
Rick Mather Architects, 2000
Rail: West Dulwich, North Dulwich

Dulwich Picture Gallery is a celebrated London landmark and was England's first public art gallery, designed and completed by one of its most famous and respected architects, Sir John Soane, between 1811-14. But a public gallery that is simultaneously a mausoleum for a painting collection's founding ménage a trois is surely a strange circumstance to which architectural talent should adapt itself. Given Soane's status, it is understandable that Rick Mather's extensions and alterations are sensitive, contextural, and respectful of what exists, complementing both Soane's work and the old Dulwich College buildings forming a back-drop to the Gallery. Mather's design strategy at once leaves Soane's pavilion alone and stands back from it, whilst simultaneously entangling it in a new architectural composition that reaches out to the boundaries, engages the old Dulwich College buildings (especially the Christ's Chapel), the existing gateway and boundary brick walling, whilst introducing a new site concept focused upon the

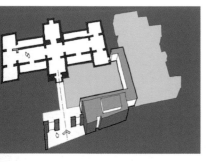

empty space between the buildings (in fact, a lawn) rather than the buildings themselves. The built device that is employed is an old-fashioned one: the idea of a cloister that wraps around the perimeter of the site, runs along the older College buildings and connects to the gallery pavilion (see plan below). In fact, it is more of a 'half-cloister'

because one half is implied rather than constructed. Nevertheless, it acts as a kind of tactful armature off which the other buildings hang, whilst the cloister itself provides an alternative means of access or egress to the gallery. A new café, new exhibition space and education rooms are neatly insinuated into and around this perimeter device. And as visitors perambulate this corridor they are given superbly framed views of the gallery building before they reach the side entry door to the gallery. This simple cloister / corridor becomes the key architectural piece binding the assembly of parts. But it is the green lawn – the void at the heart of this equation – that becomes the new spatial heart of the architectural parts. In this sense the idea of a cloister has been used cleverly and given its traditional role. The older gallery spaces themselves have been entirely refurbished, the roof-lights renewed etc.

*The facilities around the part-cloister have a distinct and artful charm, and one experiences real pleasure in the architectural perambulation to the Gallery's side door.*

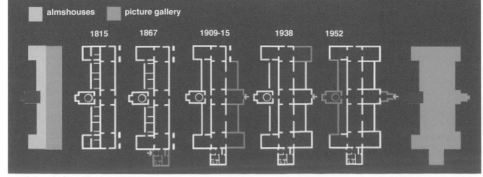

almshouses    picture gallery

1815    1867    1909-15    1938    1952

## Kingsdale School

Alleyn Park SE21
Leslie Martin/dRMM, 2004
Rail: Gipsy Hill

What to do: old '60's wreck of a school; building that needs updating? You cover over its central courtyard with inflated pillows and locate a new school hall for 1000 students right at the heart, crossing the court with a new bridge to promote better flows. The outcome is an iconic gesture that has them standing in the aisles. The architects tell us that the scheme is of national importance: "The proposal exploits the potential of the existing building, and superimposes a vast, new transparent roof over the internal courtyard. This has facilitated new dining facilities, assembly and performance spaces, improved circulation, and social activities". But does the emperor have real clothes? It was in the Hawthorne experiments of the 1920's that behaviourists first found out that the implied flattery in attention will ensure an increase in productivity regardless of whether physical conditions are made better or worse.

---

*Other London schools worthy of the specialist's interest include:*

• **Jubilee Primary**; *Tulse Hill, SW2; Allford Hall Monaghan Morris, 2002. (It has a special emphasis on hearing impaired learning.)*
• **Kings Avenue School**, *Kings Avenue, SW4; Shepheard Epstein Hunter, 2002.*
*In addition, there is Foster's* **Business Academy Bexley**, *Yarnton Way, Erith (east of Greenwich); Foster & Partners, 2003 . . . but being a business, they don't like visitors!*
*Foster has a similar academy school in north London:* **Capital City Academy** *(below), Doyle Gardens, NW10; Foster & Partners, 2003, (Willesden Green tube).*

**7** **Stealth House.** *What doesn't show externally is the clever mix of new building work appropriating parts of the house formerly here. Otherwise, this is a good example of new work with vaguely contexturalist overtones. (But what is it about Daarth Vader / stealth planes and architectural fashions from Tadao Ando to Robert Dye? Is the stealth in the strategy of realisation, a cunning design, the styling? 122 Grove Lane, SE5; Robert Dye Associates, 2004; Rail: Denmark Hill)*

**8** *This band stand (***Crystal Palace***, SE26; Ian Ritchie Architects, 1997) is one of the better examples of architectural design in London – a witty, considered exercise in using Corten steel to blend the accommodation and protective / sound reflecting structure of this moated, summer band 'platform' into the landscaping of the park. It is redolent with C18 landscaping values and also references to Richard Serra's work, but it has an almost abstract quality, as if Ritchie had produced the simplest diagram possible and built it (a diagram for a presentational platform, protected against vandals, with massive, built-in electronic acoustic support, principally from two speaker towers at either side of the platform). It is at once sculptural and practical, heroic and intimate. But try and see it on a summer's day, when a band is playing, not in a grey London winter.*

## 9 Friendship House

Described as, 'A Modern self-catered accommodation providing 160 bedsitting rooms, with angular walls of dramatic zinc tiles and bright render enclosing a quiet courtyard with reflective pool. RIBA Award Winner 2005' Friendship House is a clever and welcome exercise in fitting single-person rental accommodation into a difficult central site — bang up against the proverbial inner London rail line. It copes by turning inward, around a landscaped central court (designed by Rummy Design), but also by providing a clear architectural diagram relating shared areas to private ones. Like any such building, there are similarities with hotels and halls of residences. The city needs many more buildings like this.

Belvedere Place, off Borough Road, SE1
MacCormac Jamieson Prichard, 2003
Tube: Borough

## 10 London College of Communications Media Centre

There are two new buildings here: the 'Teaching Block' allowed the relocation of existing media facilities in Clerkenwell to this campus, consolidating the entire college onto one site (a standard strategy these days: provide estate overheads + more students + less space + concentrated and rationalised facilities + lots of digitial technology and, of course, a few low-cost architectural branding cheerups, mix well and wrap it all up as 'new ways of learning'). 'The Street Building' — a new entrance portal — ties together all of the existing college buildings while providing a central focus for the campus as a whole. These two main components are then linked to complete the basic infrastructure required by the LCC to meet its long-term academic needs. A later second phase will involve the modification and fit-out of the new and existing spaces.

Elephant & Castle, SE1
Allies & Morrison, 2004
Tube: Elephant & Castle

# Keyworth Centre

Keyworth Centre, Southbank University
Elephant & Castle, SE1
BDP, 2004
Tube: Elephant & Castle

A Southbank University building that is a pleasant neo-Scandinavian surprise on the inside. The exterior, one has to confess, is a less than scintillating contribution to the urban fabric, but don't let this put you off the neo-Ralph Erskine interior (by a partner of BDP who used to work with the late master). It's a simple enough scheme, with a tall atrium backed by stacked teaching floors served by a double-loaded corridor, and with cores at each end. The atrium serves as a positive focal point and, instead of the proverbial 'pods', it offers stacked timber-clad meeting rooms with open decks above them. It all appears to be well-liked and used. (Although additional — and instrumentally redundant — access decks around the classroom side of the atrium would have helped to engender a buzz of usage and enjoyment.)

But why is the outside the way it is? Clearly, a practice on a tight budgetary rein has to make strategic choices. BDP are among those architectural firms who long ago formally endorsed the reality that one is either in business or out of practice — and detailing a job like this can lead to losses. But that is exactly what they've done — successfully — within the atrium. And they also put such effort into (of all places) the escape stairs. However, whatever the hidden truth to the building's muteness regarding the process engendering the reasons why its form is the way it is, the façade is bad news. The building's name ('Key-worth') belies the reality of intrinsic architectural values at odds with one another. But, otherwise, the building is indicative of what current university buildings (serving 'new ways of learning') are all about.

*If Erskine interests you, there is the Ark and the Millennium Peninsula housing to see. Other university buildings to see include those at Imperial, the LSE, Chelsea Art School and Queen Mary's, as well as Libeskind's work at the Metropolitan.*

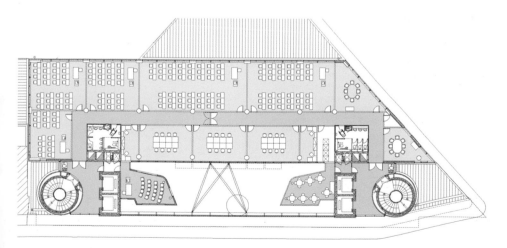

# Inner Ring

## 12 Baron's Place

More 'volumetrics'. The positive aspect of this apartment block concerns the service provided to London's 'key workers' who can't afford London's apartment prices. However, one can't but worry about varieties of 'experimentation' on comparatively deprived sectors of the community. The scheme provides very small 'flatlets' (36 sq.m. one bed, and two-person apartments of 54.sq. m.) made from units of 3.6m x 5m or 7m (Raines Dairy was 11.8m) proffered in guise of the joker's costume. But this isn't why the planners shamed the Peabody Trust (the developers) by turning down the first planning application — it was because of the size of the 'microflats'

(there's a PhD just in that discussion). Go there, have a look, compare it where neighbouring public housing and make up your own mind. Also visit some of the other Peabody projects mentioned in this guide and other modular projects listed below. No doubt their design will improve as architects realise that the issue is not displays of technical wizardry and acrobatics, but the quality of life for the people who live in these homes and don't give a damn about whether they are prefabricated or not. (In truth, they probably do; modularisation still suffers a poor public image.)

*Other newly completed modular schemes include*
*• **Wyndam Road**, Southwark. Tube: Oval. Architect: PCKO. Eighteen apartments.*
*• **Barling Court**, Larkhall Lane, Stockwell SW4. Architect: PCKO. Eight apartments.*
*Also see **Raines Dairy** (p.219) and **Murray Grove** (p.222).*

**13** *The **Foster studio** (1990) might be one of the more pleasant architectural studios in town: designed for London's most successful architect as a double-height space, 60m long and 24m wide, overlooking the river through a tall wall of glass and accessed by a long, slow stair that Alvar Aalto might have been proud of. The rest of the building is comparatively ordinary, built as speculative offices below and apartments above, in order to finance the development. Compare with the Rogers' riverside studio further west, at Hammersmith. The studio is often open during London Open House.*

*The architects of Baron's Place (above) have adopted a distinctly upbeat approach to addressing the difficulties of volumetric housing provision and disguising its atomised construction as a unity — aesthetically, as a kind of 'displacement' activity obviating the constructional realities. It's all a long way from Bucky Fuller and Archigram's dreams and there are interesting comparisons to be made with*

*Photo: Foster & Partners / Nigel Young*

## Albion

Hester Road, SW11
Foster and Partners, 2003
Tube: Sloane Square

A fascinating, eleven-storey up-market housing development adjacent to the Foster studio: a scheme of 186 apartments in eleven stories that takes a simple multi-storey block and cleverly bends it around whilst dividing the internal accommodation into a front / back split, so that every apartment has a river-facing terrace. It's effective and it works. The land side demonstrates that a latter-day car manufacturing obsession with the *derriére* is cross-cultural and has spread from France and Brazil to the Foster Studio (as well as from the sides up and over onto the roof). But is it a cute back-side? And is the effect helped by the acrobatic, neo-Richard Seifert V-legs propping the whole thing up? The lower areas include shops, a restaurant, art gallery, swimming pool and gymnasium for the use of residents.

Photo: Foster & Partners / Nigel Young

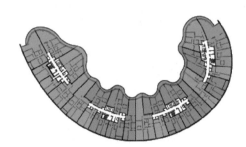

*The adjacent social housing block (45 one and two-bedroom apartments run by Peabody) and office block to the south of the main Albion structure are also quite elegant in a Miesian, 1950's manner.*

# Inner Ring

**15** Around the corner from the luxury of Montevetro is this housing association design (2–4 **Gwynne Road**, SW11; Walter Menteth Architects, 1999; Train: Clapham Junction) that sparkles like a Mediterranean jewel transported to south London. Eight units are gathered together into a garden pavilion beside the railway line, surrounded by 500 mm 'gabion' walls (dry-stone encased in mesh). White walls are played off against bright colours and slim aluminium window details. It is simple, cheap and cheerful, formal whilst still domestic, considerate and sensitive to both client and users. If only London had more like it . . . (Compare with Pete Barber's work in the East End.)

There is a Building Regulations logic that drives this aesthetic toward a Mediterranean look — also see Peter barber's housing in the East End.

**16** **Montevetro** was a rather controversial block. The name means 'glass mountain' and the neighbours were certainly intimidated by the very idea of it — which is not dissimilar in concept to CZWG's Cascades (see p.162): a stepped apartment block with roof terraces and river views for all apartments. Sitting alongside **St. Mary Battersea** (1777), the 103 units (including penthouse owned by Marco Goldschmied, a RRP partner) are organised as a slim block divided into five parts, with access towers on the land side and full views on the river side. A key aesthetic device is the use of terra-cotta cladding, first used by Renzo Piano on apartments in Paris, and now a proprietary system and common London feature. The irony of this private, gated community is that it should come from Lord Rogers of Riverside, left-wing promoter of popular causes. You can't get in, but don't worry: you can get close on the river side walkway. (Church Road, Battersea, SW11; Richard Rogers Partnership, 1999)

**17** The original church of **St Mary's, Barnes**, in Church Road, SW3, suffered arson damage in 1978 and Edward Cullinan gave it a new architecture as well as a new, complex roof and extensions in a vaguely ad hoc, Arts & Crafts manner so typical of his work. Although the church's original architecture was reformed, the best of the historic fabric was retained in a design process closely involving the local community. The aim was to produce a space for congregation and worship that could continue the tradition established on the site in the eleventh century, but without pastiche.

## Arthur Road House

**18**

82 Arthur Road, SW19
Terry Pawson Architects, 2002
Tube: Wimbledon Park

Pawson's house is a delightful, robust addition to just another inter-war London surburbia of semi-d's — truly an 'ornament' to Wimbledon. He makes the most of the narrow, sloping site and provides a fitting end to the street and a most elegant plan (which he describes, enigmatically, as 'a modern reworking of Sir John Soane's terrace in Lincoln's Inn Fields' (meaning a series of inter-locked volumes that play with perceptions of space, compressing and then opening out in unexpected directions to create a sequence of changing and ambiguous volumes). At 5m (one room) wide and 80m long, the house has a concrete substructure, with timber framed and clad tower, and steel framed rear section clad in engineering brick. The rear has a vaulted and grassed roof, with a fully glazed end, opening out into the garden.

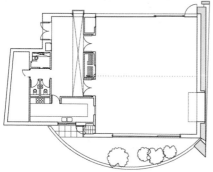

## St Mary's Church Garden Hall

**19**

30 St Mary's Road, SW19
Terry Pawson Architects, 2002
Rail / Tube: Wimbledon

St. Mary's is a 230 sq.m. building that provides a nearly square hall divisible into two separate rooms and is for use by the church and the local community. The main space is arranged to make visual connection to the lawns in front of the hall and a new curved walled garden to the rear.

 The design of the hall draws material cues from the adjacent grade II listed St. Mary's Church. The hall echoes the knapped flint and limestone of the church by using smooth white ashlar limestone, with a contrasting base of slate dry-stone wall facing onto the road. The scheme incorporates a 'light-bar' constructed from translucent glazing, an element that is inspired by the powerful use of light by church builders of the past, and provides a glowing counterpoint to the massive stonework.

**20**   *Ted Cullinan's Lambeth Health Centre of 1984 (Monkton Street SE11; Tube: Lambeth North / Kennington) was exemplary as a local hospital building, but also served as the nearest anyone in this country ever got to 'deconstruction' as an architectural aesthetic. (Which is not too close.) It is full of the old Cullinan touches and caring attitude, including local-made ceramics on the exterior depicting healing herbs. On the south-facing garden side there is a strong relation between building terrace and the garden itself.*

## 21 Understatement in Wandsworth

86-96 Garratt Lane, SW18
Sergison Bates, 2004
Rail: Wandsworth Town

This is a 1930's paint factory refurbished and extended to provide a mixed use development comprising apartments, a health centre and light industrial units. Located behind a large shopping centre and on a small river that leads into the Thames, the mixed-use development is a refreshing addition to the area and comes from architects excited by (the potentially paradoxical notion of) architectural 'everydayness', who describe their work as "so quiet you could almost walk past it, and yet it becomes more interesting the longer you observe it". This sounds very English. The adopted stance is given as 'natural' and always understated: a feigned, born-to-the-poise tradition of sound and cultured good taste that knows of no necessity to self-consciously contrive and project a pose. Blatant egotism is repugnant. As an inter-personal value this suggests a self-confident ease of communication suggesting authentic attentiveness and considerateness — the kind of charming relationship lower classes like to have with ostensible betters who are perceived to strike an aspirational bench-mark. And, architecturally, it can work — proffering a relief from 'customary' fashionability and base creaturely concerns. But one's experience is always contextural and whether an entire city area possessing such qualities would be hugely soothing or deeply irritating is a moot point. We have learned appetites for spectacle and those architects who don't provide it for their clients walk a precarious career path. Whatever: this work at Garrat Lane nevertheless exhibits a bald note of pure quality and is worth experiencing for that simple reason as an exceptional voice midst London's architectural cacophony.

*Parallels can be drawn with the work of Caruso St. John; the contrast is the likes of BedZed and Alsop's work.*

**22** *The **Putney Bridge Restaurant** building (Embankment, Lower Richmond Road, SW15) is by Paskin Kyriakides (1997) and is a welcome addition to the riverside scenery around here (a good place to go at Boat Race time). Opposite — on the east side of the bridge — is an example of extensive remodelling to a former office building by Patel & Taylor (see right).*

**23** ***Putney Wharf**, on the east side of Putney Bridge, is the extensive refurbishment, re-cladding, etc. of an old 'shoe-box' office building past its sell-by date, but deemed suitable for the contemporary residential market. (You have to use your imagination.) The architects were Patel & Taylor, 2004 (who also did the architectural work at the Thames Barrier Park).*

**Outer selections**

*The following buildings are all slightly further out from the centre, but still readily accessible.*

## Outer selections

**24** Another one to dislike because of its theatricality — as if most architecture wasn't by nature theatrical. The reality is some 10,000 sq.m.. of contemporary offices arranged as a complex of small buildings — but are most office blocks a mere external dressing upon a facility manager's conventionalised equation? Within a more 'pop' / Ron Herron / Hollywood tradition (and among lay people) these buildings are admired for their cleverness and reassurances. Perhaps the project's real crime is a denial of the modernist zeitgeist? And who last gave that much thought? Ah, 'progress' . . .? OK, I understand: if you're an architect, you still hate them because they also deny a spirit of challenge that dares to fracture conventions rather than endorse them . . . We could go on and on with this one. (Hill Street / Bridge Street, Richmond; Erith & Terry, 1986-88; Tube: Richmond).

**25** The **Charles Cryer Studio Theatre** by Edward Cullinan (1991), in the High Street, Carshalton, should have been a celebrated building, but it had an unfortunate project history that dragged it out and got bogged down in changes. But you just have to look at the engaging way Cullinan has handled the problem of adapting an old theatre and transforming it into a new work of architecture to get a feel for just how well things might have worked out. It is a 'might have been', but well worth a look if you're this far south.

**26** There are two buildings to see at this office park designed as a set of blocks around a square that might be in Holborn (New Square, **Bedfont Lakes**, Staines Road (A30), south west corner of Heathrow Airport; Michael Hopkins & Partners, 1992): Ted Cullinan's somewhat less attractive venture into speculative offices; and Sir Michael Hopkins' more than successful exercises for IBM (with, one suspects, a nod toward the 1960's YRM black, steel-framed Cargo Agent's building on the Southern Perimeter Road).

**27** The interior of the **Compass Centre** (North Perimeter Road, Heathrow Airport; Nicholas Grimshaw & Partners, 1994) serves air crews 24 hours a day, seven days a week; a facility where operators track planes around the world whilst disoriented crews refresh themselves and get their briefings. The deep interiors (45m face to face, including small atria) feel tight and effective – one of the few buildings where the life of the inhabitants is truly demanding and dynamic, well served by the two accommodation wings either side of a central atrium space. The peculiar façade is meant to diminish the building's radar 'shadow', but the form is similar to another building by Grimshaw and one is suspicious of such a rationale. The interior fit-out, serving 850 employees and about 200 flight crews passing through each day, was by Auckett.

### BedZed

Beddington, Sutton (A237, Hackbridge)
Bill Dunster Architects, 2002
Train: Hackbridge; Mitcham Junction tramlink

They're not much greener than this in 2002 and there still isn't: an impressive 'zero-energy' development on a 'brownfield' site (a former sewage works), providing 82 dwellings in a mix of flats, maisonettes and 'town houses', plus 2500 sq.m. of workspace and community accommodation, including a health centre, cafe, nursery, etc. (Density is 187 people per hectare.) All this is set out in five long, south-facing rows of 3-storey buildings with narrow spaces between the rows (the 'gardens' have become 'sky gardens' on the south face; town houses have a small bridge to a roof-top garden on adjacent units, similar to the Branch Hill project). Walls are 300mm wide, stuffed with insulation; other construction is in concrete, bricks and blocks. Rainwater is used, baths are low-volume, toilets are double flush . . . and the entire scheme is served by a central heat and power plant. Nothing, it seems, has been overlooked in promoting a sustainable way of living (including schemes for community electric vehicles).

Wherever possible, natural, reused and local materials and contractors were employed — argued to increase local employment, cut down on transport costs, reduce pollution and reinforce local identity. (Grand claims crying out for justification, but BedZed takes itself very seriously e.g. everything is carefully researched and materials are sourced, whenever possible, within a 35m radius.) The roofs provide photovoltaic panels and are topped by cowls that scoop in fresh air and discharge used air (employing a heat-exchanger in the process — a functional but rather Mickey Mouse feature that proclaims the development's green credentials). This is, by the way, a Peabody Trust development and many of the houses are part-owned or rented.

A few years on (the brief was given in 1998) Dunster and BioRegional, their associated consultants, have gone on to all kinds of similar schemes, although the client — the Peabody Trust — sadly feels reluctant to experiment further in this direction.

# Outer selections

## 29 Waterside

Harmondsworth (off the A4 / Bath Road)
Take exit 14 on the M25
Neils Torp Architects, 1998

This is the office as house of a large corporate family wearing security badges – an independent, autonomous and self-sufficient place referring to a global community. The design is the sibling of a similar building in Stockholm, both of them being a village of office pavilions strung along a shared mall. They are both impressive, but the BA building takes the conversation further, integrating the spatial concepts into contemporary strategies of space-time management, non-territorial working patterns, cultivated cafe-work, and similar themes that make up a latter-day theory of office practices. The central street is a huge success and a place whose ambience only the Ark, in Hammersmith, can compete with. However, the interiors of the office pavilions leave something to be desired and are not so radical. On the outside, design excellence continues in the form of extensive landscaping whose idyllic qualities are only disturbed (not inappropriately) by the roar of aeroplanes taking off.

## 30 Stockley Park: sanitised arcadia

Furzeground Way, Hillingdon (North side of Heathrow Airport)
Various architects, 1990–2000

Stockley is a successful '80's business park on the northern edge of Heathrow. DEGW did the research and briefing; Arup Associates were the master planners and the architects for many of the early buildings in a place where issues of typology loom large within an equation of two-storey development and 25% ground coverage. SOM have buildings on the west side of the scheme; Foster, Troughton McAslan, Ian Ritchie, Geoffrey Darke, and Eric Parry have buildings on the east side. Everyone struggled with the same developer constraints that offered tenants a carefully structured, shell-and-core option (a suburban, low-rise version of Canary Wharf — or vice versa). This strategy culminates in recent Arup buildings at the western edge, where ingenious geometrical variations strive to creatively cope with the realities of architecture as a building type set within a landscape that is the undoubted feature lending the place its character of acceptability.

And the landscape is the real, hidden achievement: the reclamation of a heavily polluted area of land and its transformation into the business park and a local authority golf course to the north. Ducks and flowers flourish above the barriers that keep a frightening toxicity at bay. It's a beautiful place where people bring the kids on Sunday to feed ducks and carp.

But it is also a place where buildings hide behind bushes, globalised tenants identified only by discrete signs labelled with acronyms and offering instructions with regard to acceptable behaviour. Luxuriant nature hides security cameras and the stealth of guards who slowly cruise in neo-military vehicles looking for those 'who don't belong'. The entertainment of sanitised arcadian landscape beauty lulls the mind into contentment and the illusion that all is well in the world. Somehow, even the dull, constant background sound of aeroplanes is comforting. It is very clever, very modern, and rather strange . . . But it is, nevertheless, a classic example of this genre. Make a visit, then escape back to Soho in order to discuss it midst the sex shops, bums, homeless, and ethnic offers. These might constitute their own variety of theatre and inauthenticity, but I know where I want to hang my hat.

**31** *Homewood*, in Esher, was designed by Patrick Gwynne as a young and promising architect then working with Denys Lasdun at the office of Wells Coates. At 24, Gwynne persuaded his father to allow him to design a new family home on their land (the existing family house was, apparently, too near an increasingly noisy road). Daddy agreed and Patrick lived there ever after — after his parents died, turning the place into a pad for himself and boyfriend, who together held, we're informed by the guides, rather entertaining dinner parties (featuring, for example, a central table lamp that flashed when Gwynne considered a speaking guest was getting boring!). Completed in 1938, the house is clearly inspired by a mix of Corbusier (Villa Savoye) and Aalto (Villa Maira) and is as good as it gets as an example of English Modernism of the period. It's a simple enough place, with spacious principal rooms on the first floor — separated into a living wing and a sleeping wing — plus servants and study, garaging etc. on the ground. And the surrounding gardens are very pleasant. It all makes quite a contrast with London's East End and underscores the capital's westward orientation. Overall, it's not on a par with the European masters and has none of their originality, but it's good stuff and well worth a visit, most especially for the 1950's and '60's modifications (very James Bond and all that in Gwynne's study) rather than the '30's references. You have to book through the National Trust (see their web site for details) and prospective visitors gather at Claremont Landscape Garden, outside Esher.

Also see Erno Goldfinger's house in **Willow Road,** Hampstead. Another comparison to make is with the 1930's parts of **Eltham Palace** (Court Yard, Eltham SE9; an English Heritage property).

# Others in West London

*Some other west London older architecture to visit. The more historic tends to be themed and packaged, so you have fight to get to the architecture itself:*

• **Hampton Court Palace**, East Moseley, 1514–1882. Former royal palace; large complex including work by Wren and William Kent. Train to Hampton Court. Photo: top left.

• **Chiswick House**, Hogarth Lane and Burlington Lane, W4, designed by Lord Burlington (1725–29), who also designed Burlington House (The Royal Academy) and, in this instance, was inspired by Palladio's Villa Rotonda. There is an earlier gateway here, of 1621, by Inigo Jones. Photo: top right.

• **Osterley Park**, Isleworth. A remodelling by Robert Adam (1763–67), this time of the entire house. Photo: second from top.

• **Syon House**, London Road, Brentford. Internal remodelling by Robert Adam (1761–68).

• **Pitshanger Manor**, Sir John Soane, 1801- 3. Mattock Lane and Ealing Green, W13; Tube: Ealing Broadway. Now a museum.

• The **Palm House** at Kew Gardens was designed by Decimus Burton (1844-48) and is a marvellous iron and glass structure in the Royal Botanic Gardens. The Gardens also now include a recently completed glass house (the **Alpine House**) by Wilkinson Eyre (2005). Photo: right.

• **Leighton House,** Holland Park Road, W11. George Aitchison, 1877 - 9. Tube: Holland Park. Some delightful interiors.

• **Voysey House**, 1902. Barley Mow Passage, W4; Tube: Chiswick Park of Turnham Green. Fine, former Sanderson's factory. Image: third from bottom.

• **Hoover factory**, Wallis, Gilbert & Partners, 1931 - 5. Western Ave.; Tube: Perivale. Now a supermarket, but still a landmark and indicative of London's westward suburban ex[pansion in that era. Photo: second from bottom.

• **Peter Jones** department store, 1935 - 7; Crabtree, Slater& Moberley. Sloane Square, SW1; Tube: Sloane Square. Good recent refurbishments by John McAslan..

• **World's End Estate**, SW10; Tube: Sloane Sq (and bus west). Eric Lyons, Cadbury-Brown, Metcalfe & Cunningham, 1967 - 77. Tall brick towers.

• **Commonwealth Institute**, W8; Tube: Kensington High Street. Robert Matthews, Johnson-Marshall & Partners, 1960 -2. Dramatic hyperbolic-paraboloid roof to an exhibition building erected to celebrate the Commonwealth countries.

• **Hillingdon Civic Centre**, High Street, Hillingdon; Tube: Hillingdon. Robert Matthews Johnson-Marshall & Partners, 1973 - 8. Piles of brick with neo-vernacular undertones, disguising a rather large building; at the time, this was the future of civic architecture (post the 1960's). Photo: bottom right.

*Right: Banksy graffiti. Photo: Martin Hartmann.*

# Index

# Index

# Index

# Index

*Below: View from New Concordia Wharf toward
Tower Bridge and the City, with the former Natwest
Tower and 'the Gherkin' in the background and,
in the foreground, a 1920's warehouse recently
converted into apartments (with a bar / restaurant
at ground level). The concrete building on the right
is a 1960's hotel at St. Katherine's Dock.
Right: car workshop in Wembly.*

## Population

In 1100, at the time of the Norman conquest, the population of London was about 15,000, growing to about 80,000 two hundred years later. By 1600 it had grown to 200,000 and, by the time of the Great Fire in 1666, had expanded to 375,000 — by then a European curiosity divided into three areas: the historic City; a suburban development that stretched along the Fleet Street / Strand axis to Westminster; and outlying areas of market gardens and the like to the north, east and south of the Thames in Southwark (an area that the Commonwealth defenses had enclosed between 1643-47).

John Summerson described an air-view at about 1615 as follows: *"Below us is the constant ribbon of the Thames. . . London is one of its shallower curves, a tesselation of red roofs pricked with plots of green and the merlon-shadowed patches which are the lead roofs of churches. Within the blurred margin, the line of the ancient wall takes the eye . . . Away to the west, clearly separate, is Westminster. The abbey church and the cloister are distinct . . . Round them is a red-roofed colony, less compact, less imposing, and much smaller than London. . . Between London and Westminster a line of buildings fringes the river — the palaces along the Strand . . . like Oxford colleges . . . whose great highway and approach is the river itself. . . Within a few years two great rectangles crystallise north of the Strand, in Covent Garden and the fields of Lincoln's Inn; and the houses around them are conspicuous by trim discipline — uniform, ungabled fronts."* And of the post-1666 developments he remarks: *"Long before the charred patch [of the Great Fire] glows again with fresh brickwork there is commotion in the west. The streets around Lincoln's Inn, Covent Garden, and St James' fill up with houses. Squares spring into being in Gray's Inn Fields and Soho, and packed streets close in upon them; new streets shoot northwards, eastwards and westwards".* After 1720 he comments: *"We notice the shabby gabled streets in the inner west end slowly yielding to neatly parapeted rows . . . now the brickwork tends to be grey and brown rather than red. Whitehall becomes truer to the colour of its name, the slow operations for a new bridge are seen at Westminster. But someone at the top of St Paul's Cathedral would still (on a clear day) have been able to see the entire city".*

Between 1700 and 1750 the population rose from 674,500 to 676,750. But by 1801 it was around 0.9-1.1m, most of them living in terraced housing, many in the fashionable 'Georgian' squares and terraces of west London. The city was rich, powerful and sprawling. By 1831 the population was 1.66m and in 1861 it was 3.323m and the railways were extending the urban area ever outward. About this period Summerson comments: *"1801-3 coincides with the making of the first docks . . . to the dock area come line upon line of brown cottage streets, each carrying the east-end invasion further towards the Essex fields. . . . [T]he perimeter of London has been moving at a ramping, devouring pace. Every outward road, now, is lined with terraces and villas. In the wedges of country between, streets and squares are filling in. London's satellite villages are villages no longer: Hackney, Islington, Paddington, Fulham, and Chelsea are suburbs. . . . [C]an London still grow- and yet be a humane city? . . . The Victorian age provides an answer. Iron fingers point to the stucco terraces*

*in Euston Square, to the fields of Paddington, to Bishopsgate and Southwark".*

By 1921 the population was 7.5m, split between central terraces and apartments, and the new suburbs of detached and semi-detached villas served by rail and road networks. By 1951, it was 8.2m, but by this time the definition of London was increasingly blurred and confused by extensive suburbanisation served by rail and road networks (the peak population was reached in 1939, at 8.6m). London was now an extensive south-east region in which outer residential areas were separated from the heartland ('Greater London') by a 'green belt' where development was not permitted. In 1965 administration of this area was taken over by the Greater London Authority (GLC), later removed by Thatcher's government in 1986. It was not until 2001 that London had its own Mayor and Greater London Authority.

## Characteristic building materials

Before the Great Fire of 1666 and subsequent building regulations which sought to reduce fire risk, most buildings were of timber. After that time new building regulations ensured that the common materials were brick, stone, clay and slate (for roof tiles). Yellow 'stock' bricks, white Portland stone, and grey slate roof tiles still dominate much of the metropolis, particularly the older buildings. The most characteristic building material is the yellow 'stock' brick. Originally, this was hand-made and came from the London area itself, with some supplies coming up the river from Kent. By the early C19 most sources had been expended but the new canal system (late C18) enabled the metropolis

to be supplied from outlying areas — producing a proliferation of brickfields along the banks of the Grand Union Canal that led one commentator of 1811 to describe London as surrounded by a 'ring of fire'. By the 1840s and '50's machine-made bricks were being brought by rail from sources in the near Midlands (e.g. Bedfordshire). The Portland stone came from the Portland island off the south coast of Dorset and arrived in London via the Thames.

# London notes

### Architectural Periods and Styles
*It may be imprudent, even potentially misleading, but it is also useful and convenient to divide London's architectural history into a series of distinct periods:*

### Early
Roman -1615. Not much remains of this period, either before the Norman Conquest (symbolised by the Tower of London) apart from a few Roman remains and memories, for example near the Barbican and the Tower (and within quite a few City buildings, including the new ones for Merrill Lynch).

### Taste, Regularity and Romance
1615 — 1820: from Inigo Jones' introduction of Palladianism as Surveyor to the King, to the Baroque of Wren, Hawksmoor, Gibbs et al, through another Palladian revival and a transformative period of 'Georgian' development characterised by the squares and terrace types developed in the late C17. The period — racked by religious dissent, revolution and rebellion — manifest the Industrial Revolution and articulated notions of Beauty, the Sublime and the Picturesque, ending with the building of docks and warehouses, John Nash's work on Regent Street and Regent's Park, and Sir John Soane's house — perhaps a fitting memorial to this remarkable period.

### Tumult and Improvement
1820-1920: a radical period characterised by stylistic battles that polarised the Greek with Gothic, the utilitarian with the romantic, and populated inner London with endless rows of terrace housing and the first social housing developments, all of it served by new transport systems such as the train, the underground and the omnibus. The period saw the introduction of new building types and a fusion of architecture, engineering and instrumental intent. Good neo-Gothic architecture is epitomised by William Butterfield's All Saints, Margaret Street and George Street's Law Courts in the Strand. Although the highlight of the period was the great 1851 exhibition — much celebrated as one of the sources of modernism (and inspiration for the Dome) — some historians see it as the sunset of British engineering expertise. The period ended with Empire bombast and the Germanic royal family adopting the English name of the House of Windsor, new sensibilities toward dying crafts and old buildings, and nostalgia for what became known as (an implicitly anti-Palladian and baroque) 'Wrenaissance', with many 'grand manner' buildings populating the City.

### Inbetweens
1920-1945: an intermediate period between the wars when the instrumental values of the C19 were being translated into a new Modernism on the Continent, but with very little evidence in London (except for excellent fore-runners of what to was to come, such as Tecton's Finsbury Health Centre and Highpoint flats, Erno Goldfinger's home in Hampstead, and Gwynne's Homestead). A contrast was perhaps epitomised by the late work of Edwin Lutyens, now undertaking 'grand manner' commercial work rather than the country houses he became famous for in the period before WWI (e.g. Brittannic House in Moorgate and the Midland Bank HQ in Poultry).

### Art Leading the Facts of Science
1945-70: a time when art (as architecture) was attempting to lead the facts of science in the service of a progressive and optimistic Modernism that had caught up with influences from Scandinavia (Alvar Aalto), France (le Corbusier), and the USA (the Chicago of Mies, the New York of SOM, and the California of Charles and Ray Eames et al), much of it informing large urban redevelopment programmes (exemplified by the work of Camden's architects). Brutalism was discovered and Pop Art invented. The LCC's Royal Festival Hall is an outstanding building from the beginning of this period and Denys Lasdun's National Theatre of the end. In between are iconic housing schemes such as the Brunswick Centre, Alexander Road, and Trellick Tower.

### Post-Modernism, Hi-tech and the Invisible hand
1970-90: when socially oriented architectural programmes were withdrawn and commerical ones took over, culminating in the boom years of the later '80's and the redevelopment of the former Docklands. Architectural 'post-modernism' arrived as a US import in the mid 1970's to supplant an earlier socially-oriented modernism that had evolved into the Hi-tech (these two forming the major polarisation of the period, both fueled by City deregulation in the mid '80's). Typical buildings of the period are by Terry Farrell (Embankment Place and MI6), Robert Venturi (Sainsbury Wing), Jim Stirling (Clore), and Richard Rogers (Lloyd's). Broadgate (SOM and Arup Associates) and Canary Wharf (Cesar Pelli et al) embody urban change. The stylistic battles (which had included a 'Deconstruction' conversation that hardly touched UK practice) died overnight in the 1990-94 recessionary period, and a new era began with architects now enjoying an orientation toward continental rather than American values.

### Grand Projets and community
1990-now: a period initially dominated by millennium *grand projets* such as Rogers' Dome, Herzog & de Meuron's Tate Modern, the London Eye and a proliferation of other projects from Foster's office (e.g. the Millennium Bridge and City Hall), as well as outstanding stations on the Jubilee Line by a range of architects (e.g. Canary Wharf and Westminster stations) and many new commercial buildings that, in effect, continued the boom years of 1970-90 (e.g. Foster's 30 St. Mary Axe). Canary Wharf strode into a second phase; the City continued to change and sought tall symbols of its success; the masses and the media discovered architects, designers and modernist tastes whilst larger the pattern of residential accommodation made an historical flip from houses to apartments (especially in Docklands, but good examples also include Albion and Montevetro in west London). There has also been a short boom in socially-oriented architecture e.g. Peckham Library, the Idea Stores, Stratford Circus, Plashet School bridge, and the Laban Centre, together with a host of other educational and health projects exploiting a Labour government's proclivity for public expenditure. With the promise of the Olympics in 2012, construction emphasis remains in the east of London and controversy still colours the issue of the provision of residential buildings (where? what mix? density? costs? families?).